Transforming the Finance
Function to Add
Company-Wide Value

Pearson Education

In an increasingly competitive world, it is quality of thinking that gives an edge. An idea that opens new doors, a technique that solves a problem, or an insight that simply helps make sense of it all.

We work with leading authors in the fields of management and finance to bring cutting-edge thinking and best learning practice to a global market.

Under a range of leading imprints, including *Financial Times Prentice Hall*, we create world-class print publications and electronic products giving readers knowledge and understanding which can be applied, whether studying or at work.

To find out more about our business and professional products, you can visit us at www.business-minds.com

For other Pearson Education publications, visit

www.pearsoned-ema.com

MANAGEMENT BRIEFINGS
EXECUTIVE BRIEFING

Transforming the Finance Function to Add Company-Wide Value

MARGARET MAY

FINANCIAL TIMES
Prentice Hall

London   New York   San Francisco   Toronto   Sydney
Tokyo   Singapore   Hong Kong   Cape Town   Madrid
Paris   Milan   Munich   Amsterdam

PEARSON EDUCATION LIMITED

Head Office:
Edinburgh Gate
Harlow CM20 2JE
Tel: +44 (0)1279 623623
Fax: +44 (0)1279 431059

London Office:
128 Long Acre, London WC2E 9AN
Tel: +44 (0)207 447 2000
Fax: +44 (0)207 240 5771
Website: www.business-minds.com

First published in Great Britain 1999

© Margaret May 1999

The right of Margaret May to be identified as author
of this work has been asserted by her in accordance
with the Copyright, Designs, and Patents Act 1988.

ISBN 0 273 64313 0

British Library Cataloguing in Publication Data
A CIP catalogue record for this book can be obtained from the British Library.

All rights reserved; no part of this publication may be reproduced, stored
in a retrieval system, or transmitted in any form or by any means, electronic,
mechanical, photocopying, recording, or otherwise without either the prior
written permission of the Publishers or a licence permitting restricted copying
in the United Kingdom issued by the Copyright Licensing Agency Ltd,
90 Tottenham Court Road, London W1P 0LP. This book may not be lent,
resold, hired out or otherwise disposed of by way of trade in any form
of binding or cover other than that in which it is published, without the
prior consent of the Publishers.

10 9 8 7 6 5 4 3 2 1

Typeset by Boyd Elliott Typesetting
Printed and bound in Great Britain

The Publishers' policy is to use paper manufactured from sustainable forests.

About the author

Margaret May FCMA is a managing director of a firm of consulting CIMA (Chartered Institute of Management Accountants) members, Management Accountants in Practice, known as MAP, based near Gatwick. MAP specialise in advanced management techniques designed to prepare organisations to change the present and manage the future.

Following a career in finance and administration in both the private and public sectors, working for, among others, British Steel, North West Securities (Bank of Scotland), Cheshire Police, Southern Electricity and Bowthorpe Holdings, she moved into general management, running the Thermoplastic Sheet Division of Doeflex plc. She entered consultancy, forming MAP with other CIMA practising members, in the early 1990s and has specialised in the development of process/activity-based techniques, performance management, performance improvement, information management and change management, concentrating particularly on the practical aspects of implementation.

In addition to her consultancy work, Margaret is a regular seminar and conference presenter, visiting university lecturer and a member of CIMA Council since 1994. She currently sits on the Appointments, Membership, Student Affairs and Technical Committees. Her recent publications include articles in *Management Accounting*; a chapter in the Gee/CIMA *Handbook of Management Accounting*; and IFAC-published research entitled *Preparing Organisations to Manage the Future*.

Contents

List of figures	xi
Acknowledgements	xiii
Foreword	xv
Introduction	xvii

PART 1 WHY THE FINANCE FUNCTION NEEDS TO CHANGE — 1

1 Problems with the traditional finance function — 3
1.1 Introduction — 5
1.2 Outdated financial computer systems focusing efforts on processing and spreadsheets — 5
1.3 Insular approach — 7
1.4 Traditional costing methods have become inappropriate and misleading — 7
1.5 Focus on traditional budgetary control with no clear links between strategy, operations, resource allocation and performance — 9
1.6 Emphasis on backward-looking financial measures — 10
1.7 'Top-down control cycle' organisational culture — 11
1.8 Public-sector requirements — 14

2 The need for transformation of the finance function — 17
2.1 Introduction — 19
2.2 Demonstrating the ability to be customer focused and service oriented while delivering best practice and best value — 20
2.3 Impact of technology — 21
2.4 Moving from processor to value-adding function — 21

	2.5	The necessity for finance professionals to transform their roles to support and facilitate decision making and assist value creation throughout the business	22
	2.6	Utilising methods of planning, budgeting and resource allocation linked to process outputs, business strategy and priorities	23
	2.7	Introducing non-financial performance measures alongside financial measures and qualitative alongside quantitative	24
	2.8	Control of the organisation's integrated information and performance-management strategy	25
	2.9	Best Value	26

PART 2 VALUE-ADDING TOOLS AND TECHNIQUES   29

3 Value-based management   31

3.1	Introduction	33
3.2	Rappaport's theory	34
3.3	Shareholder value calculation models	34
3.4	EVA example	36
3.5	Embedded VBM	38
3.6	Inter-business unit charging	39
3.7	Risk management	40
3.8	Case study – VBM at British Aerospace	43

4 Balanced scorecard   51

4.1	Introduction	53
4.2	Measures that drive performance	53
4.3	Weighting the balanced scorecard	54
4.4	The ten commandments of implementation	56
4.5	Key learning points of best practice	57
4.6	Links to quality frameworks	58
4.7	Case study – Eurotunnel	61
4.8	Case study – Manchester Council Housing Department's information strategy	61

5 Activity/process-based techniques — 69

5.1	Introduction	71
5.2	Hierarchical process/activity analysis	73
5.3	Costing	78
5.4	Performance improvement	85
5.5	Performance management	91
5.6	Case study – Process-based performance improvement in Lund University Hospital	102
5.7	Case study – ABT and benchmarking at Metropolitan Housing Trust	106

6 Benchmarking — 113

6.1	Introduction	115
6.2	Types of benchmarking	115
6.3	Data-gathering methods	117
6.4	Phases of the benchmarking process	118
6.5	The Benchmarking Code of Conduct	120
6.6	Benefits of benchmarking	121
6.7	Case study – Tower Hamlets benchmarking	121

7 Information management — 127

7.1	Introduction	129
7.2	Defining the business requirement	129
7.3	Formulating a company-wide information strategy	130
7.4	Evaluating enterprise-wide software	135
7.5	Activity/process/value-based software	137
7.6	Case study – ABM systems design at Anglian Water	143
7.7	Case study – Data warehousing at Nationwide	148

PART 3 TRANSFORMATION OF THE FINANCE FUNCTION — 153

8 How to plan and implement the necessary changes — 155

8.1	Introduction	157
8.2	Establishing the transformation project	158
8.3	Analysis of the present finance function activities	159
8.4	Develop the vision for the future of the finance function	162

8.5	Create the change strategy	166
8.6	Align staff skills and competencies	166
8.7	Implement the transformation	169
8.8	Monitor success and results of implementation	170
8.9	Case studies – Worldwide excellence in finance	170

9 Outsourcing and shared service centres 173

9.1	Outsourcing	175
9.2	Shared service centres (SSC)	181
9.3	Case study – Outsourced shared services at the BBC	186

10 The finance function as facilitator of change, adding company-wide value 193

10.1	Introduction	195
10.2	Achieving successful change	195
10.3	How not to do it	197
10.4	Case study – Company-wide ABC and BPR at ABB	198

PART 4 EXECUTIVE SUMMARY 203

References 215

Index 221

Figures

1.1	Changes in cost composition	8
1.2	Barriers to strategic implementation	10
1.3	The 'top-down' control cycle	11
1.4	Stifling innovation memorandum	12
1.5	The 'bottom-up' empowerment cycle	13
2.1	Transformation of the finance function	19
2.2	Integrated performance management	26
3.1	VBM integrates management processes	39
3.2	BAe – Jetspares	45
3.3	BAe – Value driver map yielding performance indicators	46
3.4	BAe – Value impact of a 1% movement in top 10 KPIs	46
3.5	BAe – Characteristics of KPIs	47
3.6	BAe – Identification of KPIs	48
3.7	BAe – The initial management view of moveability on KPIs	48
3.8	BAe – Potential value creation	49
4.1	The balanced scorecard	54
4.2	EFQM Business Excellence model	59
4.3	The Malcolm Baldrige National Quality Award	59
4.4	MH – Balanced scorecard outcomes	63
4.5	MH – Housing demand and rehousing	64
4.6	MH – Graphical trends	65
4.7	MH – Geographic 'drill down'	65
4.8	MH – Balanced scorecard functional perspectives	66
5.1	The development of activity-based techniques	71
5.2	Organisation structure hierarchy	73
5.3	Process/activity hierarchy	74
5.4	CAM-I cross	74
5.5	The systems design and delivery subprocess	75
5.6	Data collection form	77
5.7	How ABC differs from traditional costing	79
5.8	ABC – Help desk	83
5.9	Customer profitability	84
5.10	Help desk pricing	85
5.11	Value chain	88
5.12	The procurement process	89
5.13	Cause and effect analysis	90
5.14	Process improvement lifecycle	90
5.15	Activity budgeting	93
5.16	Balanced performance measures	95

Figures

5.17	Alternative service levels	97
5.18	Priority-based budgeting rating scale	98
5.19	Priority-based budget – security	98
5.20	Departmental priority budget	99
5.21	Earned value activity analysis	101
5.22	Actual activity analysis	102
5.23	Lund – Competing demands	102
5.24	Lund – Activity-based costing	104
5.25	Lund – The complete picture	104
5.26	Lund – The medical process	104
5.27	Lund – The patient added value	105
5.28	Lund – Allergy clinic core processes	105
5.29	MHT – RRP activity costs	107
5.30	MHT – RRP regional activity costs per order	108
5.31	MHT – Average costs for repairs and maintenance administration	108
5.32	MHT – RRP cost drivers	109
5.33	MHT – Repairs and maintenance budget – traditional versus ABC	111
6.1	Tower Hamlets – Phase 1 List of activities and published reports	122
7.1	AW – User network	144
7.2	AW – Billing and collection process (micro)	144
7.3	AW – Billing and collection process (macro)	145
7.4	AW – ARTS 2000	146
7.5	AW – Process guide	146
7.6	AW – QPR system	147
7.7	AW – QPR efficiency analysis	148
8.1	Sales invoicing process	161
9.1	BBC – Overview of the arrangements	188
9.2	BBC – MedAS can deliver all components of finance and IT services	188
9.3	BBC – There are a variety of service delivery models	189
9.4	BBC – Examples of in-house v outsourced service delivery	190
9.5	BBC – Outsourcing service delivery models	190
9.6	BBC – Outsourcing contracts can be complex	192
9.7	BBC – Different (and conflicting) agendas exist within an organisation	192
10.1	The impact of change	196
10.2	The boat race	197
10.3	ABB – The development of product cost structure	199
10.4	ABB – Improvement potential	199
10.5	ABB – ABC working team structures	201
10.6	ABB – Linking the plans	202

The author and publisher have made every effort to seek permission for the figures used in this book.

Acknowledgements

The author would like to thank the following for their help, advice and contributions in the form of case studies, all of which she gratefully acknowledges:

- Management Accountants in Practice Limited (MAP), her employers, who have kindly consented to the use of seminar material being used extensively in this publication.
- Miriam Alcock for technical IT advice on Chapter 7, Information management.
- Tony Bryan and Rogan Dixon for their contribution of the British Aerospace case study on value-based management in Chapter 3.
- Hilary Vaughan and the Departmental Management Team at Manchester City Council Housing Department for approving the use of their balanced scorecard client case study in Chapter 4.
- George McMorron, for allowing use of the Metropolitan Housing Trust client case study of activity-based techniques on its reactive repair process in Chapter 5.
- Dr Ulf Hallgarde of Lund University Hospital for allowing the case study on process-based performance improvement at the allergy clinic to be illustrated in Chapter 5.
- Mike Howes for writing the case study on the Tower Hamlets benchmarking project, originally published by IFAC in 1997 and reproduced in Chapter 6.
- Abhai Rajguru for writing the Nationwide case study on data warehousing, originally published by IFAC in 1997, and for giving permission for the use of the Anglian Water client case study on ABM, both in Chapter 7 on Information management.
- Richard Hartt of MedAS and Penny Lawson from the BBC for contributing the outsourced shared services at the BBC case study in Chapter 9.
- Andy Daniels for writing the case study in Chapter 10 on company-wide ABC and BPR at Asea Brown Boveri (ABB).
- Ian Kleinman of Reuters and Colin McIlwaine of the University of Ulster for their helpful comments on the draft of this book.
- Andrew Mould, former commissioning editor of the FT Management Briefing series, who 'persuaded' me to write this book.
- The editorial and production team at FT Prentice Hall for their assistance in finalising the book for publication.

Any mistakes or shortcomings are, of course, the author's responsibility.

Foreword

Ian Kleinman, Finance Director, Global Sales and Operations, Reuters

The approach of the millennium is cause for reflection on the past and quite a few predictions about the future. We see this almost daily in articles and television programmes. Two common themes which are discussed are the final arrival of the global village, already heralded by Marshall Machluan some thirty years ago, and the ever increasing rate of change. Both of these trends are directly influenced by technology. The global village could only exist because of the current all pervasive nature of electronic mail and the internet. Similarly, the increase rate of change reflects to a large effect the impact of new industrial technologies, as well as commercial technologies, such as electronic commerce. Just think of their influence on products, costs, processes and even ways of doing business.

A similar process of reflection and review is taking place in business. At a basic level, companies are urgently reviewing the preparedness of their own and bought in technologies to handle potential millennium bug problems. But the more forward-looking companies are also taking the opportunity of such reviews to re-think their underlying business strategies and what impact any resulting changes will have on their structures and operations.

We already noted that the world is becoming a more open and fast changing place. But there are factors which are adding even more urgency to such reviews. Firstly, many firms are increasingly finding themselves in a very competitive global, or, in some cases at least, regional marketplace. The fall of the Iron Curtain, the creation of the Eurozone, NAFTA and other regional trading zones, are offering companies larger marketing opportunities than ever before, and at lower cost. Combined with this, there has been a dramatic acceleration in the deregulation of markets and industries. This is often driven by the needs of governments to both improve their financial position by selling off state-owned assets, and to ensure that their economies remain competitive internationally. Similarly, the growing presence of international markets, particularly financial markets, as well as multinational companies mean that capital and human resources are flowing more freely than ever to where the best returns can be found. The pressure for best returns is also being directly influenced by ever more active shareholders.

But probably the most important driver for change in business is the impact of technology. Technology is not only breaking down barriers to entry, it is also fundamentally changing the rules of the competitive game. There is no longer any need to have fully owned integrated operations. Companies can have almost complete freedom of location and can provide immediate responsiveness to customer demand. One only has to look at some well-documented case studies in the use of electronic commerce technologies to see the actual impact achieved. Take Dell for example. Its factory in Limerick, on the west coast on Ireland, supplies custom built PCs all over Europe. It takes some $15m daily of customer orders over its own website and call centres, and then passes on details, of which components it needs and when, to suppliers through its extranet. Both customers and suppliers are plugged into the whole process. The results from such a transparent and electronic process are clear: more accurate and timely hand-offs between customers, the company and its suppliers, lower costs for all and therefore increased satisfaction for all. A truly win-win-win situation.

So what does all this mean for the finance function? Margaret May's book is a timely reminder to us all that the finance function, like all other functions, has to react to the opportunities as well as the challenges posed by the changes already mentioned. So profound are the changes that no less than a transformation is required. From what to what you may ask. In simple terms, I would say from a specialist control function with its focus on historical financial data to one of a business partner focussed on the future, using its skills to take a holistic view of the business, both internally and externally.

The next question is how to achieve this transformation? Margaret May provides us with a practical blueprint. First she takes us through the case for change. It becomes apparent from this that finance needs to reposition itself within the organisation. To achieve this repositioning, the function needs to re-tool itself. Margaret May takes us through the latest ideas and techniques being applied in leading-edge finance departments. Finally, she examines various alternatives on implementation of the transformation.

If you are currently working in a finance department, consider this. Assume that you are at a funfair but there is only one attraction, a carousel. You have three options.

- to watch
- to jump on
- or to wait until the carousel is moving and then try to jump on.

Once you are on the experience is exhilarating and rewarding. If you try to get on once its moving, it is not only difficult but also dangerous. The longer you wait to get on, the faster the carousel goes, and the more dangerous it gets. Or alternatively, you could stand on the sidelines and watch the world go by. Which option would you take?

Introduction

Over the last 15 years companies have faced unprecedented change and inevitably this has placed new demands on finance functions. As we enter a new millennium, it is no longer acceptable to spend over 80% of the finance function's resources on transactional processing and control activities utilising outdated financial computer systems, without adding significant company-wide value. Hugh Collum, Executive Vice-President and CFO of SmithKline Beecham, is quoted by KPMG as saying:

> *Accountants could go the way of coal miners! A mighty industry that once employed three quarters of a million and helped bring down a government today employs fewer than SmithKline Beecham. I believe that accountants in industry could go the same way if they do not realise the fundamental changes they need to make.*

In research carried out by Price Waterhouse in 1997, 'maximising shareholder value' stood out as the number one priority of chief finance officers (CFOs) worldwide. The challenge is to link strategy successfully to operational goals and set measures and targets that ensure that added value is achieved. Performance-management frameworks must incorporate far more than measures; they need to incorporate processes that ensure that the necessary change occurs to execute the strategy.

The finance function must be transformed to take the lead role in building and running such a framework that links, in a meaningful way, strategy, operations, resource allocation and performance measurement, in addition to facilitating the necessary changes. It is ideally placed to undertake this challenge because it is the only part of the organisation that holds the key, pivotal role linking shareholder demands with business strategy and operational performance.

In the empowered organisational structure of today's companies, the finance function must demonstrate its ability to be customer focused and service oriented, while delivering best practice and best value company-wide. The modern finance professional will be embedded within the business, with his effectiveness and performance measured, not by how many invoices or journals have been processed but by what value has been created within the strategic business unit, in which he/she has become an indispensable team member.

In Part 1, problems are identified with traditionally run finance functions and arguments put forward as to why transformation is unavoidable for both the private and public sectors alike. All parts of the organisation are under pressure

Introduction

to improve performance, deliver more with less, work smarter not harder and add value on a continuous basis. Many one-off initiatives are undertaken by organisations to that end, often with each department trying different approaches, using different firms of consultants, resulting in much duplication of effort and uncoordinated results. The finance function is not only *not exempt* from these pressures, but should be taking the lead in facilitating one single, coordinated company-wide performance-improvement initiative. But first it must transform itself into a more cost-effective, business-process-integrated, customer-focused, service-oriented, value-adding function and demonstrate its worth beyond doubt to the whole organisation. Costs of the finance function will need to fall by one-third on average and 50% of the activities in that transformed finance function must be switched to decision support and adding value company-wide.

In Part 2, the modern tools and techniques of performance improvement, performance management and information management are explained and illustrated with case studies and examples. Emphasis is put on the necessity of linking the corporate strategy, driven by generating value, through a balanced scorecard of financial and non-financial measures, to an activity/process-based model of company operations. Such a holistic information and performance-management system, which is accessible to all, ensures congruent behaviour and is necessary to facilitate informed decision making and accurate measurement of achievement. The key to success in the building of these systems is the identification of the relevant information and measures from the masses of data being produced around the organisation and the ability to cascade it down the organisation, reinforcing the links with strategy and value creation.

Part 3 concentrates on the practicalities of how to transform the finance function to fulfil this new value-adding role, considering the new competencies and skills required by the modern finance professional and the changes in structures and organisation that may accompany it. Finance staff must become an integrated and indispensable part of the strategic business units and offer higher levels of service than ever before. The ways in which second-generation outsourcing deals are overcoming the conflicts of interest and the failure to encourage cost efficiencies that plagued earlier contracts are considered along with the undoubted benefits of shared service centres, whether national or global, covering one or more processes, sourced internally or externally. The final chapter considers the role of the transformed finance function as facilitator of change, adding company-wide value.

As a practising consultant throughout the 1990s, through MAP, I have specialised in the practical aspects of implementation of these value-adding tools and techniques. In this book I have therefore attempted to convey, not only *why* change is inevitable for survival of the finance function and *how* to make the necessary transformation, but *what* value-adding tools and techniques you will need to adopt to effect the change company-wide. My approach, as always, is practical, explaining the techniques, their origins and uses and illustrating throughout with examples and up-to-date case studies.

As a member of the Chartered Institute of Management Accountants Council, I firmly believe that the finance function and finance professionals can achieve the momentous transformation required in order to remain in a pivotal position within the organisation in the next millennium. For those students training to become accountants in business, CIMA, together with the other accountancy bodies, is changing its syllabus, training and membership criteria to cater for this new role. For those hundred thousand qualified accountants in the UK currently working in business, in both the private and public sectors, the responsibility must rest with you, as none of the professional accountancy bodies presently imposes continuing professional education and development on members in business. You will need to be proactive in facilitating and driving these changes over the next five years to ensure that the management accountancy profession remains in demand in the UK for at least another 100 years.

Part 1

Why the finance function needs to change

- 1 Problems with the traditional finance function   3
- 2 The need for transformation of the finance function   17

1

Problems with the traditional finance function

- 1.1 Introduction 5
- 1.2 Outdated financial computer systems focusing efforts on processing and spreadsheets 5
- 1.3 Insular approach 7
- 1.4 Traditional costing methods have become inappropriate and misleading 7
- 1.5 Focus on traditional budgetary control with no clear links between strategy, operations, resource allocation and performance 9
- 1.6 Emphasis on backward-looking financial measures 10
- 1.7 'Top-down control cycle' organisational culture 11
- 1.8 Public-sector requirements 14

1.1 INTRODUCTION

Over the last 10–15 years businesses have experienced exceptional levels of change, attributed to new and difficult challenges, varying in detail from industry to industry and from private to public sector, including such factors as:

- changing patterns of customer demand
- increases in customer bargaining power
- pressure on cost
- impact of technology
- strategic alliances
- new emerging markets
- globalisation
- government legislation
- highly liquid capital markets.

As organisations look to respond to these challenges and become truly 'world class', they inevitably place new demands on their finance functions. According to the Hackett Group's on-going benchmark study,[1] on average a typical finance function costs 1.4% of company revenues, with transaction processing and control activities consuming 84% of these costs. The range between the lowest and the highest finance function cost is large, with first-quartile companies having costs as low as 0.4% and fourth-quartile companies having costs as high as 7.4% of company revenues.

1.2 OUTDATED FINANCIAL COMPUTER SYSTEMS FOCUSING EFFORTS ON PROCESSING AND SPREADSHEETS

Many firms that installed computers during the 1970s and 1980s failed either to integrate these financial and other resource management related transaction processing systems with their business strategy, or to keep abreast of technology changes. Developed in an age of mainframe programming languages, the systems are troublesome to document, costly to maintain and difficult to change as business conditions evolve. This has resulted in many finance systems and processes becoming standalone and requiring very large amounts of expensive manual intervention.

A survey conducted by Tate Bramald Consultancy in 1996 for CIMA/JBA[2] revealed that 83% of UK management accountants surveyed use spreadsheets to produce their management accounts, compared to 13% who use enterprise information systems (EIS). These findings are confirmed by a report produced by Bournemouth University for IBM.[3] This research found that more than 75% of finance professionals believe that their personal computer (PC) is essential for business, but only 45% take full advantage of the networked collaborative applications available; the rest use their PCs merely to compile spreadsheets and other basic financial documents. Highly labour-intensive rekeying of data from source systems into spreadsheets for reporting is still the norm.

Those accounting operations associated with transaction processing and traditional duties typically consume over 80% of the resources in finance, leaving less than 20% for company-wide value-adding activities. Coopers & Lybrand's pan-European[4] finance function benchmarking survey defines the main finance function activities grouped as follows.

Accounting operations/transaction-processing activities include:

- accounts payable
- customer billing, accounts receivable and credit control
- travel and expense claims
- fixed assets
- general ledger accounting
- payroll and time recording
- accounts consolidation.

Decision support and control activities include:

- strategic and business planning
- budgeting and forecasting
- cost accounting
- investment appraisal
- performance reporting and analysis.

Financing and stewardship activities include:

- corporate finance
- treasury and cash management
- tax
- risk management
- internal audit
- stakeholder relations
- management of the finance function.

1.3 INSULAR APPROACH

Over the last two decades, finance, aided in part by separate computer systems, managed to adopt an insular approach to its function within the business. Located at head office, concentrating on its financial, control and statutory obligations, it had far too frequently lost sight of the need to produce relevant, timely, meaningful information for the business. This had been, in part, a consequence of the drive in the 1970s to merge costing, management and financial accounting systems into one super, integrated system.

Management information became the financial accounts, slightly modified, compared to budgets and then issued as the monthly management accounts pack. This information had little relevance to the operational managers of the business. This inevitably resulted in the growth of informal information systems all over the organisation, with each department having its own dedicated team producing the management information that it needed to run the business.

Finance, shut away, dictated what the business needed in terms of information and rarely ventured outside to talk to 'its customers'. The concept of the operational managers being internal customers of the finance function was not considered until the early 1990s with the advent of quality initiatives organisation wide. In the modern organisation, all departments have had to adapt to the idea of providing a service to their internal customers, and all too often the finance function has lagged behind in making this cultural leap.

As a result, the information produced by traditional finance functions often lacks credibility in the business. American Professor Robert Kaplan[5] said:

> *Management accounting cannot exist as a separate discipline, developing its own set of procedures and measurement systems and applying them universally.*

1.4 TRADITIONAL COSTING METHODS HAVE BECOME INAPPROPRIATE AND MISLEADING

Introduction

Costing systems developed in the 1960s, which allocate overhead costs primarily as a percentage of direct labour costs, are no longer appropriate in the world of the 1990s. Figure 1.1, Changes in cost composition, illustrates why it was reasonable in the 1960s to allocate indirect costs of 25% of total costs including material as a percentage on to direct labour, which was also in the region of 25%.

However, by the 1980s the sharp changes in the proportion of the make-up of business costs show indirect costs of 45% being allocated as a percentage on to direct labour of only 5%, which can no longer be considered to be appropriate, producing costings that are inaccurate and misleading.

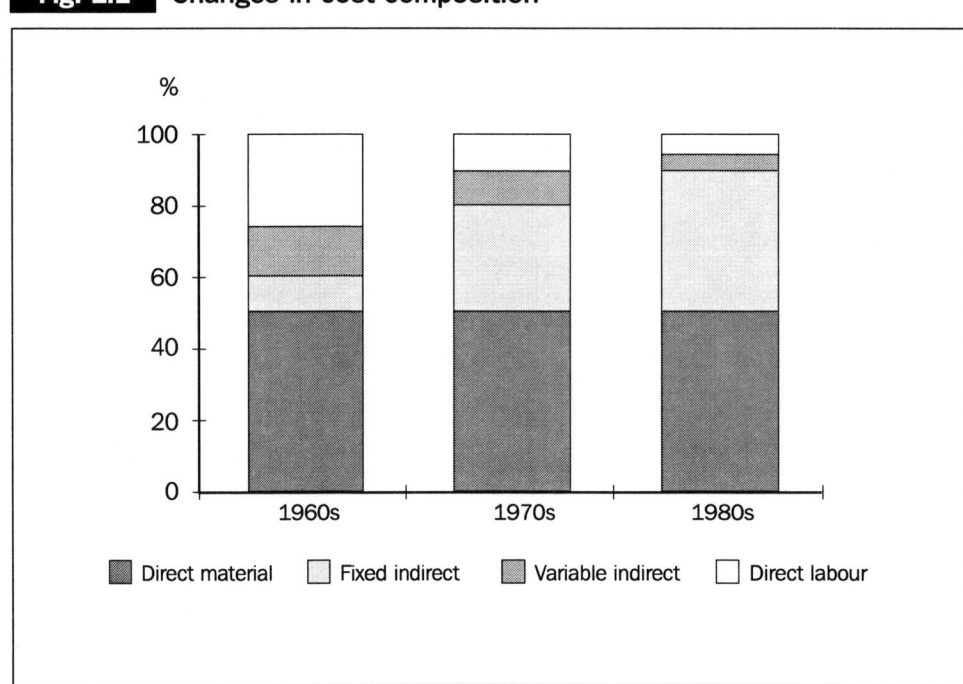

Fig. 1.1 Changes in cost composition

Direct material Fixed indirect Variable indirect Direct labour

A book written in the 1980s by American Professors Kaplan and Johnson,[5] called *Relevance Lost: the rise and fall of management accounting*, clearly identified this problem. Evidence that this practice continues was provided by a CAM-I[6] survey in the late 1980s, which showed that over 80% of companies in a man-paced environment still allocated costs based on direct labour.

The reasons for the changes in composition of the average business's costs, from direct to indirect, are due to many factors affecting organisations over the last three decades. These include:

- the introduction of more, increasingly sophisticated information technology (IT), within both the operational and administration areas of the business, requiring a massive infrastructure
- advanced automation techniques within production and operational areas, requiring considerably fewer direct employees and more indirect
- the introduction of just-in-time and other quality philosophies within the workplace, changing working practices
- the faster throughputs now achieved within the modern factory

- the greater choice and diversity of products being offered to customers and being produced in the same factories
- the need for complex marketing and sales functions to service the new breed of customer.

Signs of the need to review the costing system

- Lack of use of official costs being used in product and pricing decisions.
- Unofficial cost information being used due to lack of confidence in the information provided.
- Sales rise but profits fall.
- Expected cost reductions do not materialise.
- Customers 'cherry pick' products.
- Decisions being taken by operational managers to outsource the production of components to save high overhead costs, which have been allocated via the outdated costing system.

1.5 FOCUS ON TRADITIONAL BUDGETARY CONTROL WITH NO CLEAR LINKS BETWEEN STRATEGY, OPERATIONS, RESOURCE ALLOCATION AND PERFORMANCE

The traditional finance function is focused on running the organisation by means of traditional budgetary control techniques. These budgets are set based on what is usually a very lengthy process, taking up to six or eight months in some businesses and involving operational managers in a very time-consuming process, but still not linking resource allocation to output volumes or value added. More usually, resources are allocated based on such factors as who had what last year and which directors are most powerful within the organisation. Under these traditional budget-led regimes, rigid adherence to whether cost centres are within the pre-set budget limits is maintained on a monthly basis, irrespective of changes in demand for products or services within individual cost centres or the business as a whole.

If costs need to be reduced within this traditional budgetary framework, then all departments are instructed to reduce their costs by the required percentage. These arbitrary 'across-the-board' cuts are made irrespective of which departments are carrying out high-priority or customer-facing services and which are already being run in a very efficient, cost-effective manner. After several years of such arbitrary cost reductions, many organisations are finding that the long-term health of their business is being endangered.

Figure 1.2, Barriers to strategic implementation, summarises these shortcomings. The corporate vision is not fully understood by all staff; there is a failure to link the corporate vision and strategy to departmental and individual goals; also a failure to link strategy to resource allocation – this is traditionally done based on history, not on what outputs are required; and the traditional budgetary control feedback is usually a comparison of actual cost-centre expenditure against budget, with no direct link to outputs achieved. These are typical symptoms of the barriers, which can be traced back to this short-term, financial framework.

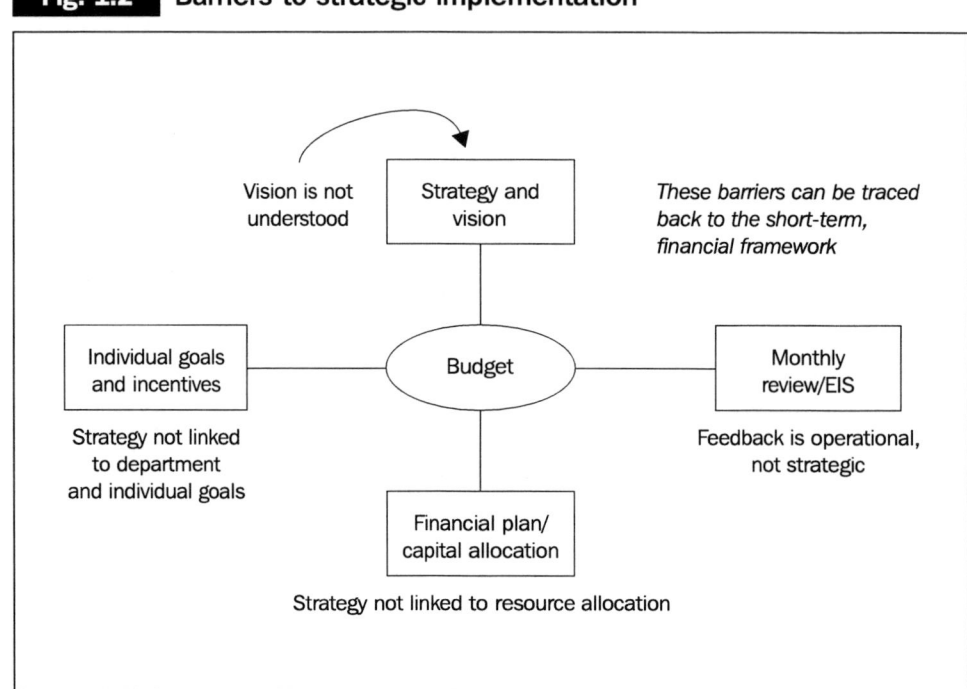

Fig. 1.2 Barriers to strategic implementation

Vision is not understood — Strategy and vision

These barriers can be traced back to the short-term, financial framework

Individual goals and incentives — Budget — Monthly review/EIS

Strategy not linked to department and individual goals

Feedback is operational, not strategic

Financial plan/ capital allocation

Strategy not linked to resource allocation

1.6 EMPHASIS ON BACKWARD-LOOKING FINANCIAL MEASURES

Performance-management systems controlled by the traditional finance function exhibit many of the following characteristics:

- too inward focusing
- too historical, lacking predictive power
- reflecting the business functions and structure, not processes

- reinforcing of wrong behaviour
- focusing on inputs not outputs
- often either too summary in nature or mistaking data for information
- based on the way the company worked before change
- too financially oriented.

1.7 'TOP-DOWN CONTROL CYCLE' ORGANISATIONAL CULTURE

Until the early 1990s, most publicly owned organisations were focused on short-term results, often driven by the stock market demanding improvements in share price and dividends year on year, without interest or regard for long-term strategies, growth or value generation. This resulted in senior managers running the business based on financial and accounting information, which they used to plan the next cycle of required results and then to instruct the workforce accordingly, requiring them to manipulate processes and cajole customers to achieve them. This can be seen from Fig. 1.3, The 'top-down' control cycle, taken from Johnson's *Relevance Regained*.[7]

Fig. 1.3 The 'top-down' control cycle

Read down from here → Ownership of accounting information

Empowers

top management

to plan, analyse and transmit instructions to the workforce

who manipulate processes and cajole customers to achieve accounting results

feedback

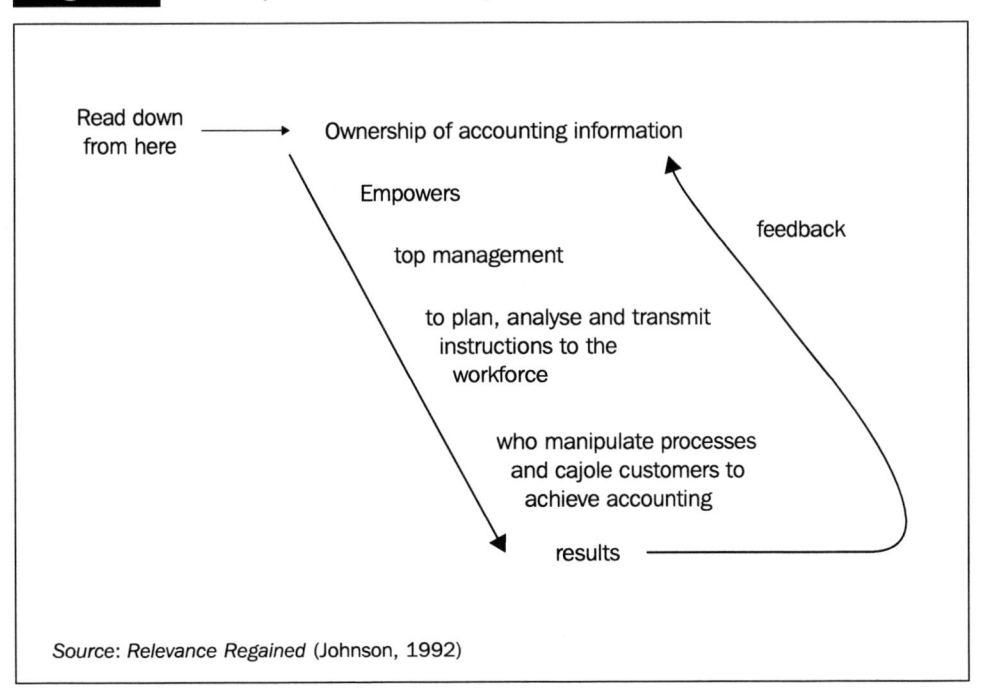

Source: Relevance Regained (Johnson, 1992)

Typical characteristics exhibited by a top-down control cycle organisation can be seen in Fig. 1.4, Stifling innovation memorandum.

Fig. 1.4 Stifling innovation memorandum

MEMORANDUM

To: All senior executives

Subject: **10 RULES FOR STIFLING INNOVATION**

1. Regard any new idea from below with suspicion – because it's new.
2. Insist that people, who need your approval to act, first go through several other levels of management to get their signatures.
3. Express your criticisms freely and withhold your praise. Let them know that they can be fired at any time. (That keeps people on their toes.)
4. Treat identification of problems as a sign of failure in order to discourage people from letting you know when something in their area is not working.
5. Control everything carefully. Make sure that people count anything that can be counted frequently.
6. Make decisions to reorganise or change policies in secret without any consultation and spring them on people unexpectedly. (That also keeps people on their toes.)
7. Make sure that requests for information are fully justified and that it is not given out to managers freely.
8. Assign to lower-level managers, in the name of delegation and participation, responsibility for figuring out how to cut back, lay off, move people around or otherwise implement threatening decisions that you have made. And get them to do it quickly.
9. Do not forget to launch a *new* cost-cutting initiative at least twice a year. This will score you points with the directors and leave the staff wondering what is going to happen next.
10. And above all, do not forget that you, the higher-ups, already know everything important about the business.

Shareholders in the 1990s have become far more sophisticated within this process and are now demanding that boards of directors take a much more comprehensive approach to managing their companies in order to maximise total shareholder value over time. They require a management approach that involves focusing all levels of the organisation on creating value in the commercial marketplace, through identifying appropriate drivers and incorporating them into a clear strategy and thereby realising value in the capital marketplace. Evidence abounds of those companies not delivering the required returns to shareholders being put under pressure to do so by institutional shareholders. Equally, the new breed of ethical shareholder and customer have demonstrated adequately how they are also concerned with factors other than financial issues and will vote with their feet if ethical and environmental standards are not adhered to.

Most organisations in the late 1990s have made a conscious effort to switch their culture to that depicted in Fig. 1.5, The 'bottom-up' empowerment cycle, again taken from Johnson's *Relevance Regained*. This illustrates that in the new global age customers have so much choice that they are forced to be responsive and flexible and must empower their workforces to learn and make changes that continuously improve processes capable of better satisfying their customers. Moving to an empowerment culture takes time, requires determination and considerable change by organisations, and it can be seen that those who persevere are the ones who are the most successful. In the process of these changes, far too often the finance function lags behind the rest of the organisation in making the necessary adjustments, when it ought to be leading the change by transforming the way it operates as a function and the business operates as a whole.

Fig. 1.5 The 'bottom-up' empowerment cycle

satisfying customers
to learn and make changes that
continuously improve processes
capable of
                                    feedback
workforce
to be responsive (listen) and flexible
(change quickly) by empowering the
companies
to choose among global opportunities
and requires
customers
empowers
Read up ⟶ Ownership of information
from here

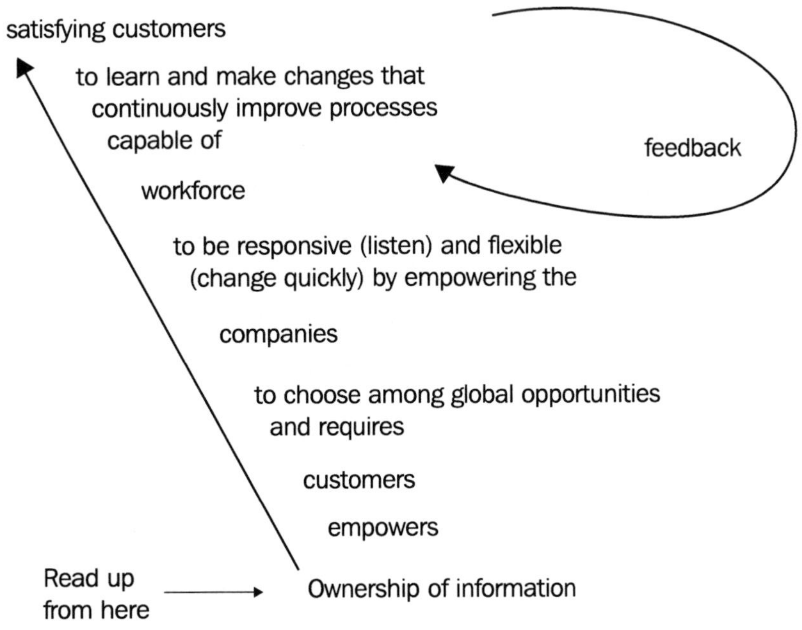

Source: Relevance Regained (Johnson, 1992)

1.8 PUBLIC-SECTOR REQUIREMENTS

Over the last two decades the public sector has been subjected to unprecedented transformation and change, with initiatives including:

- Financial Management Initiative
- Next Steps and Citizens Charter
- Competing for Quality
- Continuity and Change
- Resource Accounting and Budgeting

leading to:

- greater competition
- fundamental management reform
- contracts and service-level agreements
- financial and quality targets
- clear framework of objectives and resources.

These incorporate the use of many of the value-adding tools and techniques explained in Part 2 of this book, including activity-based techniques (ABT) and benchmarking.

In the Green Paper on Resource Accounting,[8] the Chancellor of the Exchequer reiterated his commitment to a continuing programme of radical improvement in the way that the public sector manages itself. He states:

> *Only by taking a progressively more business-like approach can the Government continue to bear down on cost to the taxpayer of delivering public services whilst improving service standards through the Citizens Charter . . . The proposals are probably the most important reform of the Civil Service accounting and budgeting arrangements this century . . . To implement the changes successfully will require the development of new skills, and commitment and leadership from managers at all levels in the Civil Service.*

The proposal to apply resource accounting, which includes the accruals concept, coherently to the whole of central government will require new systems and additional skills, both for those operating the systems and for managers and staff who use the information provided. Resource accounting and budgeting give departments a clearer picture of input costs and their activities. Utilising ABT allows government organisations to take this one stage further and include an explicit link between a detailed analysis of input costs according to departmental objectives and outputs.

With a new government the change continues and the local government 'Best Value' initiative will become effective in 2000, changing the Compulsory Competitive Tendering (CCT) regime to one that requires demonstration of best value, by utilising the value-adding tools and techniques described in Part 2. (*See* Section 2.9, Best Value.)

2

The need for transformation of the finance function

- 2.1 Introduction 19

- 2.2 Demonstrating the ability to be customer focused and service oriented while delivering best practice and best value 20

- 2.3 Impact of technology 21

- 2.4 Moving from processor to value-adding function 21

- 2.5 The necessity for finance professionals to transform their roles to support and facilitate decision making and assist value creation throughout the business 22

- 2.6 Utilising methods of planning, budgeting and resource allocation linked to process outputs, business strategy and priorities 23

- 2.7 Introducing non-financial performance measures alongside financial measures and qualitative alongside quantitative 24

- 2.8 Control of the organisation's integrated information and performance-management strategy 25

- 2.9 Best Value 26

2.1 INTRODUCTION

Gregory Hackett of the Hackett Group said:

> *By the year 2005, the finance function as we know it will have changed beyond recognition.*

The challenge for the finance function is to become more cost effective, embedded within the business processes, customer focused and service oriented, adding company-wide value, reacting quickly when responding to ever-changing needs. This can only be achieved by transformation. The question is not whether the organisation's business units will each have a new style 'business analyst' as part of their core management team, but whether that person will be a finance professional or from another management discipline with some acquired financial skills. The pure financial content of this new role will form less than 50% and the requirement for the new strategic value-adding skills will dominate the choice of individuals selected for these roles. This is a challenge not only to every finance professional but also to the accountancy bodies responsible for their training.

Fig. 2.1 Transformation of the finance function

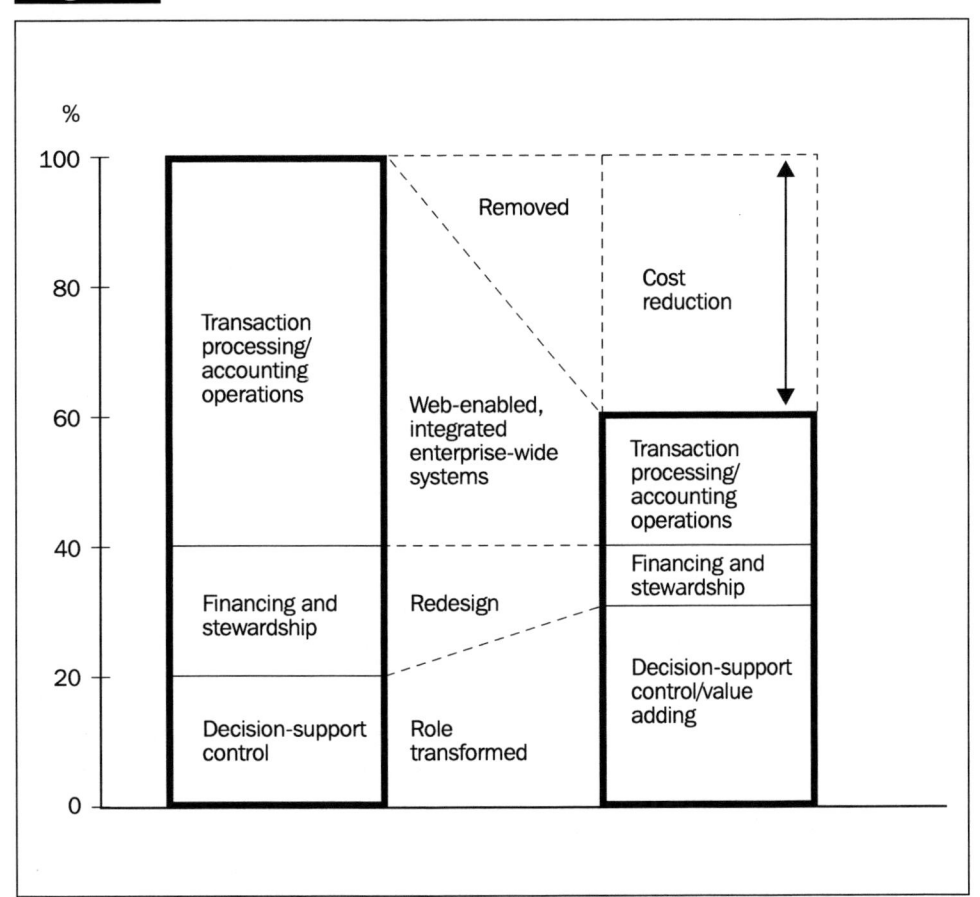

In the process of transforming the finance function, time-consuming transaction processing is being reduced by the introduction of new, web-enabled, integrated enterprise-wide computer systems, reducing costs by up to one-third. The resultant freed-up, financial resources can be retrained to work with operational managers to add company-wide value in their new roles as 'business consultants', 'business analysts' and 'technical specialists'. Figure 2.1, Transformation of the finance function, illustrates the change that needs to take place, with decision support, control and the new value-adding activities making up 50% of the slimline finance function. Traditional financing and stewardship activities will need to be redesigned to reduce costs to half their previous average levels. As the diagram shows, costs of the new transformed finance function as a whole need to be reduced by almost a third to compare with what is now regarded as upper-quartile best practice.

2.2 DEMONSTRATING THE ABILITY TO BE CUSTOMER FOCUSED AND SERVICE ORIENTED WHILE DELIVERING BEST PRACTICE AND BEST VALUE

In the next millennium, all parts of the organisation must be able to demonstrate visibly that they are using best-practice methodology, delivering best value and are cost effective and efficient. All parts of the organisation that are responsible for delivering services, like the finance function, must develop a service-oriented culture, focusing on the customer's requirements, utilising internal service-level agreements (SLAs) wherever practicable. The finance function should, as part of its new transformed role, be driving this initiative throughout the business and therefore should be leading the way, by example in undergoing the change before the rest of the company. This change is not just one of introducing and learning new techniques and utilising new tools, but involves a complete change of mindset, requireing a flexible and responsive approach, with newly developed skills in selling as well as delivering services.

How this change needs to take place is covered later in this book, including the following:

- The necessity to benchmark with other organisations carrying out similar activities to learn, establish best practice and continually improve is described in Chapter 6.
- Why it is appropriate for part or all of the function to be evaluated under outsourcing or be transferred to a shared service centre (SSC) or both is looked at in Chapter 9.
- The process of the finance function undergoing the necessary transformation utilising business process reengineering (BPR) and other value-adding

techniques is examined in Chapter 8. The finance function's role in facilitating this change for the rest of the organisation is considered in Chapter 10.

- The importance of becoming customer focused and service oriented with clearly drawn-up service-level agreements, even for internal suppliers like the finance function, is considered in Chapter 8. Only with clear lines of accountability and responsibility can performance be improved.

2.3 IMPACT OF TECHNOLOGY

The impact of technological developments on the finance function in recent years is profound and is covered in more detail in Chapter 7 on information management. The new systems are changing not only the method of operation but the whole structure of the traditional organisation. Changes have resulted in:

- not only the automation of processes but also access to data
- boundaries breaking down between finance and other functions utilising workflow techniques, e.g. finance and logistics, leading to new organisational structures, such as shared service centres, covered in Chapter 9
- new possibilities and opportunities for finance emerging from use of the internet, e.g. e-commerce.

Organisations are spending considerable sums of money implementing systems that are linked company wide. Many are switching to enterprise resource planning (ERP), but others are bridging the gap between legacy systems with middleware. Once integrated, the new investment is being targeted towards web-enablement of systems, permitting web-based processes outside the organisation, transferring the generation of transactions to suppliers and customers and removing the need to input orders or invoices within the company at all. Typically, orders can be placed by customers, which are automatically processed via workflow techniques and passed to suppliers to execute, and payment is made via electronically funded transfers (EFT), the finance function staff finding themselves involved only where exceptions occur.

2.4 MOVING FROM PROCESSOR TO VALUE-ADDING FUNCTION

Figure 2.1, Transformation of the finance function (p.19), shows what needs to be done:

- Accounting operations/processing is reduced by two-thirds via the latest computer technology, discussed in detail in Chapter 7, Information management, when the process of defining business requirements and formulating an organisation-wide information strategy is examined in addition to a section evaluating enterprise resource planning software.

- The increasing use of outsourcing and shared service centres for finance processes, particularly operations, is examined in Chapter 9.

- Financing and stewardship activities, such as corporate finance, treasury and cash management, tax, risk management, internal audit and stakeholder relations, will need to undergo reengineering to deliver improved, added-value services at half their previous costs. This is covered in detail in Chapters 5 and 8.

- Decision-support and control activities will be transformed by new value-adding tools and techniques described in Part 2, Chapters 3 to 7, and will make up half of the activities of the new finance function, which will demonstrably be adding company-wide value. The tools and techniques covered include value-based management (Chapter 3), balanced scorecard (Chapter 4), activity-based techniques (Chapter 5), benchmarking (Chapter 6) and information management (Chapter 7).

2.5 THE NECESSITY FOR FINANCE PROFESSIONALS TO TRANSFORM THEIR ROLES TO SUPPORT AND FACILITATE DECISION MAKING AND ASSIST VALUE CREATION THROUGHOUT THE BUSINESS

In the future, at least 50% of the effort of the finance function will be focused on active participation in the organisation's on-going pursuit of competitive excellence. These changes will involve huge amounts of upheaval for finance professionals, who traditionally have been content spending most of their time on processing and technical issues, not needing to venture far from the safety of their offices. Realigning and retraining of the existing finance professionals will form one of the biggest challenges in the transformation journey. This is dealt with in detail in Chapter 8.

SMAC's publication *Redesigning the Finance Function*[1] believes that the new finance function will require the skills to:

- deliver analytically, strategically and value-added oriented services
- act as a consultative business partner and adviser
- become a participant and leader in the decision-making process
- foster company-wide continual performance enhancement.

Finance professionals of the transformed function will typically fall into three categories, to which, wherever possible, existing staff will be deployed based on their strengths, maximising the potential for successful retraining. These three new job roles and the activities they will carry out can be described as follows:

- **Business consultants** are usually a core of shared-service corporate staff, who specialise in specific processes, models or initiatives, providing advice and support to the business units.

- **Business analysts** are generally operating from within the business units as the financial specialist on the management team. In addition to the traditional roles of the business unit financial controller or management accountant of scorekeeping and budgetary control, the analysts are at the sharp end of delivering the new decision-support and value-adding roles discussed in detail in Part 2, Value-adding tools and techniques.

- **Technical specialists** are experts in finance and accounting, who provide the traditional transaction-processing, financing and stewardship activities, using the new systems with improved reporting and control services at much reduced costs. These professionals are often located centrally and are far fewer in number than in the traditional finance function.

These new, dynamic finance professionals will become leaders of multidisciplined teams engaged in strategic and tactical planning, taking equal responsibility for the future success of the company.

2.6 UTILISING METHODS OF PLANNING, BUDGETING AND RESOURCE ALLOCATION LINKED TO PROCESS OUTPUTS, BUSINESS STRATEGY AND PRIORITIES

There is now a sense of urgency about the need to replace traditional budgeting techniques with new methods of planning, control and allocating resources, before permanent, long-term damage is done to the health of many businesses. The detailed tools and techniques are covered in Part 2. They will allow resource allocation to be made based on efficiency, priority and output volumes, with budgets based on process and activity unit costs linked to objectives, responsibilities and performance targets.

- Activity-based management accounting (ABMA), which includes priority-based budgeting (PBB), and other activity-based techniques is detailed in Chapter 5.

- Value-based management (VBM), incorporating service-level agreements (SLAs) and, if appropriate, inter-business unit charging, is explained in Chapter 3.

- The balanced scorecard,[2] linking strategy to the activity-based common data model, is covered in Chapter 4.
- Benchmarking, in Chapter 6, illustrates how comparisons with other similar organisations can be more important than traditional budgeting.
- Information management, in Chapter 7, shows how advances in IT make new methodologies possible.

These value-adding tools and techniques are the way in which a transformed finance function will facilitate management of the organisation in the twenty-first century.

According to Janet Kersnar at *CFO Europe*,[3] Diageo, the £14 billion consumer giant whose brands include Guinness and Burger King, decided in October 1999 to scrap the firm's annual budget and replace it with a totally different approach. As a result, it joined a growing band of multinationals that have abandoned what Jack Welch, the boss of General Electric, once famously described as 'the bane of corporate America'. The annual budget is time consuming, labour intensive and seemingly never ending, and is, at best, an excuse for senior managers to gather numbers that they should have at their fingertips anyway; and, at worst, one of a company's biggest competitive handicaps.

Rather than using a budgeting process and a strategic planning process with annual targets,

> *we should try to have one single planning process of which year one was important but not so important that it stops you talking about years two, three, four and five*

says Phillip Yea, Diageo's CFO. Since that decision, managers across the company's four lines of business have been studying key performance indicators (KPIs) that they want to use to track, predict and report improvements in their operations.

The overall aim at Diageo is to benchmark itself against a peer group of 20 international consumer and branded-goods companies in terms of total shareholder return. By June 2003, it wants to be among the top five companies out of the 20 in the benchmarking process.

2.7 INTRODUCING NON-FINANCIAL PERFORMANCE MEASURES ALONGSIDE FINANCIAL MEASURES AND QUALITATIVE ALONGSIDE QUANTITATIVE

The balanced scorecard (BSC), explained in Chapter 4, is a tool designed by Kaplan and Norton in 1992 and is now widely used across all industry sectors. It highlights the need to look at critical success factors (CSF) and key performance indicators for all the perspectives, including the customer perspective, the learning perspective, the internal business perspective as well as the traditional financial perspective, when monitoring the organisation's performance. It operates on the principle that the corporate vision and strategy, once clearly defined, should determine a number of outcomes that are required to ensure its successful achievement. Each outcome will have CSFs and KPIs across the business's perspectives, each weighted in terms of importance to the achievement of the outcome. The BSC has been likened to the cockpit of an aeroplane, with a similar necessity to keep all the dials and controls in synchronisation to ensure a successful flight.

2.8 CONTROL OF THE ORGANISATION'S INTEGRATED INFORMATION AND PERFORMANCE-MANAGEMENT STRATEGY

The latest technological advances mean that it is now possible to have just one holistic, organisation-wide information strategy. This means that one performance-management system is used by everyone around the organisation, with no conflicting data produced by different departments! Decision making is based on one set of good, reliable information to reduce risk, facilitated by the new breed of finance professionals, who are now devoting large amounts of time to this crucial activity. This holistic system also needs to be linked into performance at all levels in the organisation to ensure achievement of organisational goals. Figure 2.2, Integrated performance management, shows how this one holistic system links the value-adding strategy via the BSC to a detailed common data model containing activity/process-based information, incorporating quality frameworks as well as costs and operational data. This topic is covered in detail in Part 2, Chapters 3, 4 and 5, which explain how the whole performance-management and information system can be integrated. In Chapter 7, Information management, such products as enterprise information systems, decision-support systems (DSS) and data warehouses are examined, in addition to activity/process/value-based/balanced scorecard and enterprise resource planning packages.

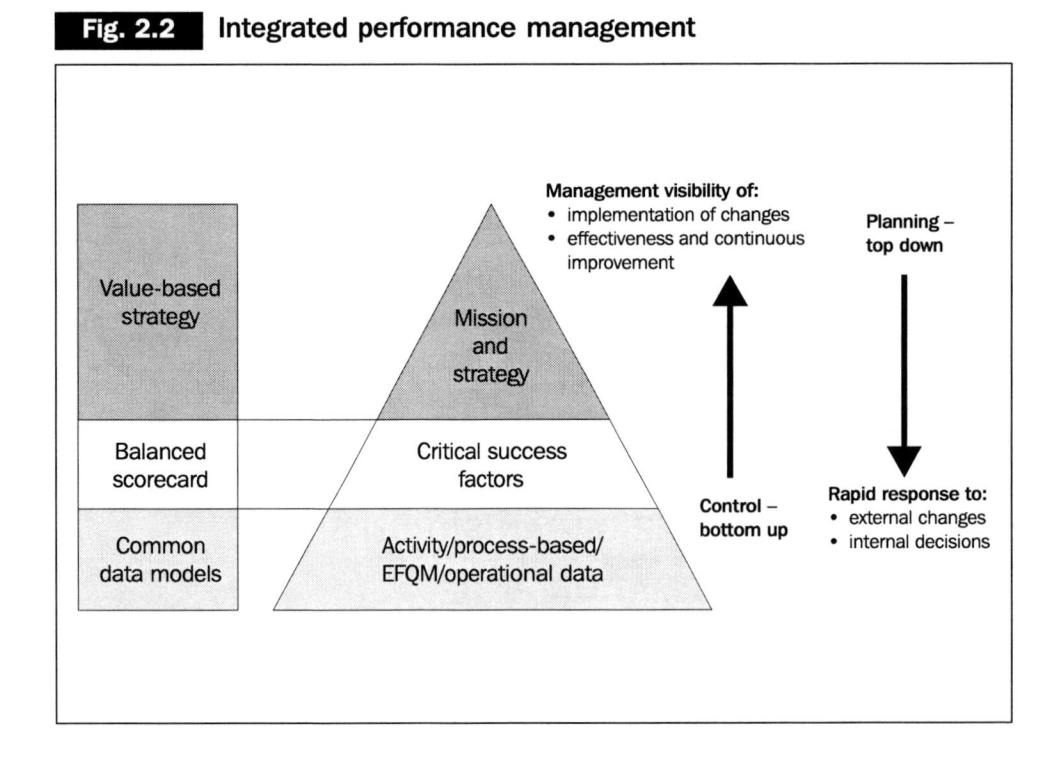

Fig. 2.2 Integrated performance management

A diagram showing:
- Value-based strategy / Mission and strategy (top)
- Balanced scorecard / Critical success factors
- Common data models / Activity/process-based/ EFQM/operational data

Management visibility of:
- implementation of changes
- effectiveness and continuous improvement

Planning – top down

Control – bottom up

Rapid response to:
- external changes
- internal decisions

2.9 BEST VALUE

CIPFA's *Accounting for Best Value Consultation Paper*[4] explains that at the end of 1998 the government issued the Local Government (Best Value and Capping) Bill. Through this Bill, the government aims to modernise local government in England and Wales, by placing principles of best value on a statutory footing and introducing reserve powers to limit excessive council tax increases. Best Value will require local authorities to deliver services to clear standards by the most effective, economic and efficient means available. It will strengthen accountability to both local people and taxpayers generally. And it will lead to healthier partnerships between local government and the private and voluntary sectors. The Bill states that Compulsory Competitive Tendering will be abolished on 2 January 2000. In Scotland, all local authorities are now in their second year of the Best Value regime. This regime is not based on specific, newly enacted primary legislation, but is covered in guidance from the Scottish Office. A Best Value Taskforce Group has been established and this group is currently looking at what legislation is required in Scotland to implement Best Value.

The Local Government Bill states:

> *A best value authority must make arrangements to secure continuous improvement in the way in which its functions are exercised, having regard to a combination of economy, efficiency and effectiveness.*

Specifically, the new Best Value powers will:

- require local authorities to review their services over a five-year period
- require local authorities to set new and demanding targets for each service and publish these in local performance plans
- introduce new external audit and inspection arrangements to ensure that local people have confidence in their authority's performance
- give ministers wide powers to intervene where local authorities are failing to provide Best Value services
- allow ministers to remove any obstacles to local authorities working with others, including other public bodies and the private sector, to provide Best Value.

Best Value will have four components:

Fundamental performance reviews (FPRs) or service reviews

Reviews of all the local authority's services over a five-year period, which will:

- challenge
- compare
- consult
- demonstrate the test of competitiveness

with the purpose being to ensure that service delivery satisfies the citizens who pay for services and to ensure that continuous improvements will be made.

Local performance plans (LPPs)

Published annual plans will provide a clear, practical expression of an authority's performance in delivering local services and its proposals to improve. These are the principal means by which authorities are held accountable to local people.

National performance indicators (NPIs)

These include:

- council-wide 'general health' indicators
- key indicators reflecting cost effectiveness and quality of each main service, focused on what services have been delivered (outcomes) rather than what resources have been devoted to them (inputs).

Audit and inspection arrangements

There will be new arrangements to give a clear view of whether Best Value is being obtained, including rigorous external checks on the information provided by authorities in LPPs and the management systems that underpin them. Regular external inspection of performance will be established in the form of an inspectorate similar to the existing inspectorates, e.g. OFSTED.

Best Value is essentially about demonstrating to the community and the stakeholders that service provision provides value for money. To demonstrate Best Value through FPRs, LPPs and NPIs, local authorities need to present and use information based on a consistent set of principles. In short, the financial and performance information used to assess Best Value is worthless unless it is prepared in accordance with a robust and consistently applied framework of accounting.

As local authorities (LAs) review the changes needed to implement Best Value, they have identified the need to adopt value-adding tools and techniques, as described in Part 2 of this book. One police authority has specifically identified the following tools to assist in meeting this need:

- the balanced scorecard
- Investors in People
- activity-based costing and associated techniques*
- benchmarking
- Business Excellence model
- Chartermark
- value management
- business process reengineering.

* Particularly important activity-based techniques for demonstrating Best Value and offering choice to stakeholders are the use of the evaluation of alternative service levels and priority-based budgeting. Using these techniques will enable LAs and stakeholders to prioritise and make difficult choices between competing levels of service in the allocation of ever more scarce resources.

Part 2

Value-adding tools and techniques

- 3 Value-based management 31
- 4 Balanced scorecard 51
- 5 Activity/process-based techniques 69
- 6 Benchmarking 113
- 7 Information management 127

Value-based management

- 3.1 Introduction 33
- 3.2 Rappaport's theory 34
- 3.3 Shareholder value calculation models 34
- 3.4 EVA example 36
- 3.5 Embedded VBM 38
- 3.6 Inter-business unit charging 39
- 3.7 Risk management 40
- 3.8 Case study – VBM at British Aerospace 43

3.1 INTRODUCTION

In research carried out by Price Waterhouse in 1997,[1] maximising shareholder value stood out as the number one priority of chief finance officers worldwide. The challenge is to link strategy successfully to operational goals and set measures and targets that ensure that added value is achieved. Performance-management frameworks must incorporate far more than measures; they need to incorporate processes that ensure that the necessary change occurs to execute the strategy.

The finance function must be transformed to take the lead role in building and running such a framework and facilitating the necessary changes, as it is the only part of the organisation that holds the key, pivotal role linking shareholder demands with business strategy and operational performance. There is no time to waste in replacing those traditional information systems consisting of individual operational data, the management accounts pack of financial data and performance-management systems of individually set targets with no clear link to corporate strategy, added value or achievement-measurement systems.

In today's world, keeping shareholders happy is more complex than was previously the case. Institutional investors control larger stakes in companies and have correspondingly greater powers to influence events in the boardroom. This means that companies need to start valuing their businesses in the same way as their shareholders do and ensuring that decisions taken at whatever level are consistent with adding shareholder value. Not doing so can lead to many unwanted consequences, including:

- the inability to raise the necessary capital funds
- falls in share price as investors switch to higher-yielding opportunities
- the requirement for directors to justify their remuneration packages
- the risk of hostile takeover.

Traditionally, companies have measured their success using such indicators as profit margin, return on assets and return on equity, and have judged the viability of investments using discounted cashflow measures such as net present value (NPV) or internal rate of return (IRR), while the shareholder measured the company's performance using such indicators as earnings per share (EPS) and the price/earnings ratio (P/E). It is generally agreed that today, many accounting entries are made on the basis of management judgement, for example pension funding, goodwill, depreciation, deferred tax and acquisitions policies, and profit as a measure has, therefore, become complex and a gulf has opened up between it and cash-generation.

3.2 RAPPAPORT'S THEORY

In 1986, Alfred Rappaport published *Creating Shareholder Value*,[2] which finally brought together shareholders and managers with one common approach to measuring company performance that could replace all previous methods, i.e. cash-generation, because that represents fact rather than opinion. Rappaport based his theory on five drivers of cash and two other value drivers, as follows:

- Those that influence '*cash in*':
  1. turnover growth rate
  2. operating profit margins.
- Those that influence '*cash out*':
  3. the percentage tax rate actually paid
  4. the percentage of incremental revenue spent on fixed capital net of depreciation
  5. the percentage of incremental revenue spent on working capital.
- The value growth potential period – the future timeframe over which the cash drivers need to be measured for evaluation, which represents the company's perceived 'competitive advantage period'.
- The weighted average cost of capital (WACC), which takes the cost of debt and equity and weights them according to the book or projected book gearing. This is considered more representative than the 'interest' shown in the profit and loss account.

Using these seven value drivers, Rappaport's formula for evaluating shareholder value is:

> *Shareholder value = Corporate value − Debt*

where:

corporate value 5 the future free cashflow (cash in 2 cash out) that the company is expected to generate over time, discounted by the weighted average cost of capital.

3.3 SHAREHOLDER VALUE CALCULATION MODELS

Since Rappaport's book a number of different models have been developed, all building on Rappaport's proposition and value drivers. These can be grouped into three main categories.

Economic value added (EVA™)[3]

EVA is the trademark of Stern Stewart & Co, US consultants, and is a methodology that is growing in popularity, particularly in the USA, with many companies quoting EVA measures in their annual reports. This model starts with profit and then makes up to 160 different adjustments to cater for the distortions caused by accounting methodologies and management judgements. These adjustments are based on two guiding principles:

1. Investment decisions taken by the company should result in assets regardless of how they are treated in the accounts, for example training and marketing expense will be capitalised.
2. Assets once created cannot be eliminated by accounting treatments, for example goodwill written down in the books will be reinstated under EVA.

The model is calculated as follows:

$$EVA = Profit - (Net\ capital \times Cost\ of\ capital)$$

It is supplemented by market value added (MVA), which reflects the spread between the capital invested in the company and the market value of the business:

$$MVA = Discounted\ value\ of\ future\ EVA$$

where:

1 returns are expressed as the percentage of net operating profits, after cash taxes, to the economic book value of the assets employed in the operations of the business.

2 equity capital is calculated in accordance with the capital asset pricing model in order to take account of risk in the weighted average cost of debt and equity capital.

Companies using this methodology include Lucas Varity and Burton in the UK and Coca-Cola in the USA, with Roberto Giozueta, former Coca-Cola CEO, quoted by Paul Nichols in his article 'Unlocking shareholder value' as saying:

> *I get paid to make the owners of the company increasingly wealthy with each passing day. Everything else is just fluff.*[4]

Cashflow return on investment (CFROI)

Promoted originally by the Boston Consulting Group and HOLT Value Associates, CFROI is popular in the UK as it values performance using similar methods to those traditionally used in evaluating individual items of investment.

It compares future cashflows to the weighted average cost of capital, either as a sum of money or as an internal rate of return. Calculations vary, but they all strive to compare inflation-adjusted cashflows to inflation-adjusted gross investments to find CFROI. Generally, a distinction is made between replacement capital, which is regarded as negative cashflow like normal expenses, and growth capital, which is seen as genuine investment.

Cash value added (CVA™)[5]

Developed and trademarked by Swedish consultants FWC AB, this model has similarities to CFROI as it also starts with cashflow and makes a distinction between strategic and book investments. The premise is:

> *If the average discounted CVA index over 5 years = or > 1,*
> *then value is being created*

where:

1. operating cashflow demand (OCFD) = annual cashflow amounts, growing by the assumed rate of inflation to yield an IRR equal to WACC on the original investment.
2. the CVA index equals the present value (PV) of the operating cashflow divided by the PV of the OCFD.

3.4 EVA EXAMPLE

Traditional statements

(i) Profit and Loss Account	Company A £mn	Company B £mn
Turnover	635	266
Operating expenditure including depreciation	(399)	(117)
Interest	(32)	(10)
Tax	(22)	(23)
Dividends	(76)	(53)
Retained profit	106	63

	Company A £mn	Company B £mn
(ii) Balance sheet		
Fixed assets	2453	1169
Current assets	274	56
Current liabilities	(381)	(278)
Long-term liabilities	(692)	(101)
Long-term creditors and provisions	(236)	(33)
	1418	813
Shareholders' funds	1418	813

(iii) Notes

- Current assets include cash of £146mn (Co A) and £1mn (Co B).
- Current liabilities include short-term loans of £27mn (Co A) and £72mn (Co B).

Economic value added statements (assuming 8% Cost of capital)

$$EVA = Profit - (Net\ capital \times Cost\ of\ capital)$$

	Company A £mn	Company B £mn
(i) Net capital × Cost of capital		
Cash	(146)	(1)
Short-term loans	27	72
Long-term liabilities	692	101
Net capital	1991	985
× Cost of capital (8%)	159	79

(ii) EVA statements	Company A £mn	Company B £mn
Turnover	635	266
Operating expenditure includes deprec.	(399)	(117)
Tax	(22)	(23)
Profit before interest	236	149
Net capital × Cost of capital (8%)	(159)	(79)
Economic value added (EVA)	55	47
Compared to retained profit	106	63

3.5 EMBEDDED VBM

Value-based management is a comprehensive approach to managing a company to maximise total shareholder returns over time. It involves focusing all levels of the organisation on creating value in the commercial marketplace through identifying appropriate drivers and incorporating into a clear strategy, thereby realising value in the capital marketplace. It is based on the following logic:

- Publicly traded companies are in business to create wealth for shareholders.
- Creating wealth for shareholders is the key to protecting the interests of all stakeholders, e.g. employees, consumers, community, government, regulators.
- Market value is determined by investors' expectations of future cashflows.
- The ability to generate positive cashflows over time depends on profitability and growth.

While most companies are now responding to this pressure by using shareholder value analysis to drive strategic decision making and using the shareholder value calculations to determine the overall value creation of their strategic business units, few are linking this into the operational levels of the business. It is necessary to change the mindset of employees to understanding what long-term value creation means for them in the language they speak within their business units. Value is created at the point where decisions are made, and in the 'bottom-up empowered' organisation that we discussed in Chapter 1, that is at middle management level or below.

Embedding VBM principles into the business, so that all decision making is based on it, is the goal. This requires detailed activity/process-based information/models on the operations of the business, in addition to the need to integrate management processes, as shown in Fig. 3.1, VBM integrates management processes. This figure demonstrates the importance of aligning corporate governance, organisational structure, strategy, planning and budgeting, performance management and employee compensation. Linking employee compensation to value creation, rather than to accounting results or budget negotiations, is crucial for the success of the embedding process. An embedded VBM system driven by the transformed finance function will make the shift from scorekeeping to true business partner. The value created by each part of the business will become transparent, with project evaluation using value-based techniques rather than discounted cashflow (DCF), each business unit becoming a value-generating centre with targets for each value driver.

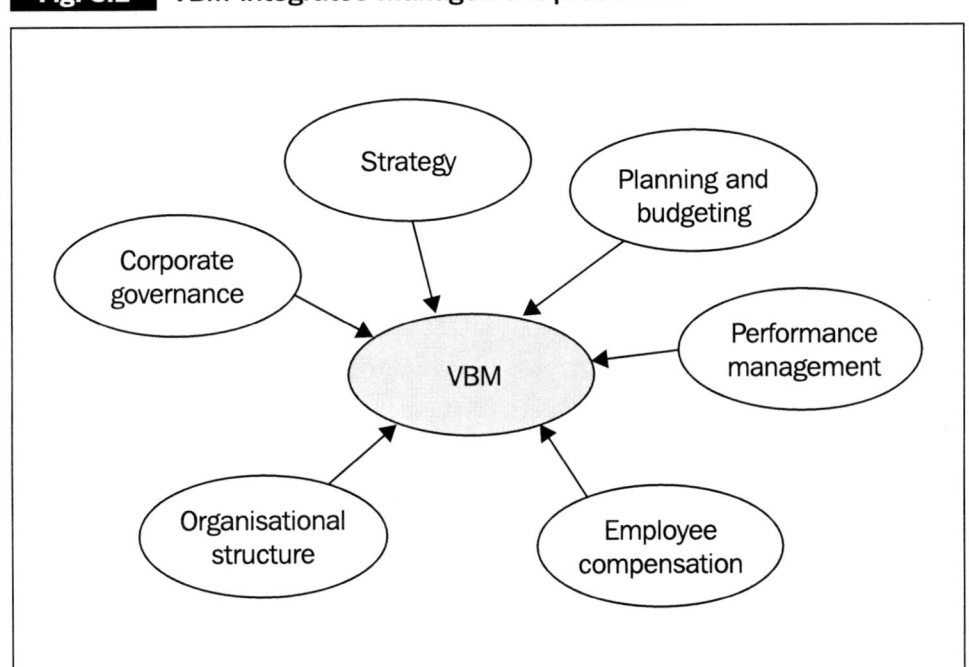

Fig. 3.1 VBM integrates management processes

[Diagram: Six ovals labeled "Corporate governance", "Strategy", "Planning and budgeting", "Performance management", "Employee compensation", and "Organisational structure" all pointing to a central oval labeled "VBM".]

3.6 INTER-BUSINESS UNIT CHARGING

Introduction

In organisations that have recognised the need to be service oriented and customer facing, the creation of business units that operate as autonomous profit centres is becoming the norm, particularly where value-based management principles have been adopted. This necessitates trading between all organisational business units, both operational and support. The setting of inter-business unit charges from support business units, such as IT and finance, requires the drawing up of service-level agreements between the supplier business support unit and the customer business units.

Service-level agreements (SLAs)

The concept of SLAs has been used by many IT departments for several years, particularly if the services have been outsourced. Similarly, the public sector has been accustomed to market testing and Compulsory Competitive Tendering over the last decade. The methodology behind setting SLAs is to use activity-based techniques, discussed in Chapter 5, to analyse the current level of service being provided and alternative levels that could be provided, in addition to the current cost of the provision, and to negotiate with customers an appropriate level of service at an agreed selling price, in the same way as you would with an external supplier. It would be reasonable within such a process for customers to obtain outside competitive quotes, if a similar service were available, to benchmark the competitiveness of the internal business unit service.

Setting 'ground rules'

A note of caution in setting these inter-business unit trading situations: it is essential that 'ground rules' be set by the organisation before negotiations commence. For example:

- It may not be feasible to allow business units to buy from an outside supplier in preference to the internal supplier, particularly in the short term.
- There will need to be rules that ensure that each business unit is not allowed to optimise its own results or profitability at the expense of other business units and/or the organisation as a whole.

If remuneration for business unit staff is linked to performance, which would be the norm under VBM, then great care must be taken with the setting of those incentives, because performance measures drive behaviour.

3.7 RISK MANAGEMENT

Introduction

If the transformed finance function is to be the driver of shareholder value throughout the business, then it must re-evaluate the way in which the organisation manages its risk. Addressing financial risk alone is no longer sufficient; a comprehensive approach to managing technical, commercial, operational, strategic and financial risk needs to be adopted by the company and facilitated by the finance function.

High-profile examples of failure to evaluate risk fully are available, such as Barings Bank where an employee was sent to prison, and Hoover's infamous 'Free flights to the USA' promotion, available to anyone who bought a new Hoover vacuum cleaner. The risk involved in offering a promotion worth at least four times the value of the goods sold was not picked up and dealt with effectively by the company's risk-management strategy and this did indeed bring dire consequences to the company, its executives and staff, despite the organisation's leading brand position. In hindsight it is easy to see the errors – but how many organisations can confidently reassure their shareholders that their risk-management strategy effectively manages the risk inherent in all their business processes?

In addition to controlling risk within the organisation, risk factors outside the control of the company need to be evaluated and incorporated into the decision-making process. Such external influences will include environmental and political issues outside the control of the company but significantly affecting it. Recent examples affecting most companies include the introduction of the euro, and the Millennium bug. An example of a specific company being hit by an environmental issue outside its control was Greenpeace's reaction and subsequent campaign regarding Shell's decision on how to dispose of an oil platform. Another environmental example would be Yorkshire Water's well-publicised problems with maintaining continuous water supplies during a summer drought. The key to maintaining shareholder confidence appears to lie in how well such situations are handled when they do occur.

The requirement is to develop comprehensive company-wide processes and policies for identifying, understanding, assessing and mitigating risk. Taking risks is a part of every organisation's normal activities, but the greater the risk, the greater the rewards, and that is recognised by shareholders in their investment portfolios. The risk-management system needs to offer assurances that controls are in place to assess significant risk and highlight strategic opportunities.

The case for integrated risk management

Traditionally, each area of risk has been dealt with independently within its own department, for example:

- treasury risks concerning exchange rates and investments
- credit risks controlled by sales ledger
- supplier risks by procurement
- insurable risks, e.g. property, employee liability
- product risks dealt with by marketing or product managers
- customer risks dealt with by the sales and account managers
- HR dealing with employment practices such as succession planning

- contractual risks dealt with by legal
- risks involved in mergers, acquisitions and other strategic decisions dealt with by strategic planning
- operations dealing with technical and health and safety risks
- IT preparing disaster-recovery contingencies and controlling system security
- change programmes dealt with project by project.

This approach is susceptible to large areas of risks not being monitored at all, either because they fall between two departments or because a misunderstanding of responsibility has occurred. Equally, the knock-on effect from one risk to another is evident in the Hoover example quoted above: a problem arose originally in offering an unsustainable promotion, but this was compounded many times over in the multitude of errors made in the handling of the problems created. This illustrates the links between risks and is further evidence of the need to adopt a holistic approach. The global, fast-moving environment of today's larger organisations, with their commercially aware shareholders, demands a different approach to risk management. In consequence, this issue has moved up the corporate agenda and become a key measure within corporate balanced scorecards.

With the drive to ever greater cost savings and increased profits year on year, the question of balance between product quality and costs of production raises questions about the risks involved in cutting corners, which ultimately must be tackled in the boardroom.

Building integrated risk management

- Assimilate information regarding the existing recognition of risk, which department takes responsibility for it and how it is assessed and mitigated.
- Collect information on historical risk problems that the company has suffered and categorise these in terms of their business impact.
- Reinforce the message throughout the company of the importance of the risk profile and the need to integrate and monitor it more closely, stressing its links to creating shareholder value.
- Set up a risk-management group, comprising the main departmental risk managers around the business.
- Evaluate existing departmental risk management and categorise materiality, identify gaps, shortcomings, inter-relationships, management strategies and improvements from a holistic viewpoint. Build new models and scenarios, linking these where possible to shareholder value calculations. This should ensure that softer risk factors linked to staff behaviour, like ineffective change management or succession planning, are considered equally alongside the more tangible risk factors such as exchange-rate losses and interest-rate changes.

- Determine and clearly set out your corporate risk strategy in a way that everyone in the organisation can understand. Document policies and procedures and train employees to 'evaluate risk' in everything they do.
- Build risk performance-measurement systems and controls to underpin the balanced scorecard's key performance indicators.
- Monitor and evaluate on a regular basis, using benchmarks, wherever practicable.

CASE STUDY

Value-based management at British Aerospace[6]

Background

British Aerospace is Europe's largest aerospace and defence company, with some 48 000 employees at the end of 1998. Turnover in 1998 was £8.6bn, with 89% of sales generated overseas, making British Aerospace the UK's leading exporter. The order book at the end of the year was over £28bn. British Aerospace has two key fields of operations: the global defence market and the commercial aerospace market.

Following a difficult period in the early 1990s that saw the share price fall to below £1, British Aerospace has undergone significant change through the disposal of non-core businesses and its role in the consolidation of aerospace and defence companies, both in Europe and internationally. The share price increased over twentyfold and the company has been working on a corporate change programme shaping the business through concentration on five values.

VBM at BAe

This programme includes the implementation of value-based management, a methodology that helps identify and set priorities for the company and ensures that the actions taken to address these priorities are those that will bring the greatest benefit.

The objectives for VBM at British Aerospace include:

- aligning internal objectives to *value creation*
- understanding where and how *value* is created
- driving improvements in *operating performance* at all levels in the business
- measuring the *important* and stop measuring the *unimportant*.

VBM can be defined as a way of linking business goals and managerial decisions to their impact on shareholder value. This process of managing the business for value provides the following benefits:

- It sets the agenda for management action through identification of a handful of key performance indicators.
- It creates a common language and objective across the group.
- It can be cascaded throughout the organisation.
- It focuses all staff on valuable tasks and highlights unproductive activities.

- It acts as an umbrella framework for other initiatives.
- It assigns priorities to the allocation of capital and resources.
- It motivates employees through incentives driven by value creation.

In the words of the Chief Executive of British Aerospace:

> *VBM methodology is fundamental to the setting of priorities in our business and ensuring that our actions are driven by value creation.*

Implementation at Regional Aircraft

VBM was trialed in the Regional Aircraft business unit at Woodford, part of BAe Commercial Aerospace, which produces the Avro RJ range of regional jet aircraft. Other Regional Aircraft activities comprise Jetstream engineering support and customer-training operations at Prestwick in Scotland, marketing of the Avro RJ and customer support for the Avro RJ, BAe 146 and Jetstream range of aircraft, both centred at Toulouse in France. The main spares distribution centre is at Weybridge, and there are marketing, customer support and spares centres in Washington, USA and Sydney, Australia. Other activities include a complete range of support capabilities, including Jetspares, aircraft maintenance and refurbishment, aircraft flight testing, engineering test facilities, customer training, specialised design services, paint finishing, information services operation, aircraft cabin crew emergency training and airport firefighter training.

An initial VBM pilot was in Avrotec, the aircraft maintenance and refurbishment business. This project ran from February to May 1997 and proved very successful, turning around a £0.5mn loss into a £2mn profit. Application of the VBM process involved an understanding of the relationship between cashflow and the Avrotec operations and the setting of key performance indicators to ensure focus on those drivers. Through a four-month rigorous process, the KPIs were identified from a combination of value driver chains and sensitivity analysis using a VBM spreadsheet model, simulating cash generation at an operational level. Attention was focused on those drivers yielding the greatest efficiency in the labour and parts process.

Following this success, attention was turned to the Regional Jet assembly process and this second VBM project ran from September to December 1997. This resulted in fewer than ten KPIs being identified and prioritised, replacing the previous 250 performance measures that were reduced to monitor status or dropped completely. This was another success story, realising efficiencies in such indirect areas as engineering change and logistics, which resulted in attention being turned to a third Regional Aircraft business, Jetspares.

The Jetspares business

Jetspares is a £20mn business, which provides a service for airlines flying the Regional Jet and 146 aircraft used, for example, in the Queen's Flight. This service provides spares and repairs as and when needed and is charged for on a 'rate per hour flown' basis. The process, which can be seen in Fig. 3.2, Jetspares, involves Jetspares holding stocks of parts in a large warehouse and a smaller number of parts at customer sites. When a part needs to be replaced, it is returned to the warehouse and a new part is immediately despatched; the worn part is refurbished and returned into store.

Fig. 3.2   BAe – Jetspares

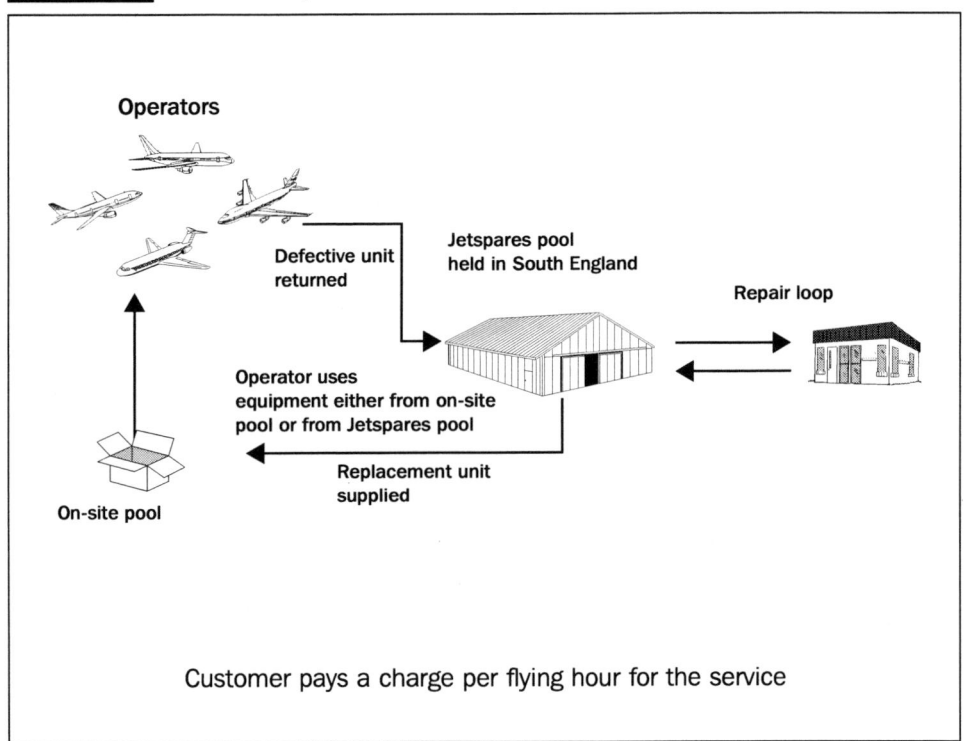

Customer pays a charge per flying hour for the service

The key steps followed within the VBM process were as follows:

1 Team interviews were conducted.
2 Financial analysis was carried out.
3 Value drivers were mapped, heavily linked to cash. Figure 3.3, Value driver map yielding performance indicators, illustrates this.
4 The VBM economic model was constructed.
5 Five KPIs were identified and respective targets set by the management team.

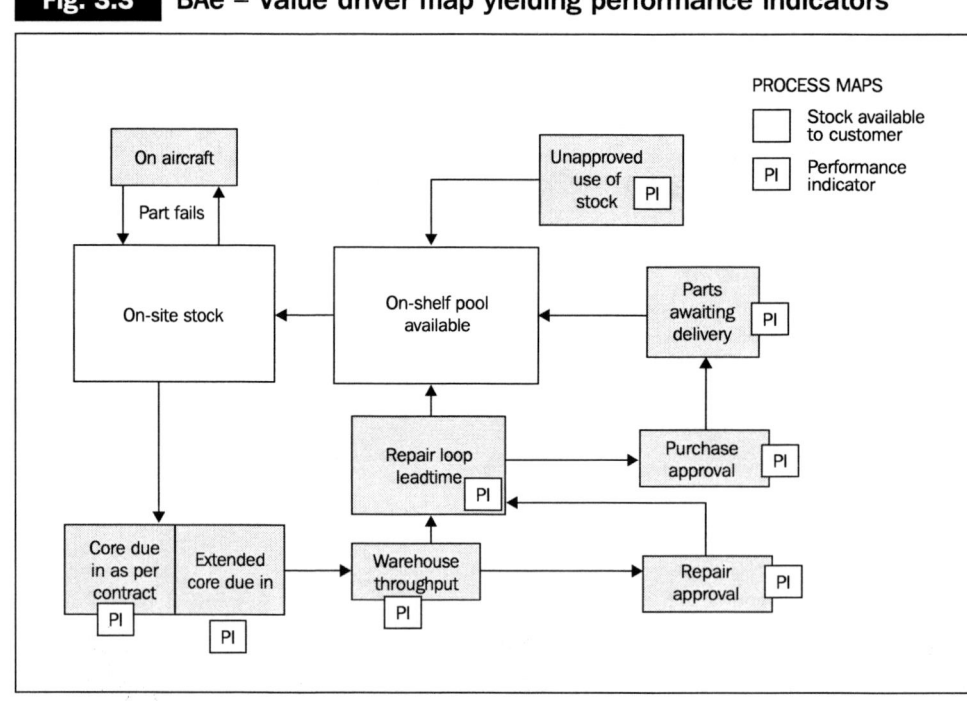

Fig. 3.3 BAe – Value driver map yielding performance indicators

The top five KPIs were selected from ten performance indicators, as seen in Fig. 3.4, Value impact of a 1% movement in top 10 KPIs. These were as follows:

- Jetspares sales rates
- reliability in terms of average time duration between failure of parts
- average repair cost per transaction
- purchase price reduction index
- repair turnaround time for defective parts.

Fig 3.4 BAe – Value impact of a 1% movement in top 10 KPIs

Figure 3.5, Characteristics of KPIs, clearly shows the characteristics that are sought in VBM KPIs, as follows:

- large impact
- controllable
- measurable
- linked to cash.

Figure 3.6, Identification of KPIs, illustrates how KPIs must be assigned priorities to determine where management's focus should be in identifying the main KPIs on which to concentrate. Figure 3.7, The initial management view of moveability on KPIs, shows that over a seven-year period the VBM study identified significant additional value for Jetspares, shown in Fig. 3.8, Potential value creation. Improving a KPI such as reliability of aircraft parts by just 1% will mean a cash saving in repair bills alone of almost £2mn over the life of the product.

Fig. 3.5 BAe – Characteristics of KPIs

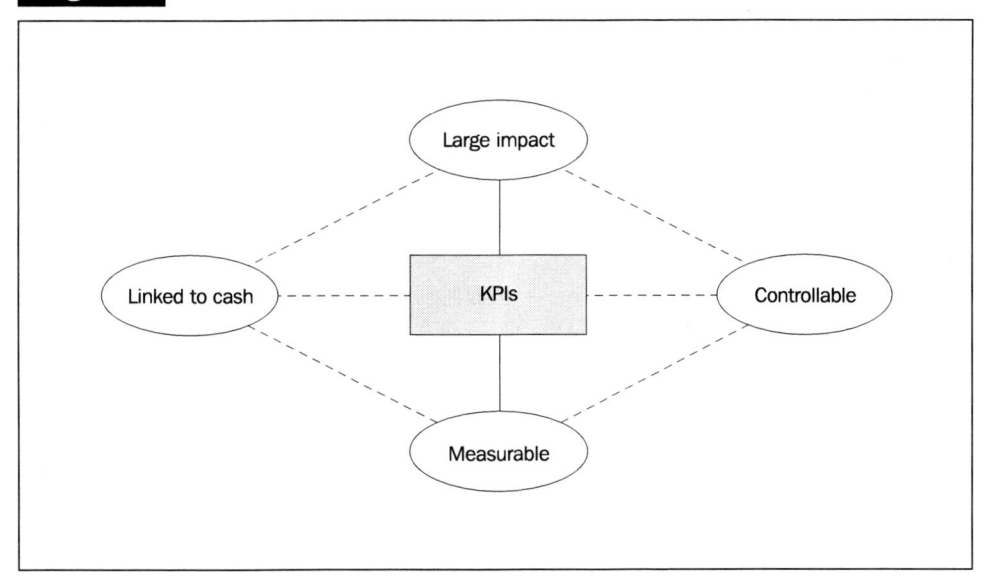

Fig. 3.6 BAe – Identification of KPIs

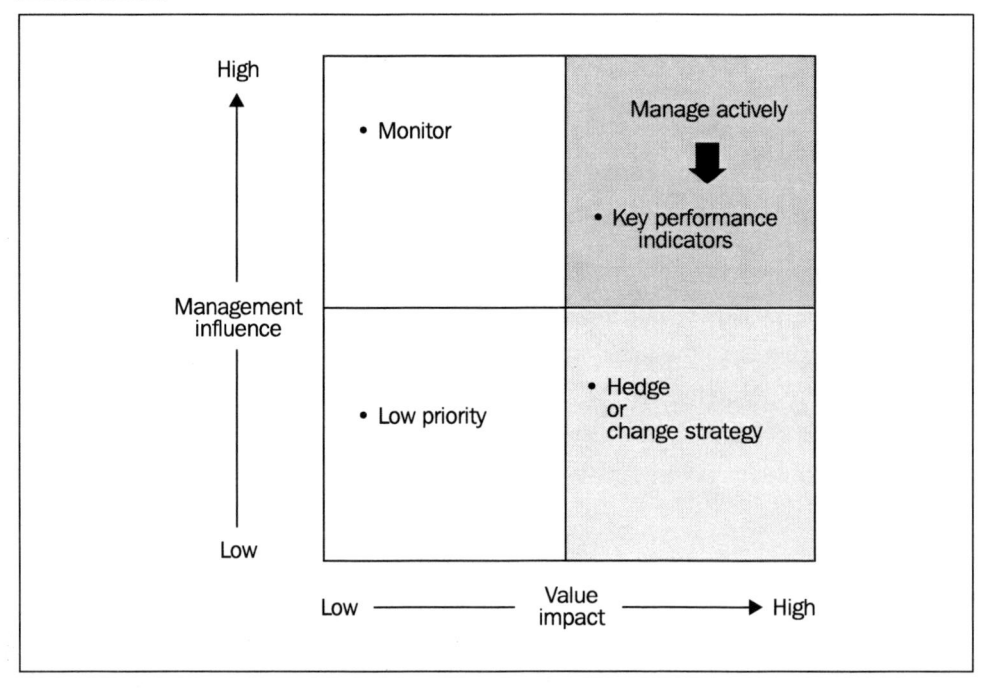

A 2x2 matrix with axes "Management influence" (Low to High) and "Value impact" (Low to High):
- Top-left: Monitor
- Top-right: Manage actively — Key performance indicators
- Bottom-left: Low priority
- Bottom-right: Hedge or change strategy

It was realised that prior to the VBM project, increases in sales were in fact destroying value; the business was operating at an economic loss. Improvements were made immediately to several processes, including working capital, reduction of stock levels per aircraft as volumes increased, and realignment of sales incentives towards cash and away from the traditional volume measures.

Fig. 3.7 BAe – The initial management view of moveability on KPIs

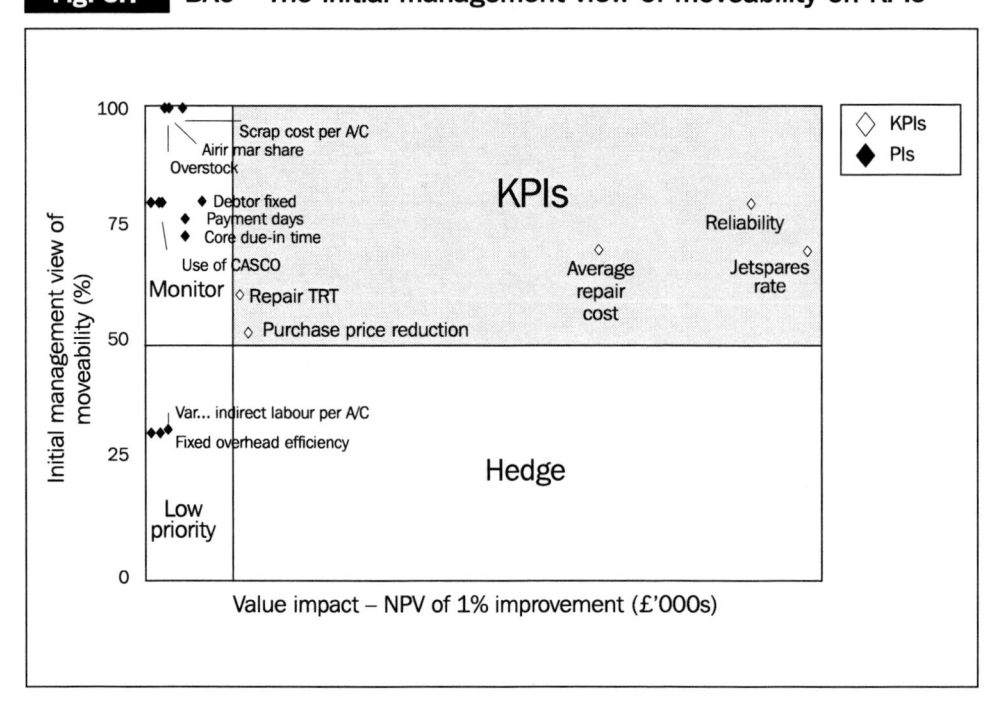

Scatter plot with Y-axis "Initial management view of moveability (%)" (0 to 100) and X-axis "Value impact – NPV of 1% improvement (£'000s)". Legend: ◇ KPIs, ◆ PIs.

Upper region (Monitor / KPIs):
- Scrap cost per A/C
- Airir mar share
- Overstock
- Debtor fixed
- Payment days
- Core due-in time
- Use of CASCO
- Repair TRT
- Purchase price reduction
- Average repair cost
- Reliability
- Jetspares rate

Lower region (Low priority / Hedge):
- Var... indirect labour per A/C
- Fixed overhead efficiency

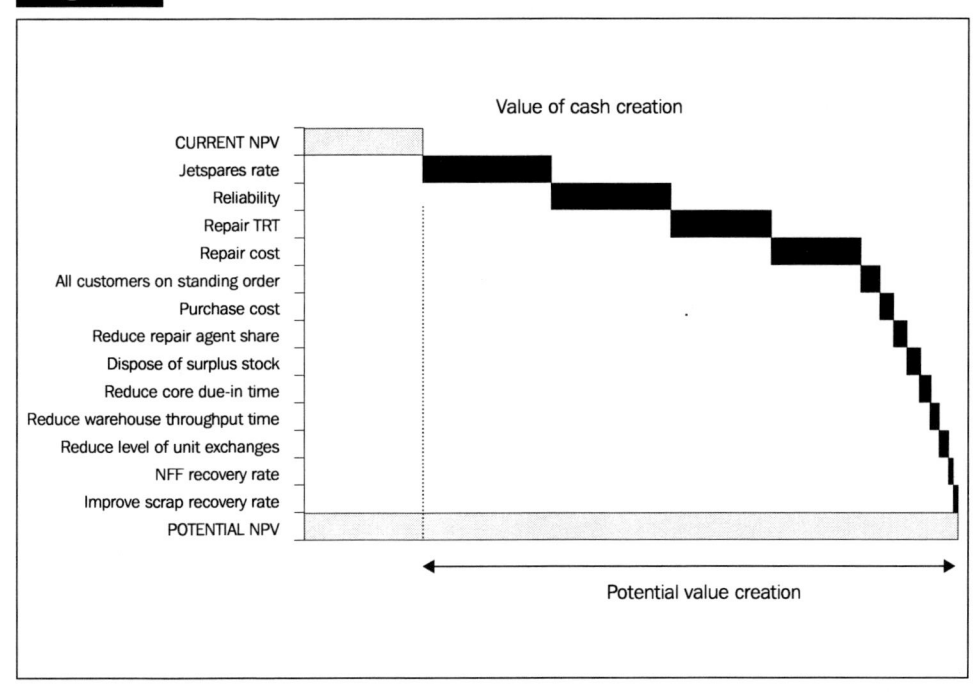

Fig. 3.8   BAe – Potential value creation

Chart showing value of cash creation with bars for:
- CURRENT NPV
- Jetspares rate
- Reliability
- Repair TRT
- Repair cost
- All customers on standing order
- Purchase cost
- Reduce repair agent share
- Dispose of surplus stock
- Reduce core due-in time
- Reduce warehouse throughput time
- Reduce level of unit exchanges
- NFF recovery rate
- Improve scrap recovery rate
- POTENTIAL NPV

With arrow indicating Potential value creation

The future

This success story proved a milestone for Regional Aircraft and encourages three further projects to be started in 1999 covering:

- sales and marketing
- purchasing and bill of materials process
- spares.

These are all being managed internally by Tony Bryan, VBM Executive for Regional Aircraft, with teams of three to four people on each project. At the same time, a series of six training modules has been developed aimed at a range of people, from team leaders participating in the project to specialist trainer training for the implementors. These training modules cover the two phases of the VBM programme:

- Phase I – Identifying KPIs in the businesses. Taking from four to six months.
- Phase II – Aligning all core management processes to KPIs, for example the reporting, budgeting and planning processes. This phase is expected to take between 12 and 36 months to complete, and is effectively a change-management programme requiring a change in behaviours and the way in which decisions are made.

The success in Regional Aircraft is mirrored across British Aerospace, with VBM implementation progressing in all its key businesses. VBM is providing valuable insights into all aspects of the business, including contract negotiations, bidding and estimating for new business, project tracking and management, manufacturing efficiency and working capital management.

VBM is a priority action for British Aerospace helping to deliver long-term sustainable growth in value for its customers, employees and shareholders.

4

Balanced scorecard

- 4.1 Introduction 53
- 4.2 Measures that drive performance 53
- 4.3 Weighting the balanced scorecard 54
- 4.4 The ten commandments of implementation 56
- 4.5 Key learning points of best practice 57
- 4.6 Links to quality frameworks 58
- 4.7 Case study – Eurotunnel 61
- 4.8 Case study – Manchester Council Housing Department's information strategy 61

4.1 INTRODUCTION

As we can see from Fig. 2.2, Integrated performance management (p.26), it is not sufficient for an organisation to decide to adopt a value-based strategy, determining what its value drivers are and what strategy outcomes are required to deliver the desired shareholder value. It is essential that it adopts a company-wide performance-management framework that monitors and, thereby, ensures that the necessary targets are achieved or deviations accounted for. At the top of this framework of measures, organisations are increasingly utilising the tool designed by Kaplan and Norton known as the 'balanced scorecard'.[1]

4.2 MEASURES THAT DRIVE PERFORMANCE

During a year-long research project with 12 companies at the leading edge of performance management, Kaplan and Norton designed a set of measures that gave top managers a fast but comprehensive view of the business. They likened it to the dials and indicators of an aeroplane cockpit – the task of navigating and flying an aeroplane requires detailed information about fuel, air speed, altitude, bearings, destination and much more, and to fly without this information would be easily recognised as dangerous to everyone aboard. Similarly, a business that attempts to manage its complex operations with just a few measures, traditionally financial, cannot hope to be in total control or be sure of making the right decisions to meet its objectives. The balanced scorecard encourages managers to look at their business from at least four different perspectives:

1. The financial perspective – How do we look to shareholders?
2. The customer perspective – How do customers see us?
3. The internal business perspective – What must we excel at?
4. The innovation and learning perspective – Can we continue to improve and create value?

Figure 4.1, The balanced scorecard, shows how to link the corporate vision to critical success factors or outcomes and key performance indicators, representing all perspectives of the business. Most companies have large amounts of information or data, usually in a form that is too detailed for senior managers to have time to digest. The idea at this level is to limit the number of measures to a minimum to ensure that the senior management team (SMT) concentrates on the achievement of the strategic goals. The 'balance' refers to balancing tension between the traditional financial and non-financial, operational, leading and lagging, and action-oriented and monitoring measures. It has the advantages of:

- bringing together in one report many of the seemingly disparate elements of the company's agenda
- guarding against suboptimisation, by forcing senior management to consider all of the measures together and ensuring that one objective is not achieved at the expense of another.

Fig. 4.1 The balanced scorecard

Financial
How do we look to our stakeholders?
e.g. profit, growth, market share, profit/employee

Customer
How do our customers see us?
e.g. price, responsiveness, product returns

Vision

Learning/innovation
Can we continue to improve and create value?
e.g. no. of skills/employee, revenue/employee, innovations

Internal business
What must we excel at?
e.g. cycle time, yield, cost/transaction

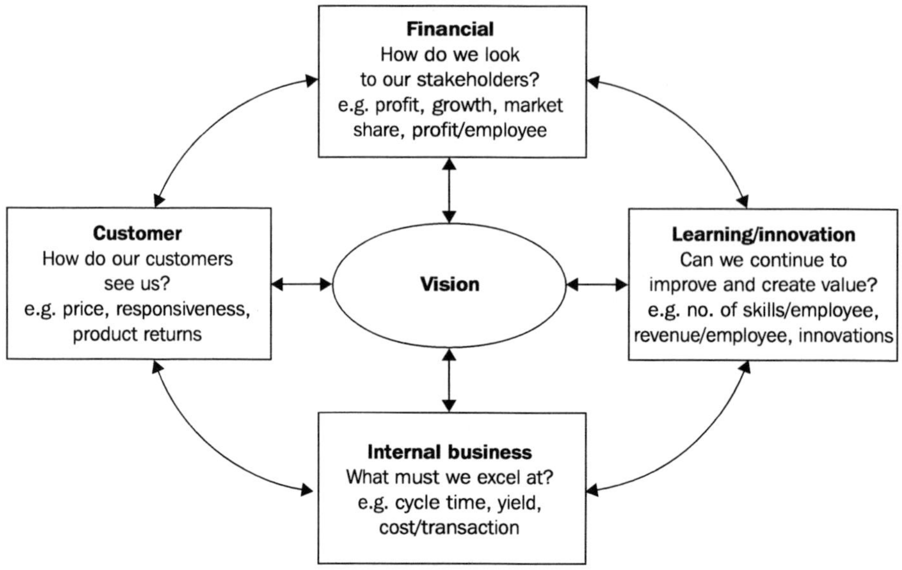

Shift from financials only to a broader set of performance measures

This can help to overcome the 'silo mentality' tendencies of some senior managers, who have traditionally pursued the objectives of their department irrespective of the effects and often to the detriment of the rest of the company. The SMT is forced to operate as a team, balancing the competing objectives to achieve the optimum result for the company as a whole.

The balanced scorecard fits in well with the 'bottom-up empowered' organisation, putting strategy and organisation, not control, at the centre. It establishes goals but assumes that people will adopt whatever behaviours and take whatever actions are necessary to arrive at those goals. The measures are designed to pull people towards the overall vision and care must be taken in setting those measures, because performance measures drive behaviour.

4.3 WEIGHTING THE BALANCED SCORECARD

The scores applied to different parts of the balanced scorecard will vary according to the importance of that measure to the overall vision. The importance placed on different measures can often vary year on year, as the emphasis changes in the achievement of goals. Weightings are commonly applied on the balanced scorecards used in managing outsourcing contracts.

Example of a weighted balanced scorecard for outsourcing the finance function

The scorecard criteria

- Provide company runs the finance company on behalf of source company for an annual fee of costs plus a margin.
- The annual budgeted amount for 1996/7 of £750 000 fee is subject to a 'risk/reward margin' based on a balanced scorecard score comprised as follows:
  - financial perspective: overall costs of running the service 30%
  - customer perspective: satisfaction of functional user groups 25%
  - business perspective: satisfaction of internal management interface 25%
  - innovation: number of process/system improvements 20%

% Margin	% Score
25	100
20	80
15	60
10	40
5	20
1	0

Score ratings agreed as follows:

Points rating	Costs incurred (£k)	Number of innovations	User/management
5	650	3	10
4	700	2	8
3	750	1.5	6
2	800	1	4
1	850	0.5	2
0	900	0	0

Annual results and scores

Measure	Value (£k)	Points	Weighting (%)	Result
Costs incurred	800	2	30	0.6
Number of innovations	1	2	20	0.4
User satisfaction rating	8	4	25	1.0
Management satisfaction	6	3	25	0.75
				2.75

Margin calculation

- 2.75 as a percentage of maximum 5 = 55%.
- 55% score equates to 13.75% margin of £750 000 planned costs = £103 125 risk/reward margin earned on the contract.

NB: Actual costs of £800 000 not used, as that would encourage higher costs!

4.4 THE TEN COMMANDMENTS OF IMPLEMENTATION

Research was carried out in Europe in 1996 by Professor Lewy of Amsterdam and Lex du Mee of KPMG,[2] using seven European companies as case studies, which resulted in findings known as the 'ten commandments of balanced scorecard implementation'. The objective was to try to understand the mixed success of the application of this simple, common-sense concept of using a balanced set of performance indicators to run an organisation. The ten commandments to be followed for successful implementation were concluded to be:

The dos

1 Use the scorecard as an implementation pad for strategic goals.

2 Ensure that strategic goals are in place before the scorecard is implemented.

3 Ensure that a top-level (non-financial) sponsor backs the scorecard and that line managers are committed to the project.

4 Implement a pilot before introducing the new scorecard.

5 Carry out an 'entry review' for each business unit before implementing the scorecard.

The do nots

6   Use the scorecard to obtain extra top-down control.

7   Attempt to standardise the project. The scorecard must be tailormade.

8   Underestimate the need for training and communication in using the scorecard.

9   Seek complexity nor strive for perfection.

10 Underestimate the extra administrative workload and costs of periodic scorecard reporting.

And when you add the eleventh commandment of

11 Do not start implementing a balanced scorecard unless you know what you hope to achieve

it makes good, sound advice that could be applied to almost any project undertaken by an organisation.

4.5 KEY LEARNING POINTS OF BEST PRACTICE

Research due to be published in full in 1999, sponsored by CIMA Research Foundation and undertaken by the University of Leeds, entitled 'Shareholder and stakeholder approaches to strategic performance measurement using the balanced scorecard',[3] has focused on 500 UK organisations in both the private and public sector. It lists key learning points for managers involved in balanced scorecard design and implementation, as follows:

Link the scorecard and content to strategy

Many scorecards are purely operational monitoring tools. Scorecards should be aligned with clear strategic objectives.

Link the scorecard to change initiatives and project evaluations

Scorecards should be used explicitly to track the effects of change programmes within the organisation.

Link the scorecard to stakeholder expectations

In the private sector shareholder interests dominate. In the public sector there often exists a complex network of stakeholders. Scorecards need to reflect stakeholder expectations.

Understand the logic of value creation

The scorecard should tell a comprehensive 'narrative' of how value is created in the organisation.

Understand end-user expectations

Scorecard design requirements are different for executive teams than for operational departments. There is a limit to the benefits of aggregation of scorecard measures up organisational hierarchies.

Link to the external competitive environment

There is a danger of making scorecards introspective. To be strategic, scorecards must be linked to monitoring discontinuities in external competitive environments.

Never believe that the numbers are more important than the issues

Numerical values of reported performance indicators are less important than the agenda for debate that they generate.

Customise the scorecard design

Best-practice organisations customise their scorecards. In some cases these become unrecognisable as scorecards.

Implementation: champion and consult

Scorecard implementation needs a senior champion or sponsor. Success is dependent on wide consultation.

Day-to-day usage: encouraging congruence

The perceived benefits of scorecard usage should encourage congruent behaviour, which may be formalised in the linkage to appraisal and remuneration.

4.6 LINKS TO QUALITY FRAMEWORKS

The Malcolm Baldrige measurement and management framework was developed in the USA in 1987, for the purpose of recognising companies that are leaders in providing increased quality and value to their customers in an internationally competitive era. Funded by the European Commission, the European Foundation for Quality Management's Business Excellence Framework was launched in 1992, with the purpose of raising the level of competitiveness throughout Europe by the identification of role-model companies and the disseminating of best practice.

Although not designed to assist implementation of strategy, these quality award frameworks are a way for companies to identify key processes. Figure 4.2, EFQM Business Excellence model, uses nine elements to assess an organisation's success against award criteria specifically with reference to quality, while Fig. 4.3, the Malcolm Baldrige National Quality Award similarly has seven award criteria.

Fig. 4.2 EFQM Business Excellence model

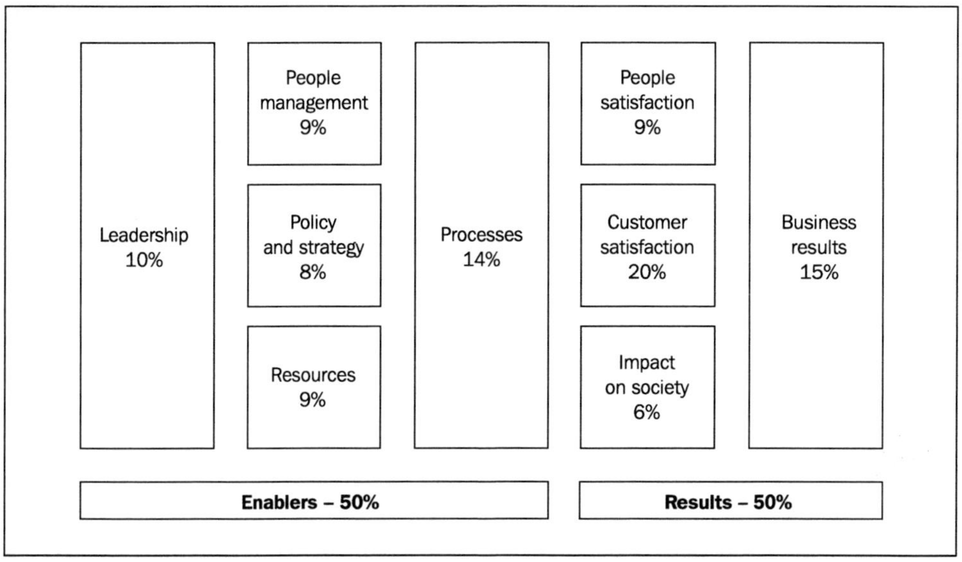

Fig 4.3 The Malcolm Baldrige National Quality Awards

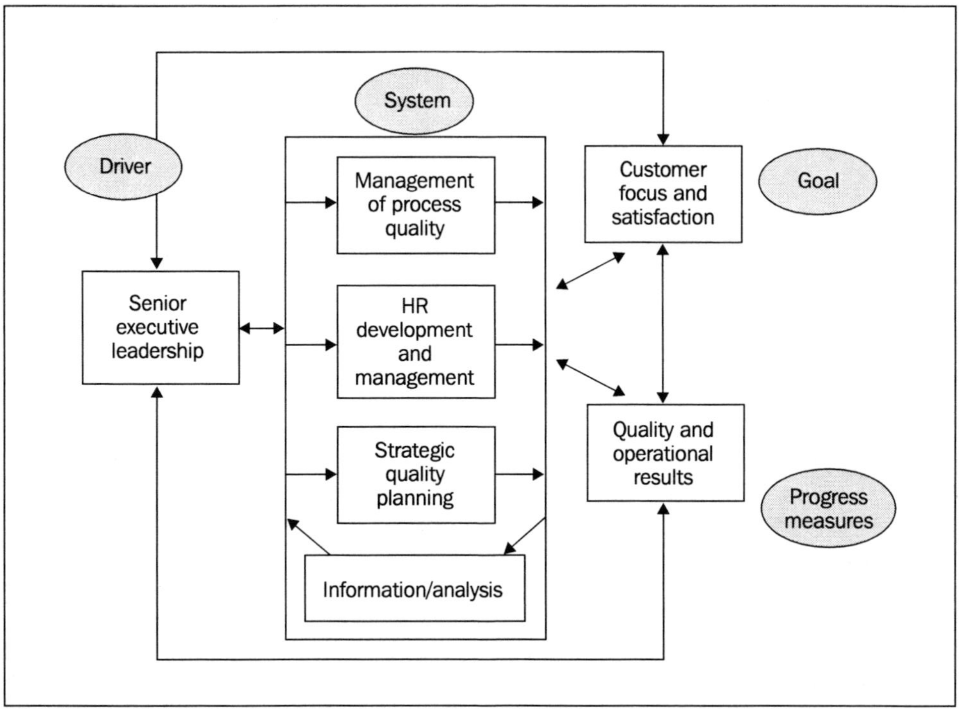

The key elements of each model are as follows:

EFQM

Enablers

		Scoring (%)
(i)	Leadership	10
(ii)	People management	9
(iii)	Policy and strategy	8
(iv)	Resources	9
(v)	Processes	14
		50

Results

		Scoring (%)
(vi)	People satisfaction	9
(vii)	Customer satisfaction	20
(viii)	Impact on society	20
(ix)	Business results	15
		50

Malcolm Baldrige

		Scoring (points)
i	Leadership	95
ii	Information analysis	75
iii	Strategic quality planning	60
iv	Human resource development and management	150
v	Management of the quality process	140
vi	Quality and operational results	180
vii	Customer focus and satisfaction	300
		1000

Because of the detail and focus of these quality models, there is considerable merit in linking this detail to both balanced scorecards and/or activity-based management systems. This has been successfully achieved in several companies, British Telecom for example, and will become widespread under the auspices of Best Value, with many local authority organisations, like the police, already using EFQM.

CASE STUDY
Eurotunnel

Eurotunnel's Technical Division adopted the balanced scorecard approach in 1997, reports Carolyn Fry in an *Accountancy Age* article, 'Rail renaissance'.[4] Improved productivity, fewer delays and greater staff satisfaction have been the result. A 'change team' supported by consultants helped set up the scorecard as part of a major financial restructuring. Eurotunnel had started life as a tunnel-building project and needed to move fast to become a business-oriented company.

The team's first move towards implementing the balanced scorecard was to work out Eurotunnel's objectives. These broadly covered four areas: financial targets, the performance of the railway, customer satisfaction, and staff satisfaction. It then broke each area down into sets of 'key performance indicators'. Examples of financial indicators include yield, capital expenditure and duty-free sales; railway performance indicators include the interval between trains, transit times, the number of stops in the tunnel, and the mean time between breakdowns. The team had to translate the KPI into targets that related to individual staff. In effect, the scorecard system they created was a 'tree of objectives', with the overall company aims at the top. At the very top, the team added a 'dashboard' to show if performance in any area was falling behind.

CASE STUDY
Manchester Council Housing Department's information strategy[5]

Manchester's vision and objectives
Manchester City Council's corporate aims and objectives give the city a clear, focused and realistic vision for the future. They are placed firmly in a 'Best Value' framework to develop and deliver services and to define the city's role in the national and regional context. They describe how the city's future will be secured. Together, the corporate strategies are delivering the vision of Manchester as:

- a European regional capital – a centre for investment and growth
- an international city of outstanding commercial, cultural and creative potential
- an area distinguished by the quality of life and sense of well-being enjoyed by its residents
- an area where all residents have the opportunity to participate – making their communities truly sustainable.

The City Council's wider economic, environmental and social strategies consolidate the corporate housing strategy, ensuring responsiveness and adaptation to local needs. This approach is essential to deliver coordinated services and create places where people want to live. Manchester Housing manages about 70 000 council homes in addition to its corporate objectives of regeneration of the city. The 1998–2001 Corporate Housing Strategy defines Manchester Housing's objectives as follows:

1. To provide a choice of desirable and affordable housing to improve the quality of life for current residents and to encourage people to come and live in Manchester.
2. To make proper provision for people who are homeless or inadequately housed and for people being cared for in the community.
3. To offer tenants a wide choice of alternative management and ownership arrangements through empowerment, effective consultation and real participation.
4. To deliver a customer-oriented, locally based, Best Value housing service that is seen as a market leader.
5. To prevent homelessness by corporate intervention.
6. To use a comprehensive approach to improve housing conditions and help communities become more cohesive.
7. To deal with the problems of low demand evident in some areas of our housing.

Manchester Housing's information strategy

Rationale

By using Business Objects and its intranet, Manchester Housing is able to bring together all of its various sources of information and present them in such a way that management can easily monitor and control all aspects of their plans. The introduction of a balanced scorecard allows all the necessary indicators that have to be controlled to be monitored by the Departmental Management Team (DMT), enabling its members to keep their 'finger on the pulse' at all times. Additionally, once defined, the performance indicators provide one of the ways for demonstrating 'Best Value' by benchmarking them against similar organisations and facilitate focused performance reviews.

Methodology

With its three-year plan objectives clearly laid down, the DMT was able to identify the key outcomes to be monitored over the next year under the following headings:

- housing demand and rehousing
- estate management
- housing investment
- Best Value
- crime and disorder
- human resource issues
- finance issues.

1 Beneath each of these outcomes is a hierarchy of critical success factors and associated measures, each with differing levels of importance to the achievement of the desired outcome, the top level of which can be seen in Fig. 4.4, Balanced scorecard outcomes.

Fig. 4.4   MH – Balanced scorecard outcomes

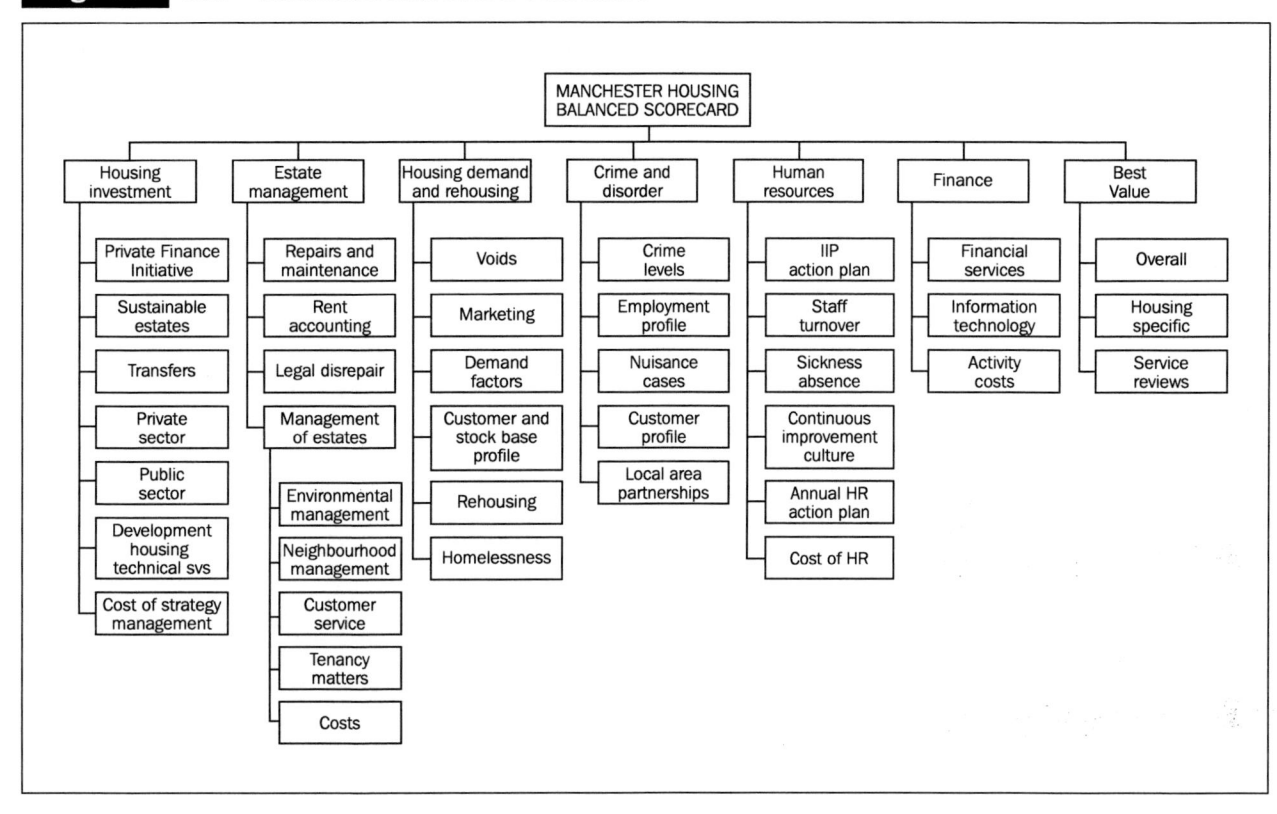

```
                        MANCHESTER HOUSING
                        BALANCED SCORECARD
   ┌──────────┬──────────┬──────────┬──────────┬──────────┬──────────┐
 Housing    Estate    Housing demand  Crime and   Human      Finance    Best
investment management and rehousing   disorder  resources              Value

Private Finance  Repairs and    Voids         Crime        IIP          Financial    Overall
Initiative      maintenance                   levels       action plan  services

Sustainable     Rent           Marketing      Employment   Staff        Information  Housing
estates         accounting                    profile      turnover     technology   specific

Transfers       Legal disrepair Demand        Nuisance     Sickness     Activity     Service
                               factors        cases        absence      costs        reviews

Private         Management     Customer and   Customer     Continuous
sector          of estates     stock base     profile      improvement
                               profile                     culture

Public          Environmental  Rehousing      Local area   Annual HR
sector          management                    partnerships action plan

Development     Neighbourhood  Homelessness                Cost of HR
housing         management
technical svs

Cost of strategy Customer
management       service

                 Tenancy
                 matters

                 Costs
```

2 The use of Business Objects (Integrated Decision Support Tool) enables each measure to be weighted. As performance indicators are not mutually exclusive to each outcome, the same indicators can occur under more than one outcome, for example customer profile, and can be given a different weighting in each outcome arm.

3 One of the detailed hierarchies beneath the outcomes can be seen in Fig. 4.5, Housing demand and rehousing. This has been weighted to reflect significance.

4 By using alerts, exceptions and trend analysis, for example see Fig. 4.6, MH – Graphical trends, only those measures that are not on target will be highlighted throughout the hierarchy. This enables DMT to see at a glance if all outcomes are going according to plan (green), or give cause for concern (amber) or need immediate attention (red) and to 'drill down' and identify the root cause of the problem.

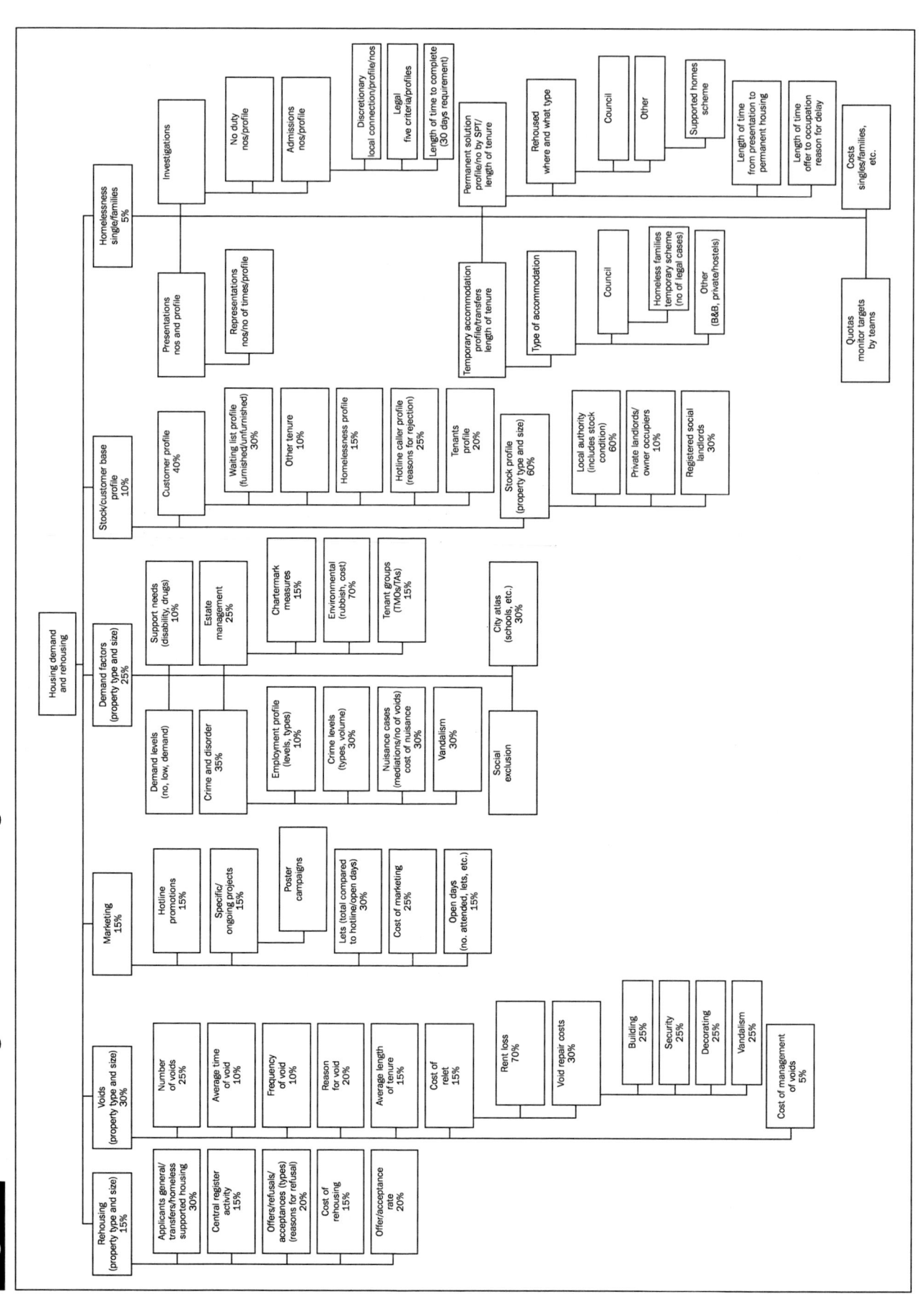

Fig. 4.5 MH – Housing demand and rehousing

Fig. 4.6   MH – Graphical trends

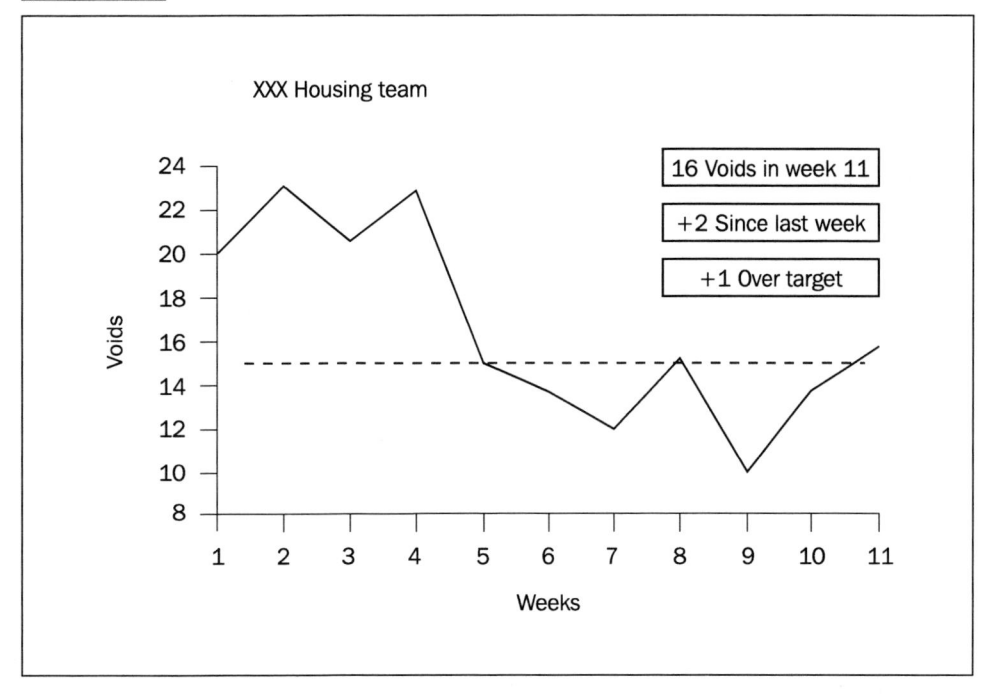

XXX Housing team

16 Voids in week 11
+2 Since last week
+1 Over target

5 Beneath each hierarchy of measures it is possible to 'drill down' geographically to regions, areas and teams to see where problems have arisen and there is variance from plan, as can be seen in Fig. 4.7, Geographic 'drill down'. The weightings, alerts and trends are shown at all levels in the hierarchy and, in fact, 'drill up' from the lowest level.

Fig. 4.7   MH – Geographic 'drill down'

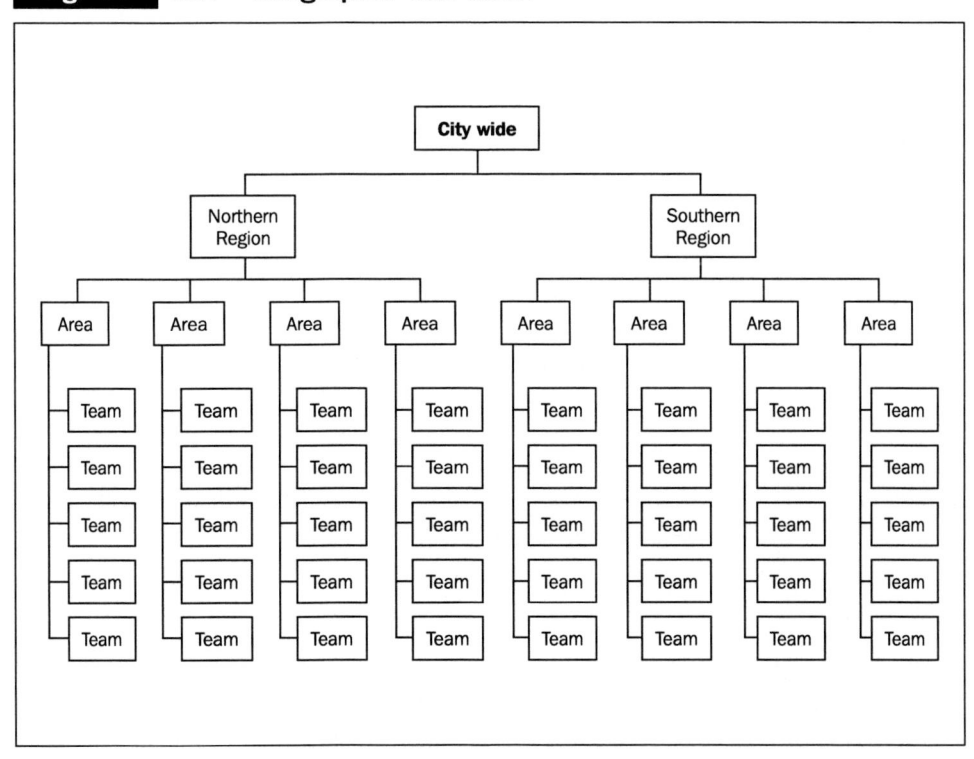

6 Other views allow each functional director to see all of the measures that relate to their areas of responsibility in one hierarchy, with exceptions and alerts drawing attention to problems needing their immediate attention, as can be seen in Fig. 4.8, Balanced scorecard functional perspectives.

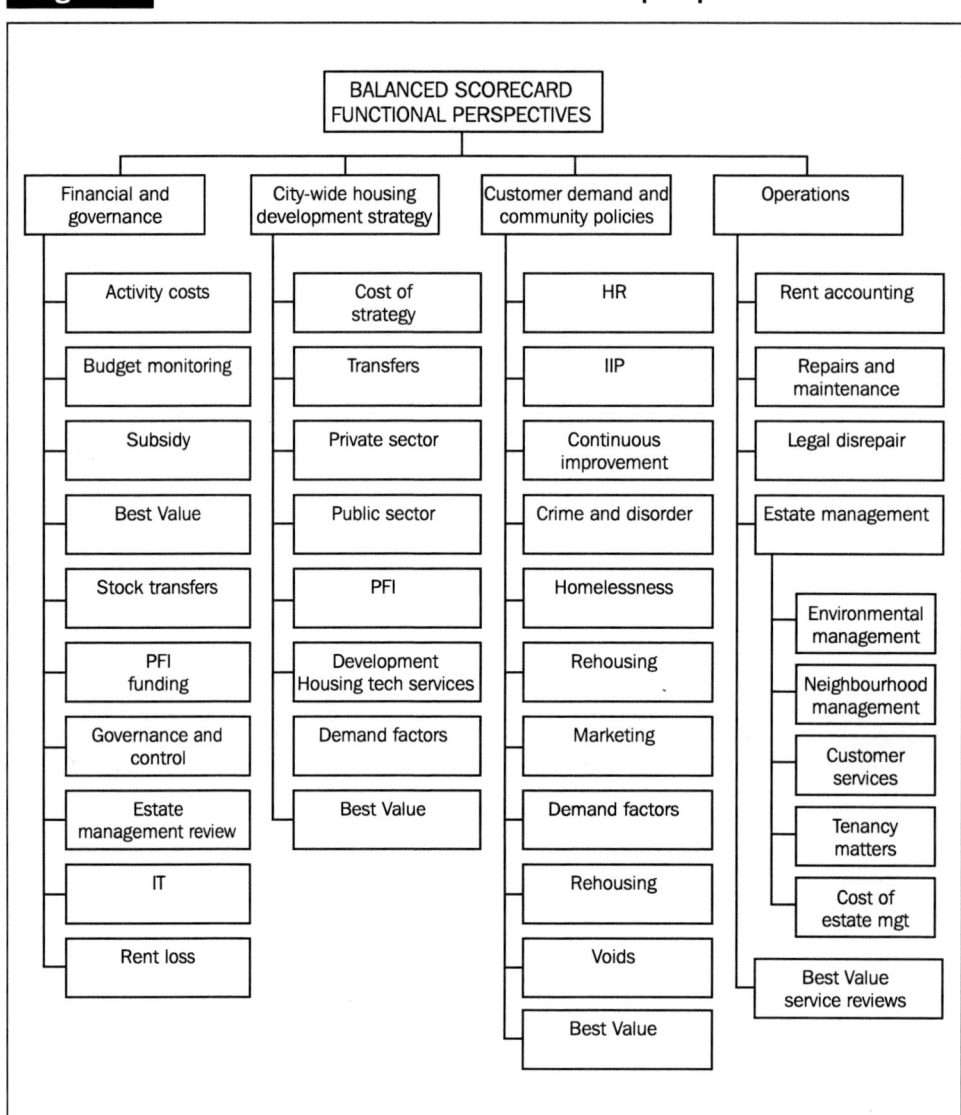

Fig. 4.8 MH – Balanced scorecard functional perspectives

```
                    BALANCED SCORECARD
                    FUNCTIONAL PERSPECTIVES

    Financial and      City-wide housing    Customer demand and    Operations
    governance         development strategy community policies

    Activity costs     Cost of strategy     HR                     Rent accounting
    Budget monitoring  Transfers            IIP                    Repairs and maintenance
    Subsidy            Private sector       Continuous improvement Legal disrepair
    Best Value         Public sector        Crime and disorder     Estate management
    Stock transfers    PFI                  Homelessness              Environmental management
    PFI funding        Development          Rehousing                 Neighbourhood management
                       Housing tech services
    Governance and     Demand factors       Marketing                 Customer services
    control
    Estate             Best Value           Demand factors            Tenancy matters
    management review
    IT                                      Rehousing                 Cost of estate mgt
    Rent loss                               Voids                     Best Value service reviews
                                            Best Value
```

7 Equally, views can be defined that cut across at any level in the hierarchy, linking any specified measures, for example a statutory KPI view. The use of the intranet not only allows these hyperlink features to be used but enables focused access across the network to be given to dispersed staff, based on password controls.

Requirement

1 Prior to the purchase of Business Objects, information was held in many different sources, some of which were not under the control of Manchester Housing. This made access difficult. Transporting all of the relevant information into a single data warehouse

will enable information to be accessed. Business Objects also has the ability to access information held by individual departments (internal or external), as long as access is available to the server, so one of its most important roles was in pulling together information from diverse sources. However, without the balanced scorecard approach, Business Objects provided a data-rich information pool but was not sufficiently focused to enable the wood to be distinguished from the trees.

2. Having brought all of the information together into one database, it was then necessary to translate this data, often held as spreadsheets at team level, into easily understood trend information. This would show, for example, the trend over a period and against target in a graph, 'drilling up' from team to organisation level, using traffic lights to alert to any problems. This enables all staff to be aware of problems without the need for each interested party to spend inordinate amounts of time calculating the necessary facts or having to 'spot' the issues in a mass of data or statistics. Having set in place the 'rules', Business Objects is able to carry out the calculations automatically on a weekly/monthly basis, reducing the need for 'routine' paper reports to be circulated.

3. While the City Council's Service Plan is a very detailed and lengthy document, updated twice a year, it does not always hold the most pertinent information or insist on specific targets and measures. The Service Plan is related to Manchester's objectives by number, but it is not possible to weight the importance of any of the measures to contributing to the achievement of those goals. What this information strategy allows is for all the information currently held in the Service Plan to be linked directly to objectives, with clear targets and weightings indicating importance, and it ensures that all business perspectives, including finance, for example, are considered in respect of each planned outcome.

4. The need to demonstrate 'Best Value' is now a requirement and what this information strategy allows is a mechanism utilising the techniques defined in the 'Best Value' White Paper, including for example activity costing. It provides for the first stage of benchmark comparisons to be made against similar organisations, leaving the way clear for process mapping, utilising the full range of indicators identified under the balanced scorecard principles. This clear definition of performance indicators, at such an early stage, will allow Manchester to lead the way in influencing how 'Best Value' NPIs should proceed within housing. In particular, it will facilitate the *Compare* element of the four Cs of Best Value, in addition to enabling a mechanism for *Challenging, Consulting* and demonstrating *Competitiveness* in service reviews.

5. Finally, once built, the comprehensive set of hierarchical indicators, with associated targets and objectives, forms the basis of a business improvement model, enabling changes in measures, targets and objectives necessary to meet future years' Service Plans to be effected easily.

5

Activity/process-based techniques

- 5.1 Introduction 71
- 5.2 Hierarchical process/activity analysis 73
- 5.3 Costing 78
- 5.4 Performance improvement 85
- 5.5 Performance management 91
- 5.6 Case study – Process-based performance improvement in Lund University Hospital 102
- 5.7 Case study – ABT and benchmarking at Metropolitan Housing Trust 106

5.1 INTRODUCTION

In this chapter, value-adding tools and techniques are explained, based on process and activity analysis and designed to improve company-wide performance. Figure 5.1, The development of activity-based techniques, shows how over a period of just over ten years the use of ABT has developed from activity-based costing (ABC) through to, among others, priority-based budgeting (PBB) and business process reengineering (BPR). ABT fall into three broad categories:

1 Costing

- Activity-based costing
- Product/service costing
- Product/service pricing
- Market/channel/sector and customer profitability
- Transfer pricing.

Fig. 5.1 The development of activity-based techniques

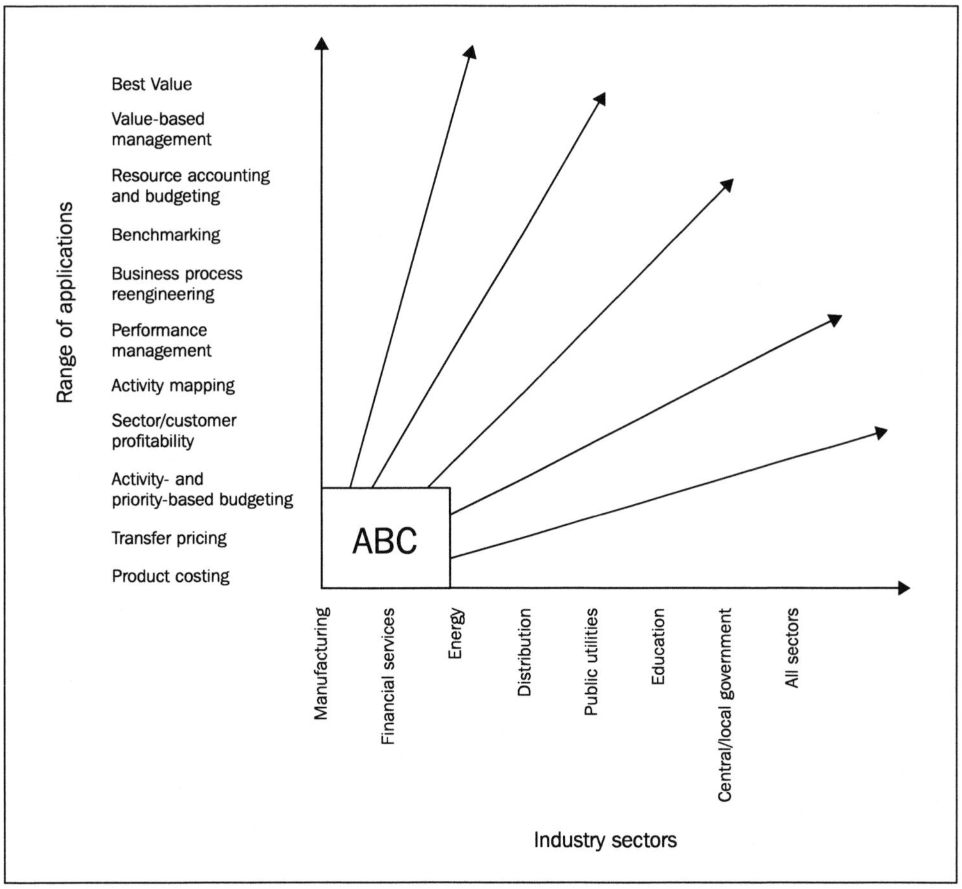

2 Performance improvement

- Process and activity mapping
- Cost reduction
- Value analysis
- Constraint removal
- Business process reengineering
- Benchmarking.

3 Performance management

- Value-based management
- Performance measurement/management
- Service-level evaluation
- Activity- and priority-based budgeting (ABB/PBB)
- Resource accounting and budgeting (government)
- Best Value (local government).

Their use now transcends every industry sector. The beauty of ABT lies in their simplicity, allowing them to be understood by anyone at any level in the organisation, and their universal application to anything that consumes resources.

A CIMA Research publication, *Activity Based Techniques – Real Life Consequences*,[1] examined 11 companies that had been using ABT for a number of years and found, among other things, the following:

- Although the businesses had typically embarked on the use of one ABT initially, often ABC for product costing or BPR for performance improvement, they went on to use an average of three techniques, usually including ABB for management and control.
- Implementation of ABT made a contribution to changing culture and improving relations between the finance function and operational departments. Noticeably, this had been assisted by such factors as the common language of ABT to discuss costs and performance.

Over the last five years, ABT have stopped being used as just one-off techniques applied for a particular purpose within the organisation and have become an all-embracing advanced planning, monitoring and control system, which encompasses quality management philosophies. In a survey in 1996 carried out by Ernst & Young and *Management Accounting*,[2] 2000 CIMA Fellows were sent questionnaires and from the respondents it was found that 21% have implemented ABT and 20% were considering implementation. Since then, the use of process/activity-based techniques as a basis for managing the business has been accelerated by the large number of enterprise resource planning software implementations within organisations and their use of a process-based philosophy. The unprecedented improvements in IT systems over the last ten years have played a large part in enabling the development and use of ABT, and this topic is covered in more detail in Chapter 7, Information management.

5.2 HIERARCHICAL PROCESS/ACTIVITY ANALYSIS

Introduction

All ABT involve analysing the business to gain a greater knowledge of what activities it performs and how those activities relate to one another (a series of activities that flow from one to another constitutes a process), in other words, understanding how the business operates. This analysis then forms the central database, which can be utilised by one or all of the numerous activity-based techniques that an organisation decides to use to improve and manage its business.

Methodology

When carrying out activity analysis for the first time, it is generally easiest to use the company's organisational structure, as shown in Fig. 5.2, Organisation structure hierarchy. The starting point is to ask a representative from each budget or cost centre within your organisation's structure of departments, directorates, functions or business units to analyse the activities that they perform and, depending on the detail required for the purpose, the tasks within those activities.

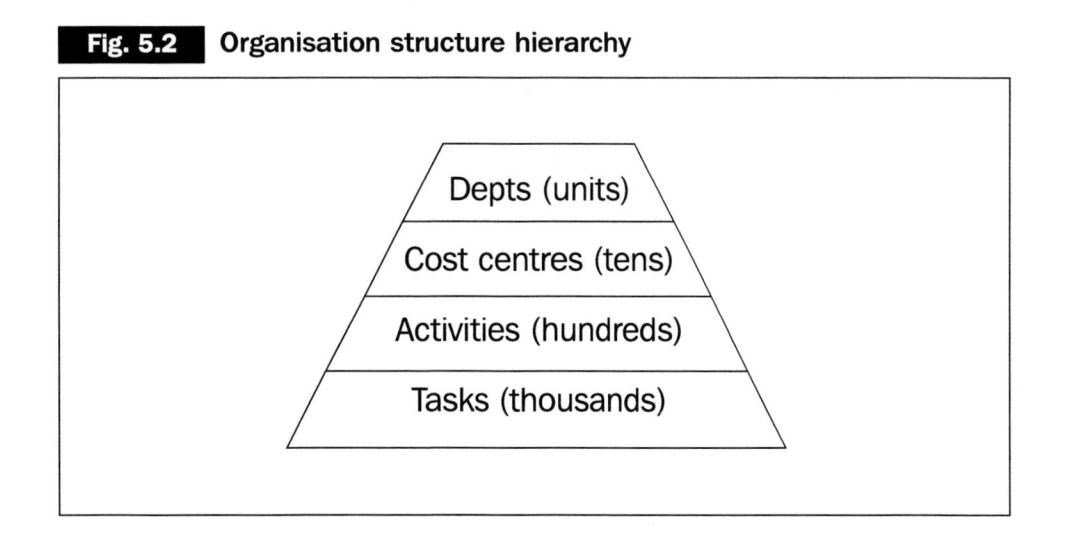

Fig. 5.2 Organisation structure hierarchy

- Depts (units)
- Cost centres (tens)
- Activities (hundreds)
- Tasks (thousands)

Then, as can be seen in Fig. 5.3, Process/activity hierarchy, the tasks and activities can be grouped into activity flows forming subprocesses, which in turn can be related to the core processes of the business. The core processes are those that define the purpose of the organisation's existence, the processes that deliver the products or services that the company is in business to provide. All activities and subprocesses carried out within the company must contribute towards these core processes in some way. The analysis carried out makes this relationship clear and provides an understanding of how the business operates. Obviously, in an actual analysis the numbers of levels in the hierarchy vary considerably, depending on the size of organisation and the level of detail required to meet objectives.

Fig. 5.3 Process/activity hierarchy

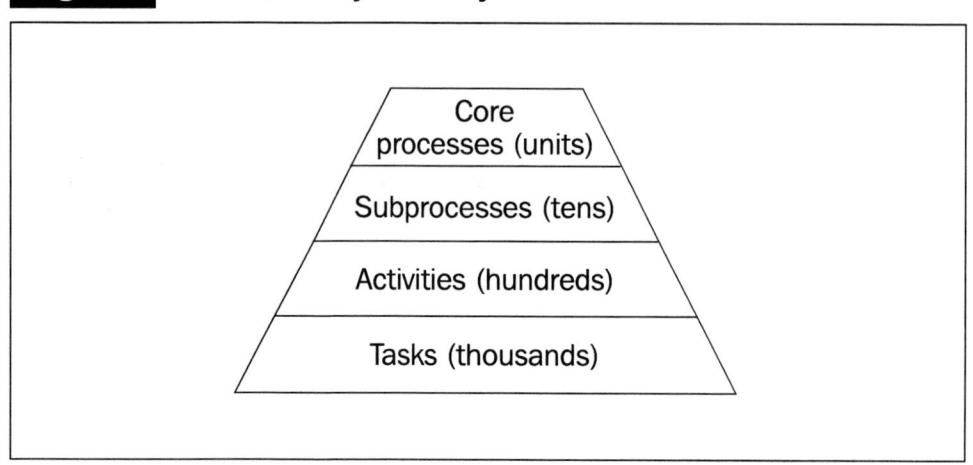

(Pyramid diagram from top to bottom: Core processes (units); Subprocesses (tens); Activities (hundreds); Tasks (thousands))

Fig. 5.4 CAM-I cross

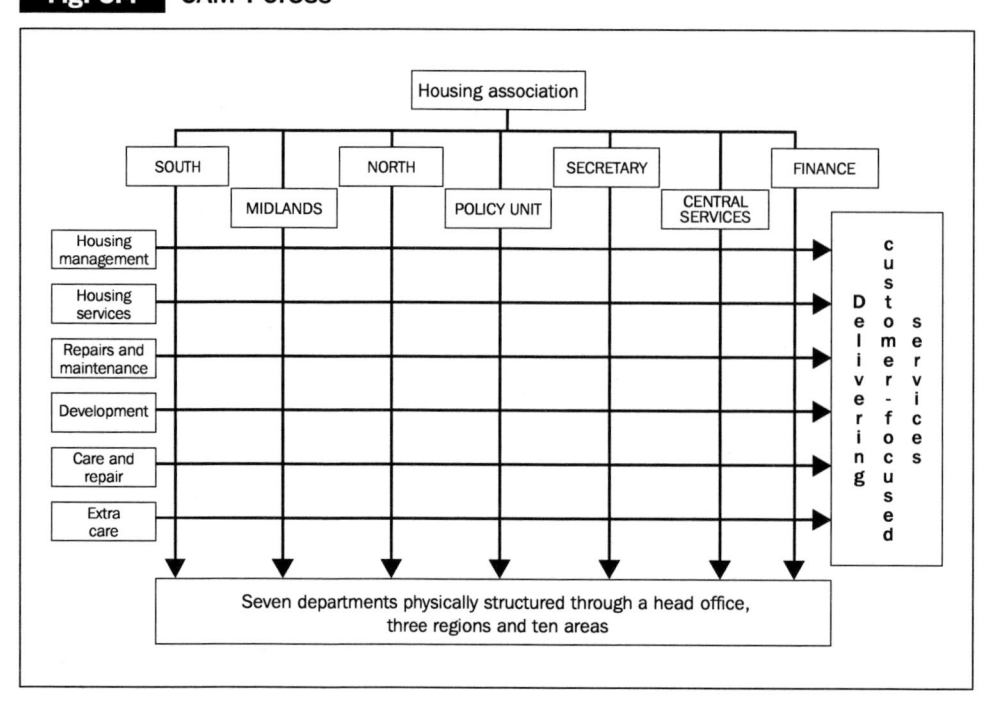

(Diagram: Housing association at top, with columns SOUTH, MIDLANDS, NORTH, POLICY UNIT, SECRETARY, CENTRAL SERVICES, FINANCE. Rows: Housing management, Housing services, Repairs and maintenance, Development, Care and repair, Extra care. Right side labelled "Delivering — focused" pointing to "customer-services". Bottom: Seven departments physically structured through a head office, three regions and ten areas.)

In Fig. 5.4, CAM-I cross, the organisational structure of a housing association can be seen going down the page and the core processes going across the page, cutting each other in a cross named after the research organisation that first defined it. This represents how all the departments within the organisational structure each contribute to the core processes via the subprocesses that they perform. Processes represent a series of activities, which produce a specified output and ignore all functional boundaries. How they interrelate and the contribution that they make to the end product or service is represented by Fig. 5.3, represented by the pyramid and built from the hierarchical analysis.

Fig. 5.5 The systems design and delivery subprocess

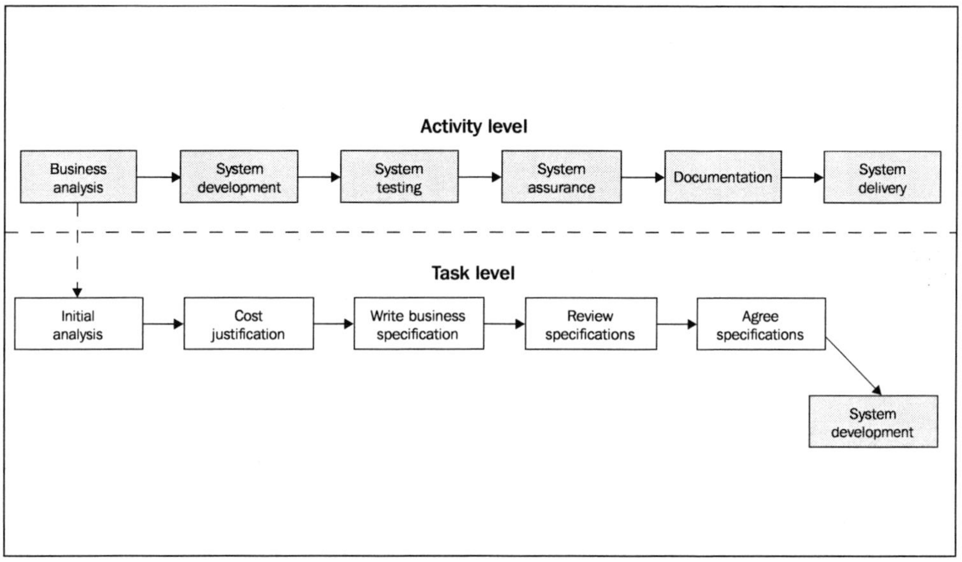

In Fig. 5.5, The systems design and delivery subprocess, this can be seen as one of the subprocesses that contributes to the infrastructure, which in turn contributes to core processes. It illustrates that the subprocess is made up of a flow of five activities, each of which in turn can be analysed into the flow of tasks that perform the activity. If required, each of the tasks could similarly be analysed into subtasks. All organisations are made up of a number of subprocesses, some of which are of a support nature and are common to most organisations, like procurement, recruitment and management information; others are specific to their industry sector, as waiting list, reactive repairs, allocations and tenancy management are to housing associations.

Collection of activity analysis information

Depending on the ABT that is being used, data needs to be collected, generally from the people carrying out the activities within each budget/cost centre or subprocess. This information could include:

- activities and tasks performed
- relationships to other activities/tasks (flows)
- inputs and outputs to and from the activities and their units of measure
- resources consumed, for example time spent, amount of office space used (resource drivers)
- basis of allocation to products or services and customers (activity drivers)
- factors that influence the activity's performance (cost drivers)
- performance measures (financial and non-financial; quantitative and qualitative)
- activity/process objectives and responsibilities
- activity classifications (core, diversionary, support)
- alternate service levels
- ideas for improvement.

It is worth noting at this point that detailed time recording and analysis by all staff on an on-going basis are not prerequisites to activity analysis. This is a popular misconception that has no foundation in practical application.

Methods of data collection

Many methods can be used for collecting data; generally, the initial analysis will be undertaken on the best data available and then specifically automated systems will be set up for on-going monitoring. Sources of existing data can usually be found in:

- timekeeping systems, particularly for identifying resource drivers
- corporate information systems, either enterprise wide or local, particularly for activity drivers and outputs and non-financial performance measures
- financial information systems, particularly for costs, assets and budgets
- HR systems, particularly for payroll and people information and organisational structures
- the department cost centre or process being analysed, particularly activities, relationships, flows, cost drivers, inputs and outputs.

Methods of collection vary considerably depending on the data required, the nature of the project and the use to which it is to be put. They include:

- observation
- storyboards – group workshops used to brainstorm activity/process analysis, useful when trying to get a quick, first cut of information

- downloading – information from other IT systems
- interviews – a popular method but one that has disadvantages of being time consuming and, therefore, restrictive in terms of the number of people that can be reached. It also depends heavily on instant responses from the interviewees. Ideal if one area only is being analysed
- questionnaires/forms – need to be explained carefully to the people who are going to complete them, with support available for questions that arise. Select one representative from each cost centre to complete the questionnaire/forms and train them in how to carry out the analysis, encouraging them to involve all the staff within their cost centre. A sample form designed for collecting basic activity and resource allocation data can be seen in Fig. 5.6, Data collection form.

Fig. 5.6 Data collection form

Activities: Handling routine enquiries, Resolving problems, Escalating problems, Management

Cost centre code: HDK
Cost centre name: Help Desk
Completed by: Joan Ayres
Date: 28.04.99

Personnel

Name	Emp. No	1	2	3	4	5	6	Fraction
Ann Williams	12341	40	28	32				1.0
Fred Smith	56782	35	25	40	10			1.0
John Shore	90123	45	32	23				1.0
Lynne Edwards	34514	55	20	25				1.0
James Roberts	78905	60	25	15				1.0
Peter Brook	1236	50	28	22				1.0
Joan Ayres	45677	40	35	15	10			1.0
Ron Jones	89018	0	30	20	50			1.0

Consumables

Code	Description	1	2	3	4	5	6	£k Budget
C2200	General travel		30	30	40			6.0
C3300	Office supplies	25	25	25	25			2.0
C4450	Publications			50	50			1.5
C3320	Photocopying		30	40	30			0.7
C2260	Car allowance				100			4.5
C4999	Internal purchases	25	25	25	25			20.0
								34.7

Once the data has been collected and analysed, always validate it by checking with the cost-centre staff and management to ensure that no errors occurred in preparation. If the collection of data has involved the selection of choices, for example of which methods of allocation to use, then it is advisable to hold a workshop of all interested parties and gain consensus on the 'preferred' methods.

Steps in building a hierarchical process/activity model

1 Decide what the model is going to be used for. As in all projects, clearly defined objectives are essential, which will indicate the level of detail required in the activity hierarchy and the software features and functionality required. For example, business process reengineering is likely to require process mapping and detailed task-level information, while activity-based costing is likely to require the ability to carry out multidimensional allocations and will require subprocess and activity detail only. It is worth noting at this stage that one of the most common problems encountered with ABC projects is that too much detail is collected.

2 Make decisions regarding use of appropriate software; *see* Chapter 7, Information management, where this topic is dealt with in more detail.

3 Design the structure of the model. The methodology will vary with the choice of software and project objectives, but decisions need to be made at this stage, for example if ABC is to be used, then what are the products/services and customers/markets/channels to be analysed? Remember that because this is a model, more than one view can be built.

4 Collect the data, as discussed above.

5 Build the model on the chosen software and validate with users. Always remember that the model is going to be utilised for decision making only if the users trust the information and, therefore, they need to be involved and consulted at every stage. The role of the transformed finance function in this process is that of information facilitator, not data owner.

6 Update, review and report regularly, depending on the ABT being used.

5.3 COSTING

Introduction

The ability to calculate accurate product and service costs and evaluate the profitability of pricing strategies and customers is essential in any organisation wishing to be competitive in the twenty-first century. Chapter 1, Problems with the traditional finance function, and Fig. 1.1, Changes in cost composition (p.8), illustrated the problems that organisations are encountering in continuing to utilise traditional costing methods, which have become both inappropriate and misleading.

Activity-based costing is now accepted and widely used as the most appropriate method of costing products and services. The sophistication of IT tools now allows multidimensional allocations to be carried out with ease, making the building of ABC models relatively straightforward. The software is discussed in detail in Chapter 7, Information management. Figure 5.7, How ABC differs from traditional costing, shows that the main difference with ABC is that, instead of collecting overhead costs into one or more central pools to be arbitrarily allocated to all products and services by a percentage on-cost, generally based on labour, it allocates resources to activities, prior to allocating activity costs on to products and services based on actual usage.

Fig. 5.7 How ABC differs from traditional costing

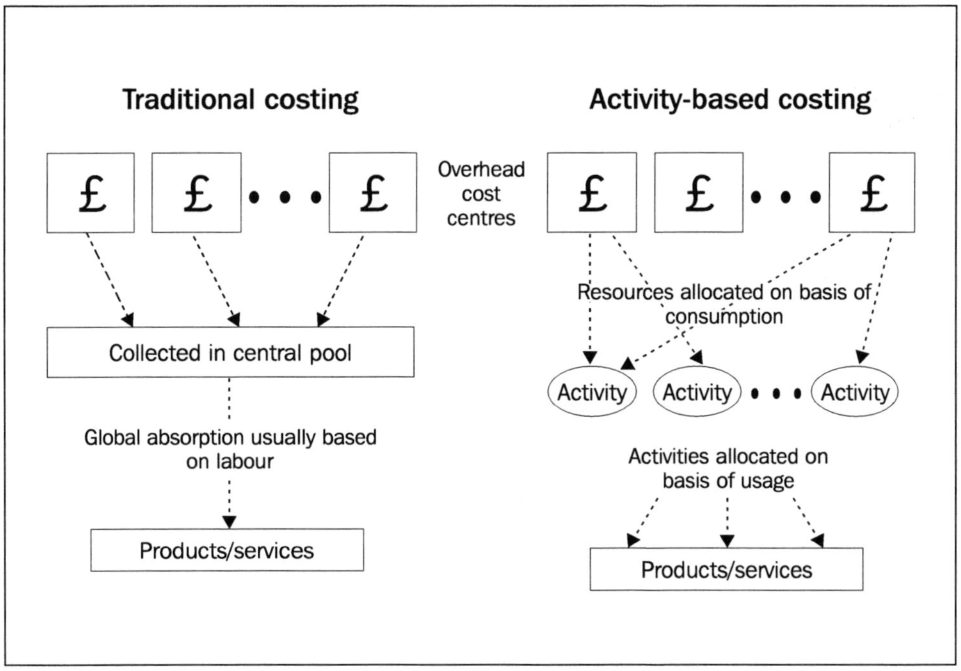

By doing so, as seen earlier in the chapter, it enables the business to understand the costs of the activities it performs and to identify their interrelationships. For example, if the overhead cost centre was Finance, the three activities shown in Fig. 5.7 might be 'Financial operations', 'Payroll' and 'Provision of management information'. ABC then allows each of these activities to be allocated according to how they are being used, by identifying their activity drivers and where they are being used. Payroll would have the number of employees as its activity driver and be allocated equally to all employees, while Financial operations would probably use the number of invoices processed as one of its drivers and be allocated according to usage. The method of allocating resource costs to activities is by a resource driver, relating directly to the activity's consumption of resources. In the example used above, the costs of employing the finance staff would be allocated to the activities based on the time they spent on each activity; similarly, the costs of IT would be allocated according to usage, possibly per package used and/or per PC, and so on with the other resources in the cost centre.

ABC example – a problem with product costing at an insurance company

General information

To illustrate the benefits of ABC over traditional methods, a simple product-costing example is shown, where a fictional insurance company sells two products, a 'Regular' and a 'Super' policy. It has traditionally costed its policies on a volume-based overhead absorption system, using premium income to absorb overhead. It counts all costs as overhead; there are no direct costs.

Data gathered in the last financial year

Policy type	Quantity sold	Average premium*	Customer visits	Underwriting amendments	Computer enquiries
Regular	70 000	£50	1	1	2
Super	10 000	£100	5	8	6

*numbers represent income per policy

Overhead costs have been gathered by activity as follows:

	£'000s
Selling	360
Underwriting	300
Computing	140
Premium collection	100
	900

The questions

1 Calculate unit overhead costs for the Regular and Super policies by the traditional system based on value of premium income.

2 Using an activity-based product costing method and the data available, recalculate unit costs on the basis that seems appropriate to you. Explain your choice of drivers.

3 Indicate the advantages that activity-based product costing can provide to aid decision making.

The answer

1 Traditional costing system

	Quantity '000s	Unit premium £	Premium income £'000s
Regular	70	50	3 500
Super	10	100	1 000
			4 500

$$\frac{\text{Overhead costs}}{\text{Premium income}} = \frac{900\,000}{4\,500\,000} = 20 \text{ pence}/£ \text{ or } 20\%$$

Unit overhead costs

Regular £50 × 20% = £10

Super   £100 × 20% = £20

2 Activity-based product costing

Overhead	£'000s	Driver	Freq × Qty	Cost ÷ Total freq	Cost/driver
Selling	360	# customer visits	1 × 70 5 × 10	360 120	£3.00
Underwriting	300	# amendments	1 × 70 8 × 10	300 150	£2.00
Computing	140	# comp enquiries	2 × 70 6 × 10	140 200	£0.70
Prem coll	100	# policies sold	1 × 70 1 × 10	100 80	£1.25

	Cost/driver × frequency/unit		Regular £	Super £
Selling	£3.00	1	3.00	
	£3.00	5		15.00
Underwriting	£2.00	1	2.00	
	£2.00	8		16.00
Computing	£0.70	2	1.40	
	£0.70	6		4.20
Collection	£1.25	1	1.25	
	£1.25	1		1.25
			£7.65	£36.45
Compared to traditional			£10.00	£20.00
Under (over) costed			(£2.35)	£16.45

3 Advantages

The example illustrates that by introducing four distinct activities, each with its own driver, into the methodology, counting the frequency with which they occurred, it is possible to calculate the unit cost of each activity driver or activity output and allocate it to the type of policy based on the number of outputs of that activity that the product consumed. This allows the varying complexity of the different products to be represented within their costs. As a general rule, high-volume, less complex products tend to be overcosted by 10–30% (in this case 23.5%) and low-volume, more complex products tend to be undercosted by 50–400% (in this case 83%).

Choice of drivers

The choice of methods of allocation between resource and activity, known as the 'resource drivers', and between activity and product/service or another activity, known as the 'activity drivers', will vary depending on the information that is available. Wherever possible:

- Use specific data that relates to consumption.
- Use data that is already available or collected either manually or by computer, or can be easily collected by computer if not currently counted.
- Allocate at as high a level as possible in the activity hierarchy without losing accuracy, usually at activity or subprocess level in Fig. 5.3, Process/activity hierarchy (p.74). This ensures that the ABC analysis remains simple and understood by those who need to use it and that it is not overcomplex to maintain.

- Gain consensus from all parties involved in the allocation on the 'best' method to be used, in their view. If the data is to be used, their 'buy-in' will be needed. ABC models must not be built in isolation by the finance function, but instead the finance function should act as a facilitator for operations, which will own and use the data.

Figure 5.8, ABC – Help desk, is a simplistic example of how relevant resources are allocated to the help desk activity by resource drivers, then overhead activities are allocated based on activity drivers, giving a total cost for the help desk activity and a unit cost per enquiry dealt with by the help desk. The example points out that there are a small amount of other costs, termed 'business sustaining', that have not been attributed to this or any other activity because it is not appropriate to do so. Business-sustaining costs may include such things as legal and audit costs and will be collected in a pool at the centre. The difference between this pool and the pool in the traditional method of costing illustrated is that it should be minimal, around 5–10% at maximum, rather than the 50% of the traditional overhead pools.

Fig. 5.8 ABC – Help desk

Direct costs of activities	Resource drivers	Total	Per enquiry £
Personnel costs	Time spent	XXX	XX
Stationery, phone and post	Cost	XX	X
Office equipment/furniture	Depreciation	XX	X
Premises costs	Square foot	XX	X
Travel costs	Cost	XX	X
		XXXX	XX
Attributable costs	**Activity drivers**		
Management	No. of staff	XX	X
IT	No. of transactions	XX	X
Payroll	No. of staff	X	X
Purchasing	No. of invoices	X	X
Personnel	No. of staff	X	X
		XXXX	XX
Total cost excluding business-sustaining costs		XXXXX	XXX

Customer profitability

Figure 5.9, Customer profitability, shows the fourth dimension of the ABC model, beyond products and services to 'markets and customers'. By multiplying product and service costs and revenues by the volume of sales to each customer and attaching any customer-driven activities directly to the market or customer (for example, the activity costs of selling in China would be allocated directly to that market area and 'drip down' to the customers within it), the true profitability of each customer can then be ascertained.

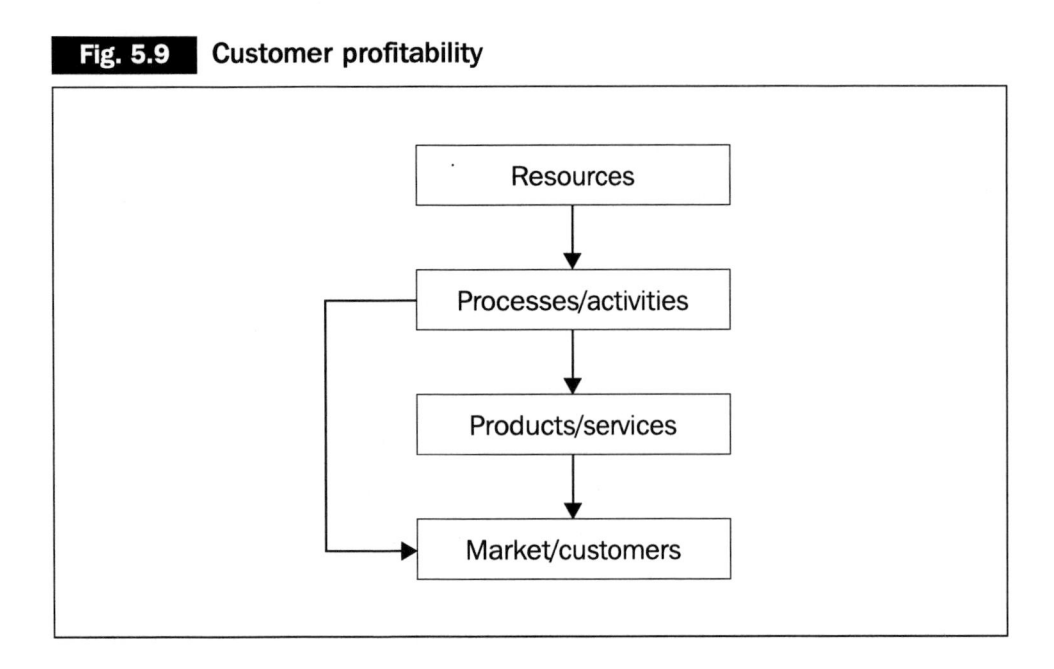

Fig. 5.9 Customer profitability

```
Resources
   ↓
Processes/activities ←┐
   ↓                   │
Products/services     │
   ↓                   │
Market/customers ─────┘
```

Pricing scenario example

An IT outsourcing company provides operational and support products and services to clients based on a fixed cost per user, per PC, etc. After building an ABC model of the costs of its services and identifying the cost drivers, it discovered that the basis of the pricing mechanism, although variable based on volumes, was often different to the way the costs were being driven, thus identifying an unnecessary risk. For example, the help desk support service is charged on a fixed price per user, but the costs are driven by two variable cost drivers (the number and the length of calls made to the help desk), plus a fixed capital cost per user for the installation of the equipment spread over a number of years. Figure 5.10, Help desk pricing, shows at what point in terms of the number of calls received the outsourcer will start to show a loss. The outsourcer's risk can be reduced by changing the pricing mechanism to reflect the way the costs are being driven; this change would also give the customer an incentive to reduce the number of calls made by its staff, taking responsibility for driving cost. By both parties working in partnership, through investing in new help desk technology, undertaking training of help desk staff and system users, the number and length of calls could be reduced to the benefit of the customer and removal of risk to the supplier.

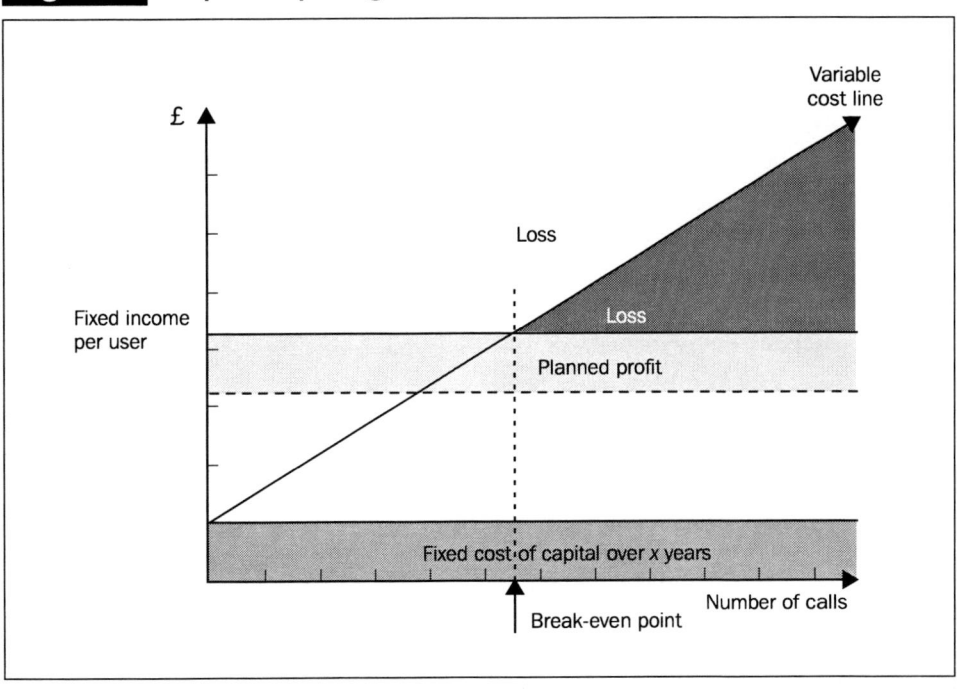

Fig. 5.10 Help desk pricing

[Graph showing Help desk pricing with £ on y-axis and Number of calls on x-axis. A variable cost line rises diagonally from origin. Horizontal lines show Fixed income per user and Fixed cost of capital over x years. Planned profit area between them. Loss region above fixed income line beyond break-even point.]

Modelling

Several of the ABC/M software tools allow 'what if' scenarios to be performed on their models to aid decision making and planning and optimise performance. It is enormously powerful to be able to back calculate, by making changes to product/service volumes and selling prices and simulating the effects on profitability and activity and resource utilisation, where fixed, variable and semi-variable indicators can be applied. Sophisticated common data models that can simulate the workings of the business are essential tools for adding value company wide.

5.4 PERFORMANCE IMPROVEMENT

Introduction

The use of activity analysis for improving company-wide performance has been good practice for over ten years. Its use to remove 'non-value-added' activity was seen as an excellent way of reducing costs, but the early focus was on activities within functional departments. Each cost centre would analyse its activities and then classify them as follows.

Primary value added or core

These are activities that are 'essential' to the being of the organisation, delivering the products or services that denote the business's existence. They add value and meet customer needs. When identified, focus on these activities will encourage enhancement, improvements in effectiveness and variation of levels of service.

Primary non-value added or diversionary

These are activities that are usually considered 'urgent' because they result from failure elsewhere. They are regarded as adding cost without adding value to the business. This category of activity needs to be eliminated, whenever possible, by getting things right first time, removing unnecessary barriers and improving methods and systems. Activities classified in this category include:

- approving
- filing
- reviewing
- preparing
- inspecting
- accumulating
- decanting
- searching
- expediting
- storing
- moving
- counting
- retrieving
- revising.

Support or secondary

These activities are considered 'necessary' to enable core activity to take place. The focus on support activities is to make them more effective through improved methods and systems and variations in levels of service and inter-business unit charging, which is discussed in Chapter 3 (section 3.6).

Activity-based cost management (ABCM)

After conducting classification or value analysis, early activity-based cost management programmes would hold workshops to discuss the analysis and find improvements by focusing on elimination of non-value-added activities at:

- cost centre level
- departmental level
- corporate level.

The understanding of what activities are performed, their classification, their cost make-up and their unit costs allows their cost drivers to be identified, i.e. those factors that drive or influence costs. For example, in a finance function such influences might be:

- system availability
- number of cost centres
- number of *ad hoc* requests
- changing business requirements
- number of upgrades made to systems
- number of system users.

Cost drivers, i.e. influencers of cost, are not to be confused with methods of allocation used in activity-based costing, which are known as activity drivers. Typical activity drivers in the finance function would include:

- number of sales invoices
- number of purchase invoices
- number of cost centres
- number of reporting periods
- number of customers
- number of suppliers
- number of PCs
- number of system users.

Removal of constraints

The result of a functional focus was that activities were optimised within their function, irrespective of the effect on the rest of the business. An example would be where attention is focused on the activity 'after-sales service', which forms part of the engineering department; *see* Fig. 5.11, Value chain. Improvements within the function would focus on quicker response times to customer calls or a faster repair cycle, not on the cause of the repair, which probably went back in the value chain to the distribution department, where there may be problems with packaging or delivery; or to production, where there may be problems with manufacturing; or to procurement, where the wrong or substandard materials may have been purchased; or sales, where the order may have been wrongly processed; or even to development, where the design of the product may be the cause of the need for 'after-sales service'. As a result, in the early 1990s it was realised that such performance-improvement initiatives should focus on processes, irrespective of functional boundaries; hence the birth of business process redesign and its big brother, business process reengineering. The latter is where an organisation also looks at all outside influences to find more innovative solutions.

Fig. 5.11 Value chain

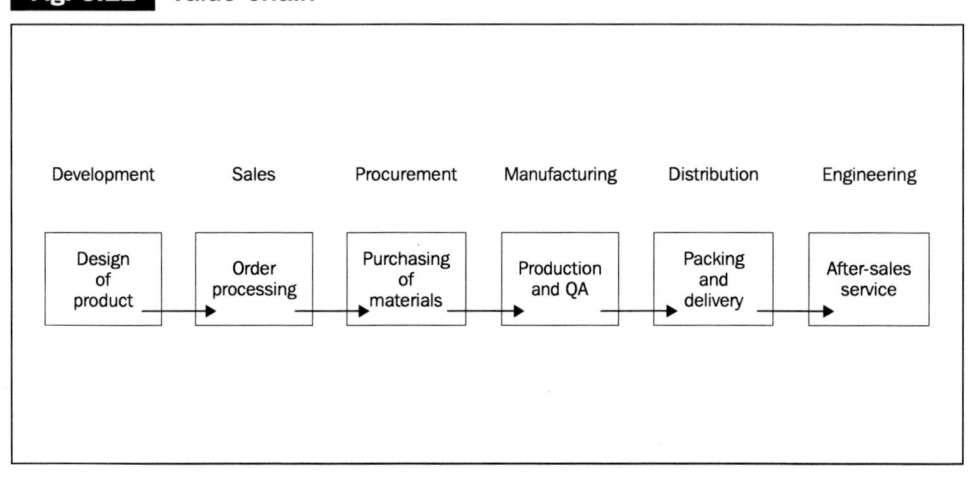

Development	Sales	Procurement	Manufacturing	Distribution	Engineering
Design of product	Order processing	Purchasing of materials	Production and QA	Packing and delivery	After-sales service

Johnson, in his book *Relevance Regained*, emphasised the need to remove constraints, i.e. practices and assumptions that cause delay, excess and variation of processes that cause work, not to optimise within them. He questioned the categorisation of non-value-added tasks as ones that must be removed and instead argued that, if the activity was being performed, then it was considered essential within the constraints that management had laid down for performance of that activity. The insistence of ABCM teams in asking workers to categorise their work as 'non-value-added' activity proved counter-productive and demotivating to staff morale. Instead, focus rightly shifted to processes and removal of constraints. Activity categorisation can still be useful within project teams, but the use of the alternative descriptions of 'core, diversionary and support' is less emotive and therefore recommended. Such classification will, of course, vary depending on the level that is being focused on, i.e. cost centre, department or corporate.

Business process reengineering

Introduction

While activity classification or value analysis still has its place within project teams, the focus of business-improvement initiatives is now rightly directed at processes. BPR has acquired something of a bad reputation since it was first proposed by Hammer[3] in the early 1990s. A statistic often quoted was that 'seven out of ten BPR projects fail', without any clear definition of what constituted either BPR or failure. The principle of examining processes to see if they can be improved by redesign is sound, but like all projects it should have clearly defined objectives and senior management backing to carry through those objectives, even if this is sometimes 'politically' difficult.

Steps in a BPR programme

1 Decide on the processes to be examined and their order of priority.

2 Appoint a process-review project team, comprised of representatives of all parts of the process to be examined.

3 Carry out hierarchical process analysis (discussed earlier in this chapter).

4 Draw process maps and graphics, showing flows, costs, cost drivers, value analysis, functional and geographic boundaries. For example, see Fig. 5.12, The procurement process.

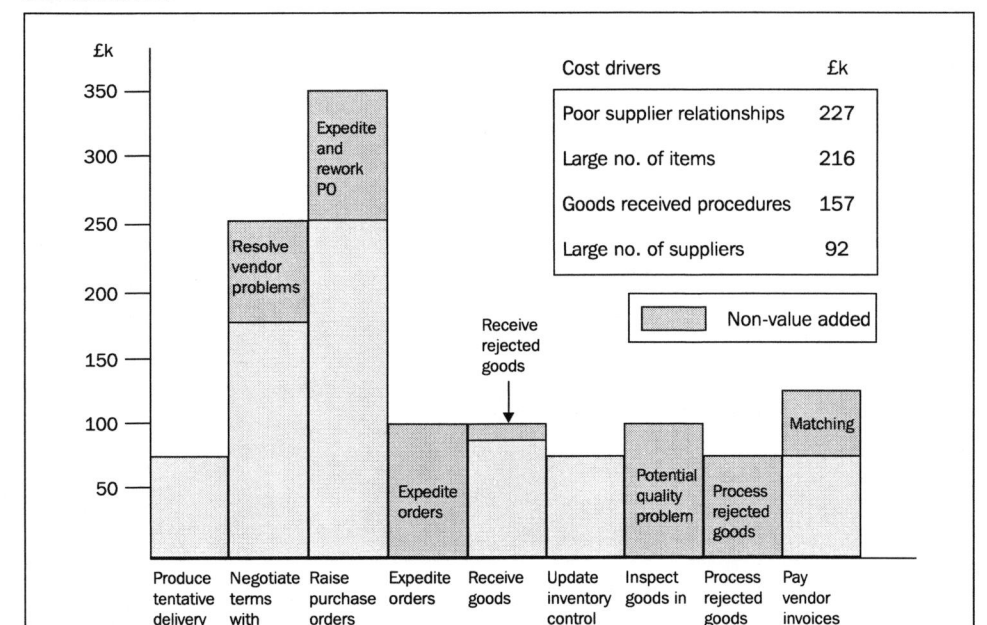

Fig. 5.12 The procurement process (1.1mn)

Cost drivers	£k
Poor supplier relationships	227
Large no. of items	216
Goods received procedures	157
Large no. of suppliers	92

5 Use other tools and techniques to illustrate all of the factors relating to the particular process under examination. For example, *see* Fig. 5.13, Cause and effect analysis, for brainstorming and analysis. This figure has been used to depict the technique while reminding analysts of the areas of improvement to look for. Figure 5.14, Process improvement lifecycle, illustrates the effect of performance-improvement ideas on the process. Some 90% of ideas from these initiatives are small and easily implemented, while 10% are larger and require more radical change, such as a new computer system.

Fig. 5.13 Cause and effect analysis

Fig. 5.14 Process improvement lifecycle

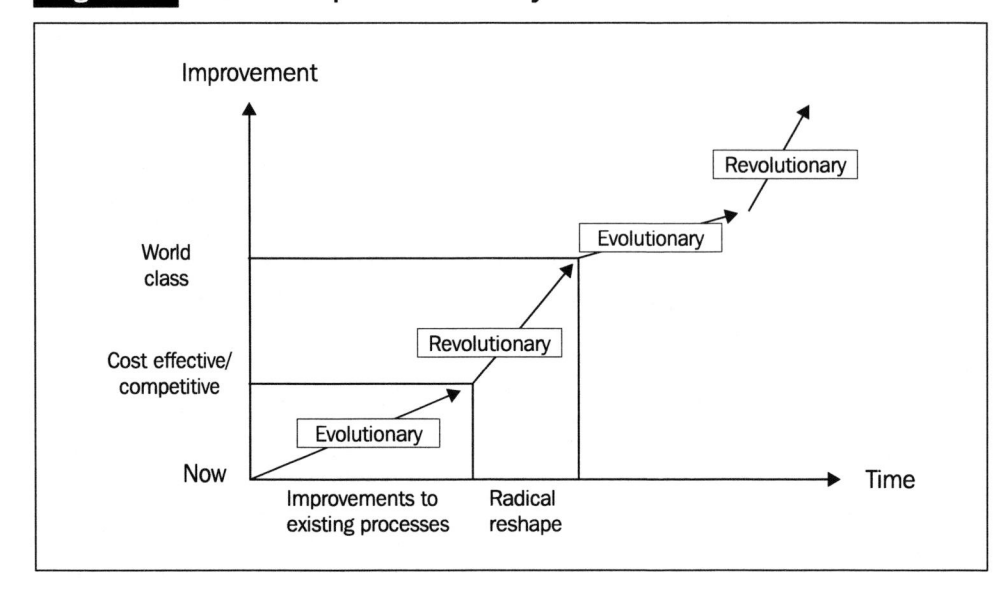

6 Hold brainstorming workshops to discuss and agree changes and establish best practice within the process. As a project leader and/or representative from finance, never attempt to tell the process representatives directly what they are doing wrong or you will encounter the not-invented-here syndrome.

7 Set implementation and performance targets and responsibilities and monitor progress.

Benefits of BPR

- A better understanding of the relationships between activities/subprocesses allowing a radical rethink of how they are performed.
- Identification of improvement ideas from people within the process, who are motivated to implement the changes.
- Cross-functional project-improving communications throughout the business.
- Involvement of all levels of staff in the process, encouraging ownership and accountability for performance.
- Building commitment to continuous improvement at all levels in the organisation.

5.5 PERFORMANCE MANAGEMENT

Introduction

Figure 2.2, Integrated performance management (p.26), illustrates the need to link the value-based strategy via the balanced scorecard measures to operational models, quality models and performance-management systems, which 'drill down' through the organisation and include balanced measures of cost, quality and time for each process/activity/task. When this has been accomplished, then one holistic performance-management system will be in place, encouraging congruent behaviour company wide. Process/activity-based management accounting (ABMA) is the management and control of the company using process/activity-based techniques. It first requires an understanding of how the business operates by analysing the organisation into activities and processes and building a model showing their interrelationships, as explained earlier in the chapter in Section 5.2, Hierarchical process/activity analysis.

The activity-based techniques discussed in this section relate not to one-off initiatives, like product costing or BPR, but to an on-going planning, monitoring and control system that facilitates controlled continuous improvement company wide. The use of one-off ABT to inform and reduce costs can be likened to a crash diet – weight is noticeably lost, but once you are off the diet the weight quickly returns. The need to maintain the necessary weight loss requires a recognition that a complete change of eating habits and lifestyle is required and that is what the use of ABMA provides for a business. ABMA is a series of related management techniques based on activity analysis, including activity-based budgeting; the need to cascade objectives down the organisation through processes and activities; the setting of a balanced set of performance measures and targets for each process and activity; the ability to evaluate alternative service levels and to prioritise them – priority-based budgeting; activity-based reporting, including earned value analysis. In Chapter 7 on Information management, the IT tools that assist in the application of these on-going tools and techniques are discussed in detail.

Process/activity-based budgeting (ABB)

Having carried out the necessary process/activity analysis and fully understood how the business operates, it is then possible to plan, monitor and control the entire business based on the activities and processes that are performed. Instead of taking the traditional approach and looking simply at cost elements – for example how many people, how much office space, and how much other resource is required to run a budget centre – activity-based budgeting allows us to examine exactly what activities are performed by the budget centre and what resources are consumed by each activity, as can be seen in Fig. 5.15, Activity budgeting. By understanding not only what each activity costs to perform, i.e. what resources it has consumed, but also what outputs it produces, for example how many systems are being developed, how many systems are being tested, then we can look at the unit costs per activity output, which enables us effectively to:

- make comparisons to other similar activities both internally and externally, i.e. benchmarking, covered in Chapter 6
- set clear measurable objectives and responsibilities for all activities (support and operational) linked hierarchically to the corporate strategy, incorporating non-financial and qualitative goals
- set clear performance measures and targets for the planning period, linked hierarchically to the balanced scorecard (covered in detail in Chapter 4), incorporating non-financial and qualitative measures
- set a clear link between and vary the budget for resources consumed in relationship to outputs produced
- examine alternative service levels for activities and processes and prioritise their importance to the business, allowing reductions in budget to be made on a basis

that relates to the importance to the business, in preference to the traditional 'across-the-board' cuts irrespective of the medium- and long-term effects, i.e. priority-based budgeting

- evaluate strategic simulations using 'what if' scenarios within the model.

Fig. 5.15 Activity budgeting

System design and delivery subprocess

Cost element report	£k
Staff salaries	500
Equipment	600
Consultancy	150
Office expenses	100
Premises	90
	1440

Activity-based report	£k
Business analysis	230
System development	250
System testing	190
System assurance	100
Documentation	70
System delivery	600
	1440

Cascading objectives and responsibilities down the process hierarchy

Introduction

Using the IT example, the setting of objectives and responsibilities can be cascaded down the process/activity hierarchy by drilling down in the same way as delegated or devolved budgeting would do. The only difference is that the association is against the activity and process hierarchy, not the organisational structure, although both can be accommodated quite easily.

Level 1 – Corporate

Objectives and responsibilities set as guidelines for the company as a whole, often linked into the balanced scorecard outcomes, critical success factors (CSFs) and key performance indicators.

Level 2 – Core processes

Objectives and responsibilities set as guidelines for each core process delivering goods and/or services to the customer.

Level 3 – Subprocesses

At this stage each core process will cascade objectives and responsibilities down to each of the subprocesses, including support, that contribute to its delivery of outputs. One such subprocess would be the systems design and delivery subprocess.

Level 4 – Activities (of the systems design and delivery subprocess)

(i)   Business analysis

(ii) System development

(iii) System testing

(iv) System assurance

(v)   Documentation

(vi) System delivery.

Level 5 – Tasks (of system delivery activity)

(i)   Transition to new system

(ii) Operating system

(iii) System support.

Level 6 – Subtasks (of system support task)

(i)   Help desk

(ii) System management

(iii) Software maintenance.

An example of an overall objective set for help desk might be:

> *To support customers in the most effective and efficient manner possible.*

Setting balanced performance measures and targets

Performance measures are the quantification of how well the activities within a process or the outputs of processes achieve specified goals. Hronec, in his book *Vital Signs*,[4] said:

> *Without performance measurement, improvement cannot be meaningful: it cannot last and only by focusing simultaneously on cost, quality and time can a company optimise its results.*

- Quality quantifies the 'goodness' of a product or service.
- Time quantifies the 'goodness' of a process.
- Cost quantifies the economics of the 'goodness'.

Traditionally, the finance function would have concerned itself solely with cost, and the quality function, through the company's quality-management initiative, would equally be trying to maximise quality without due concern for the cost implications. Figure 5.16, Balanced performance measures, shows how within this holistic, company-wide system each activity and process needs to be measured not just in cost terms, but in terms of its quality and time measures, representing a balanced view. Any change in one measure (axis) will have a direct relationship on the other measures (axes); for example reductions in cost, all other things being equal, will result in an adverse effect on time or quality or both. The measurement of these three elements defines clearly the level of service being provided by the activity.

Fig. 5.16 Balanced performance measures

Time — time taken to handle enquiry

Activity

Help desk

Cost — cost per enquiry

Quality — % of enquiries answered without referral

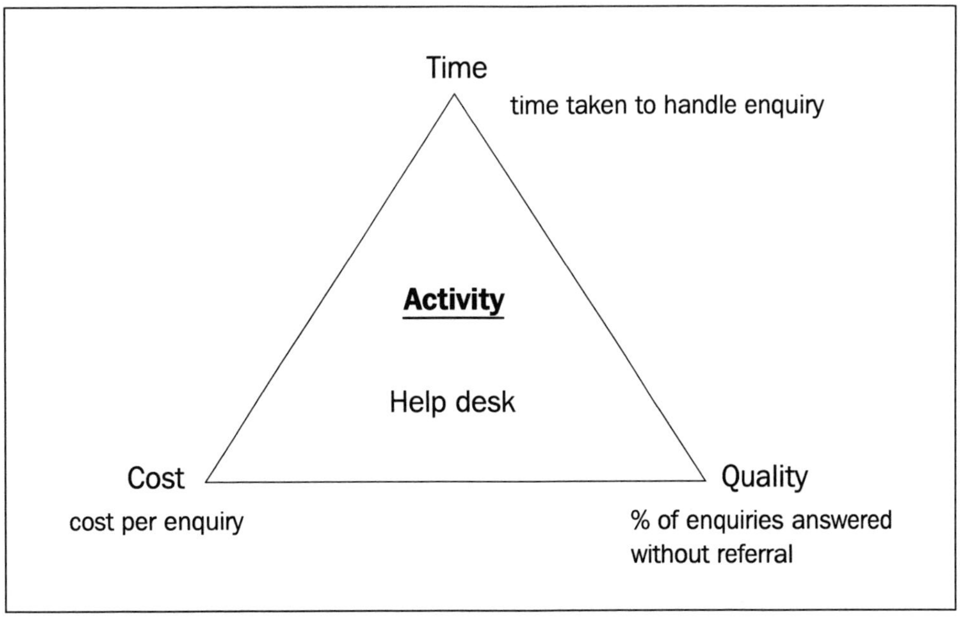

These measures and targets will be linked directly to the objectives and responsibilities cascaded down the organisation from the balanced scorecard or corporate view. In our help desk example in Fig. 5.16, the cost measure could be average cost per enquiry, the time measure, average time taken to handle the enquiry, and the quality measure, the percentage of enquiries answered without referral.

Some of the benefits of setting performance measures for all levels of activities and processes within the organisation are as follows:

- It enables the level of service being delivered by the activity or process to be defined.
- It enables the customer (internal or external) to specify his or her requirements.
- It allows a baseline to be measured and any improvements monitored against it.
- It allows 'best practice' to be identified through benchmarking.
- It facilitates the drive for change to achieve 'best practice'.

Hronec's quantum performance matrix

To use as a prompt when setting process/activity performance measures, Hronec produced a matrix of the types of time, quality and cost measures that could be set.

Cost

- **Inputs**   Unit cost of process inputs
- **Outputs**   Unit cost of process outputs
- **Activities**   Cost of performing a process activity
- **Tasks**   Cost of performing a task

Time

- **Velocity**   Speed of delivery of process output
- **Flexibility**   Ability of the process to respond to varying demands
- **Responsiveness**   Willingness and readiness to provide prompt service
- **Resilience**   Ability to change

Quality

- **Conformance** — Effectiveness of a process, i.e. meeting or exceeding customer satisfaction
- **Productivity** — Efficiency of a process, i.e. doing the right things in the correct way
- **Reliability** — Consistency of performance and dependability
- **Empathy** — Individualised attention, e.g. customer satisfaction rating
- **Credibility** — Trustworthiness, honesty
- **Competence** — Required skills and knowledge

It is possible to set time, quality and cost measures for any activity or process.

Evaluation of alternative service levels

Figure 5.17, Alternative service levels, demonstrates how, once the level of service of an activity or process like the help desk has been defined in terms of time, quality and cost measurements, alternative levels of service can be evaluated. This means that when setting budgets or discussing levels of required service with customers (internal or external), alternatives, where appropriate, can be clearly identified, measured and compared. In this example of the help desk, it can be seen that by increasing or decreasing staffing of the activity, cost and quality increase or decrease accordingly, thus providing choice as to the appropriate level of service for the business.

Fig. 5.17 Alternative service levels

Help desk activity

Higher	Cost per enquiry £5 / 95% answered without referral / 2 minutes to answer enquiry
Current	Cost per enquiry £3 / 90% answered without referral / 3 minutes to answer enquiry
Lower	Cost per enquiry £2 / 85% answered without referral / 5 minutes to answer enquiry

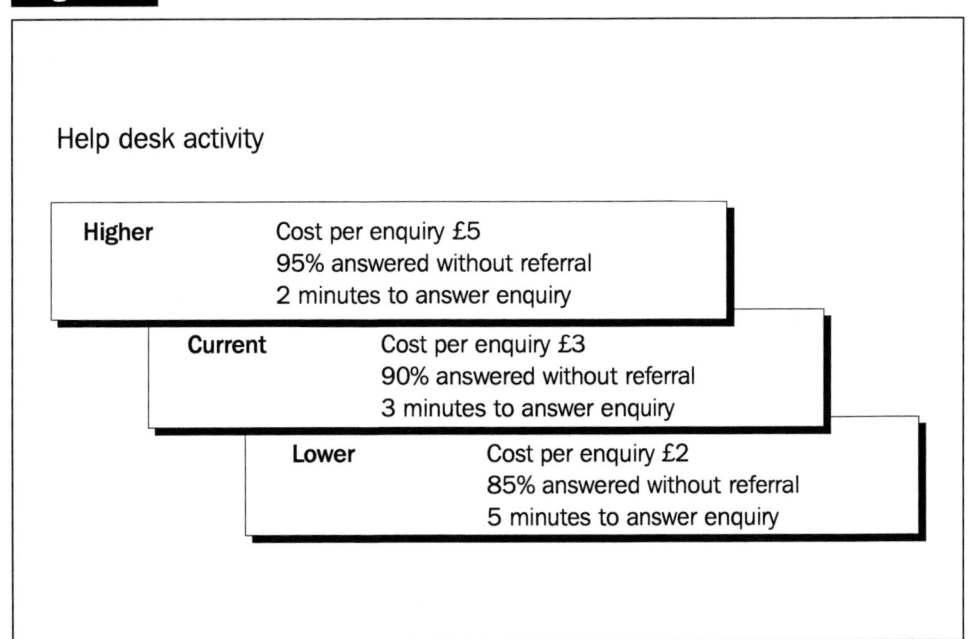

Priority-based budgeting (PBB)

By applying a rating scale like the one shown in Fig. 5.18, PBB rating scale, to the various levels of service evaluated at activity and/or process level, it is possible to rank the levels of service in order of importance to the running of the business. In this way, when scarce funds are being competed for, those that are evaluated as being more crucial to the running of the business are funded first. Ranking and prioritising of this kind have been common in capital budgeting for many years.

Fig. 5.18 Priority-based budgeting rating scale

10	Essential to the business
9	Critical – unavoidable without substantial loss or damage
8	Very attractive, important and productive increments of service
7	Important – hard to see how they could be dropped
6	Significant benefits, but could conceivably be dropped
5	Desirable, but first to be dropped if funding curtailed
4	Marginal, but first to be supported if funding increased
3	Possible, but only if much increased funding available
2	Doubtful – not sufficient justification at present
1	Unlikely ever to be funded

Fig. 5.19 Priority-based budget – security

Purpose and benefits

- Secure environment for staff
- Retain MOD contracts
- Minimise vandalism and theft
- Protect intellectual property

Changes

- Assumed
  - Remote-controlled gates
  - Combined security/reception
  - Offices monitored remotely
- Possible
  - Card key access
  - Agency personnel
- Rejected
  - Dogs

Service levels	No.	£k
1 MOD standard	11	193
2 Increased security	18	309
3 Third traffic gate	24	408
4 Reduced vandalism	27	444

Total proposed	27	444	81%
Current budget	35	548	100%

Figure 5.19, Priority-based budget – security, is an example of a priority-based budget being compiled for a security activity. It clearly sets out the objectives and goals to be achieved by the activity. It lists the ideas for change that the team has considered as ways of improving the service, some of which it is assumed will proceed and have been included in the proposal, two of which are still being evaluated and one of which has been rejected. It sets out four possible levels of service that it could deliver over the coming budget period, with their subsequent number of employees and total costs. The MOD standard is the minimum level of service possible, because the company depends on MOD contracts for its core business. It can be seen that by incorporating the assumed changes, a higher level of service is being offered at service level four at a lower cost than the current budget.

Figure 5.20, Departmental priority budget, lists the alternative levels of service for security together with the levels of service being offered by two other activities, catering and typing, which feature in the same department for budget purposes. They are ranked in order of the rating score that they achieved. This enables the departmental manager to draw a line in accordance with the resource that is finally allocated in the budget, for example if it were £500 000 then everything would be funded up to and including typing service level two, important reports, but excluding catering service levels three and four and security service levels three and four.

Fig. 5.20 Departmental priority budget

				Increment		Cumulative		
Rank	Rating	Subject	Level of service	No.	£k	No.	£k	%
1	10	Security	1 MOD standard	11	193	11	193	20
2	10	Catering	1 Room and hot water	1	15	12	208	22
3	9.1	Security	2 Increased security	7	116	19	324	34
4	8.5	Typing	1 External only	7	70	26	394	41
5	7.2	Catering	2 Sandwiches and drinks	4	50	30	444	46
6	6.7	Typing	2 Important reports	5	50	35	494	51
7	5.2	Catering	3 Basic/self-service	10	120	45	614	64
8	4.5	Catering	4 Choice and service	6	85	51	699	73
9	4.2	Security	3 Third traffic gate	6	99	57	798	83

Budgeting panels

The ranking of importance to the organisation of the alternative service levels needs to be carried out by a group of managers who are representative of the whole organisation. This is crucial to gain a balanced view. For example, if the finance function budget were being considered, it is probable that the finance manager may, quite understandably, put a higher rating score on the provision of management information than would other members of the organisation. It would depend entirely on how useful they viewed the information being provided as being. The information being produced from a traditional finance function was rarely considered to carry much importance, but that provided by a transformed finance function, one in touch with its customers, would rate more highly.

A budgeting panel needs to be formed, consisting of:

- the overall departmental/process manager (usually in the chair)
- lower-level managers from his or her department/process (as appropriate)
- managers representative of the rest of the organisation, particularly from its (internal) suppliers and (internal) customers
- the PBB project manager (usually from the finance function).

The activity/process manager would himself (or herself) be responsible, with help from the PBB manager and his or her line manager, for preparing his Budget Proposal, which would include:

- proposed activity/process budget
- proposed objectives and goals
- proposals for performance improvements
- proposed performance measures and targets
- alternative service levels, with details of their benefits and consequences
- performance to date (unless this was the first meeting of the panel).

He would attend the budgeting panel to present his proposals and answer questions directly from the panel members, prior to them ranking the alternatives and recommending:

- their ranked levels of service
- performance improvements
- performance measures and targets.

This information arms the departmental/process manager and the PBB manager with the necessary priorities when the final decision on funding is made by the company's board of directors or other final decision-making body as appropriate.

Activity-based reporting

Monitoring and reporting in the activity-based approach are based on forward-looking trend analysis, processes in control, a balanced set of performance measures at all levels, waste and unused capacity, concentrating on utilisation and output volumes, where service-level options are formally prioritised for the good of the business. The emphasis is on activities and processes not functional departments; on value-based strategy not 'last year minus' focusing instead on benchmarked industry targets. This simple and focused overall approach supports a 'bottom-up empowered' organisation with a culture of continuous improvement. The all-encompassing performance-management system is very likely to utilise the latest IT and be graphical in nature, using trend analysis, alerts and exceptions to the full. This subject is dealt with in more detail in Chapter 7 on Information management and in the Manchester Council case study in Chapter 4.

However, it is worth explaining here that activity analysis does not necessitate everyone in the organisation collecting time-recorded information on a regular basis. If time recording is the organisational culture, then this is not considered a hardship; on the other hand, it is not essential in order to report on an activity basis. Typically, a budget centre will carry out four or five activities and, as can be seen from Fig. 5.21, Earned value activity analysis, a calculation can be made for each activity based on Actual volume × Budgeted cost (a standard cost approach). This approach can be compared to Fig. 5.22, Actual activity analysis, where actual time recording and actual costs are available for each activity.

Fig. 5.21 Earned value activity analysis

Activity	Output measure	Actual output (k)	Budget cost per unit (£)	Earned value (£)	Target Cost per unit	Target EV (£k)
Process sales invoices	Invoices	1.5	16.7	25.0	10.0	15.0
Process staff claims	Claims	1.2	3.0	3.6	2.0	2.4
Banking/cash receipts	Cheques banked	3.0	0.7	2.1	0.7	2.1
Control balance sheet	Accounts	0.5	6.0	3.0	6.0	6.0
Management	Staff	5.0	1.0	5.0	1.0	5.0

Total earned value (£k)	38.7	30.5
Actual cost	42.0	42.0
Variance	−3.3	−11.5
% Effective	92	73

Transforming the Finance Function

Fig. 5.22 Actual activity analysis

Activity	Output measure (number of)		Volume	Cost (£k)	Cost per unit (£)	Target cost per unit (£)
Process sales invoices	Invoices	Budget	1.5	25	16.7	10
		Actual	1.5	27	18	
Process staff claims	Claims	Budget	1	3	3	2
		Actual	1.2	3	2.5	
Banking/cash receipts	Cheques banked	Budget	3	2	0.7	0.7
		Actual	3	3	1	
Control balance sheets	Accounts	Budget	0.5	3	6	6
		Actual	0.5	3	6	
Management	Staff	Budget	5	5	1	1
		Actual	5	6	1.2	
TOTAL		Budget		38		
		Actual		42		

CASE STUDY

Process-based performance improvement in Lund University Hospital[5]

Background

As with so many organisations operating within the public sector, the healthcare sector in Sweden has to contend with fierce demands for rationalisation and savings at the same time as the need for improving quality. Figure 5.23, Competing demands, illustrates the dilemma of competing needs and demands, where the three circles represent medical needs, patient demand and what is provided.

Fig. 5.23 Lund – Competing demands

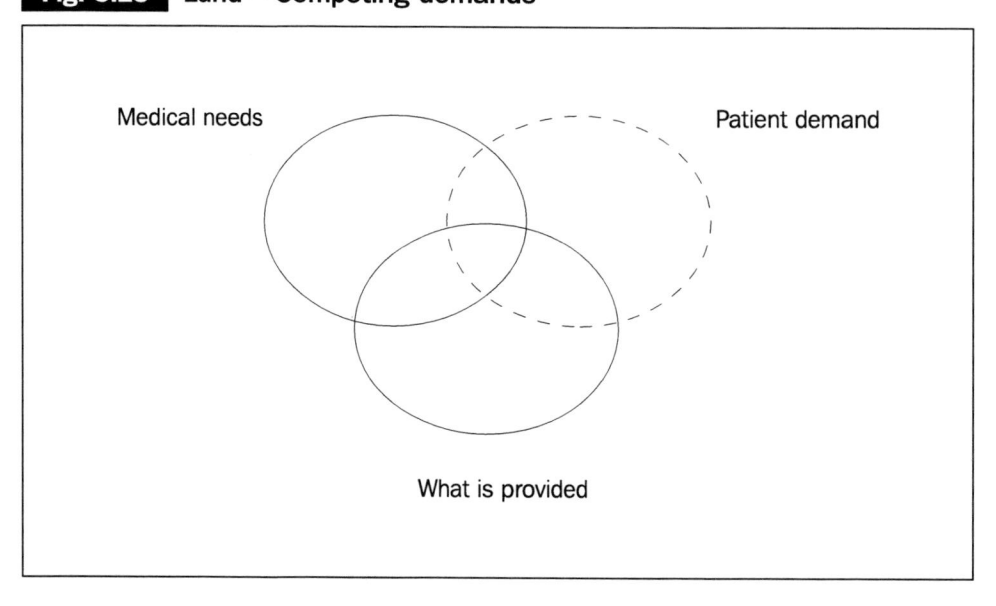

The allergy clinic is one of five clinics within the ENT (ear, nose and throat) department at Lund University Hospital in Sweden, with about 200 staff. In 1996, the ENT department faced both financial and quality problems. Because of increased allergy awareness in society, a long waiting list had developed. The ENT department also had problems with poor patient satisfaction, unacceptable waiting times and dissatisfied staff. The doctors were working hard and the nurses felt powerless to influence the situation. The assistant head of department, Dr Ulf Hallgarde, realised the need for change. The goal was to establish a new evaluation system for creating a long-term climate for improvements and better economic awareness within the organisation. He believed that an activity- and process-based analysis could provide the means to manage the necessary change. As a result, a project was initiated in which the whole organisation participated.

Methodology

The objectives of the project were defined as:

- to map and document the processes and use the same information for performance measurement
- to calculate the profitability of the services using activity-based costing
- to create a common system for management and staff, based on the process analysis, to work with change management for continuous improvements.

In the words of Dr Ulf Hallgarde:

> *With a process-based performance measurement system it is possible to achieve continuous improvements by measuring process-based measures like activity cost, leadtime or quality. The focus is upon the processes of the organisation and not on departmental costs or specific expenditures.*

Steps

1 In the first phase of the analysis, activities and processes were identified and mapped. This was done through a series of interviews and workshops.
2 The processes were then measured by calculating the activity costs, using activity-based costing, which focused on which resources are used in each activity and which activities are needed for each service/treatment, as illustrated in Fig. 5.24, Activity-based costing, and Fig. 5.25, The complete picture. This analysis generated important information about the clinic's leadtimes and the costs of quality errors, as illustrated in Fig. 5.26, The medical process, Fig. 5.27, The patient added value, and Fig. 5.28, Allergy clinic core processes, which are mapped in QPR Process Guide software.
3 Identification of basic problems.
4 Redesign of the processes.
5 Implementation of a process-based performance-measurement system for continuous improvement.

Fig. 5.24 Lund – Activity-based costing

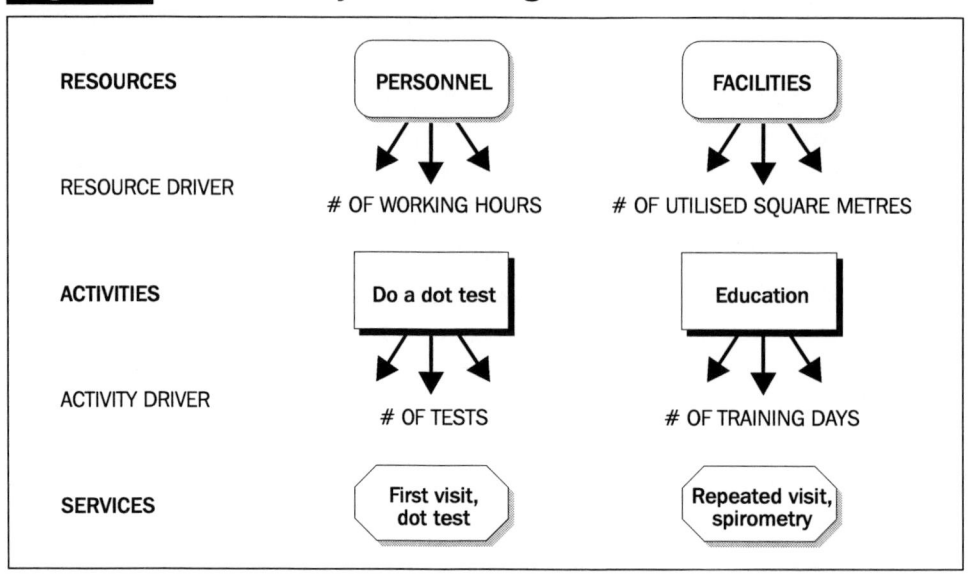

RESOURCES	PERSONNEL	FACILITIES
RESOURCE DRIVER	# OF WORKING HOURS	# OF UTILISED SQUARE METRES
ACTIVITIES	Do a dot test	Education
ACTIVITY DRIVER	# OF TESTS	# OF TRAINING DAYS
SERVICES	First visit, dot test	Repeated visit, spirometry

Fig. 5.25 Lund – The complete picture

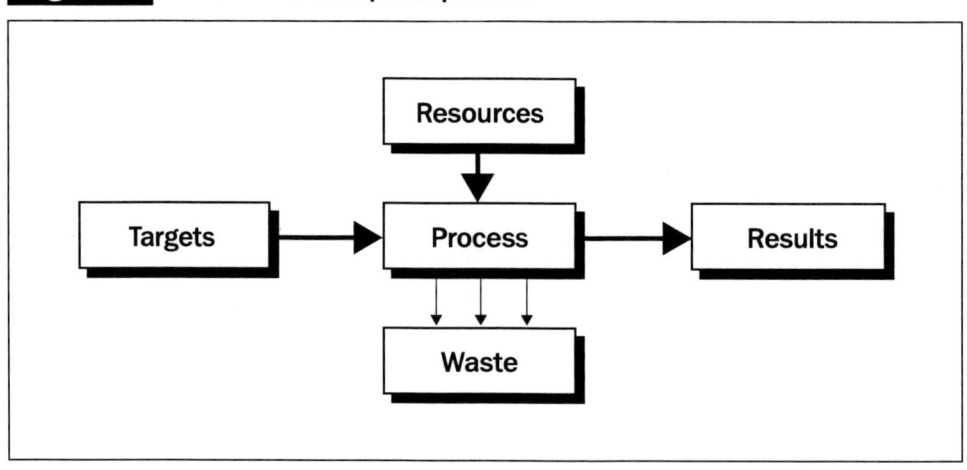

Targets → Process → Results; Resources → Process; Process → Waste

Fig. 5.26 Lund – The medical process

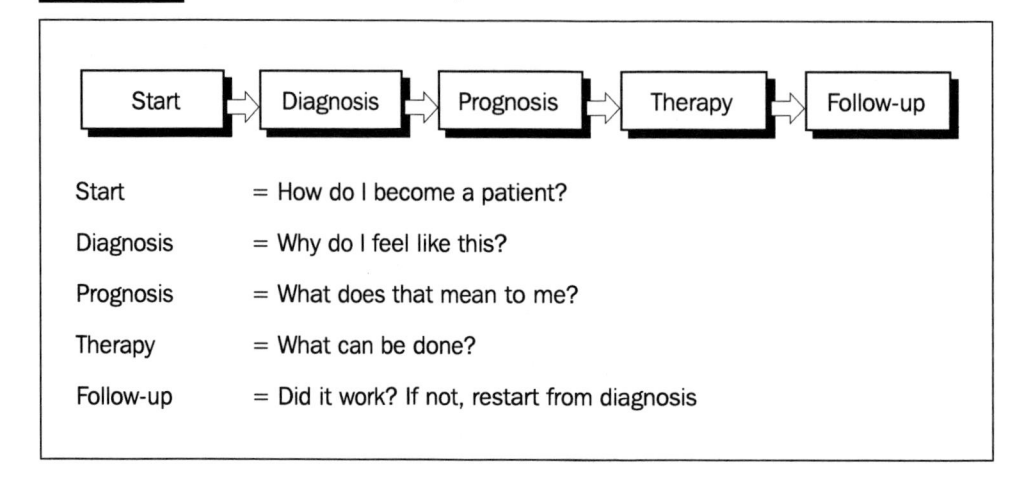

Start → Diagnosis → Prognosis → Therapy → Follow-up

Start = How do I become a patient?
Diagnosis = Why do I feel like this?
Prognosis = What does that mean to me?
Therapy = What can be done?
Follow-up = Did it work? If not, restart from diagnosis

Activity/process-based techniques

Fig. 5.27 Lund – The patient added value

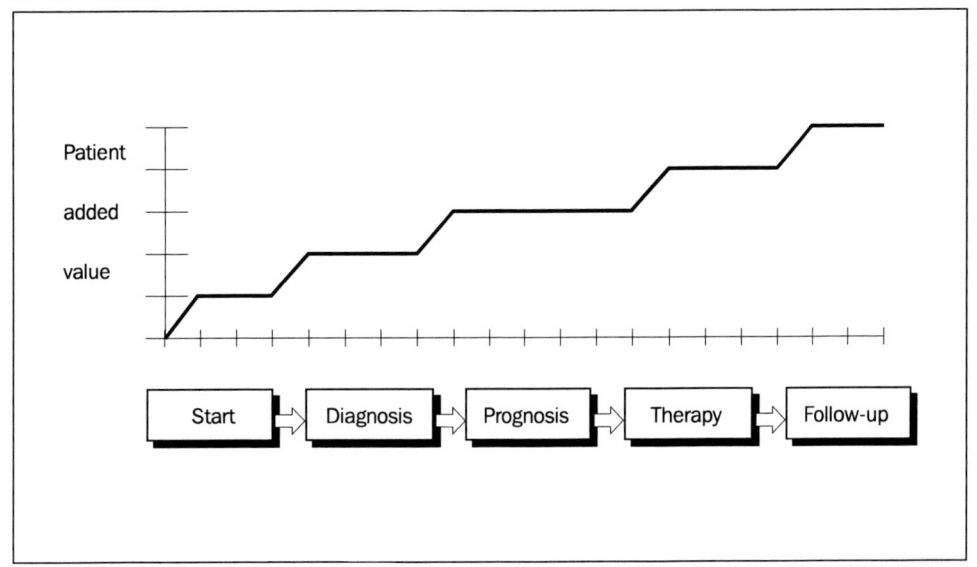

Fig. 5.28 Lund – Allergy clinic core processes

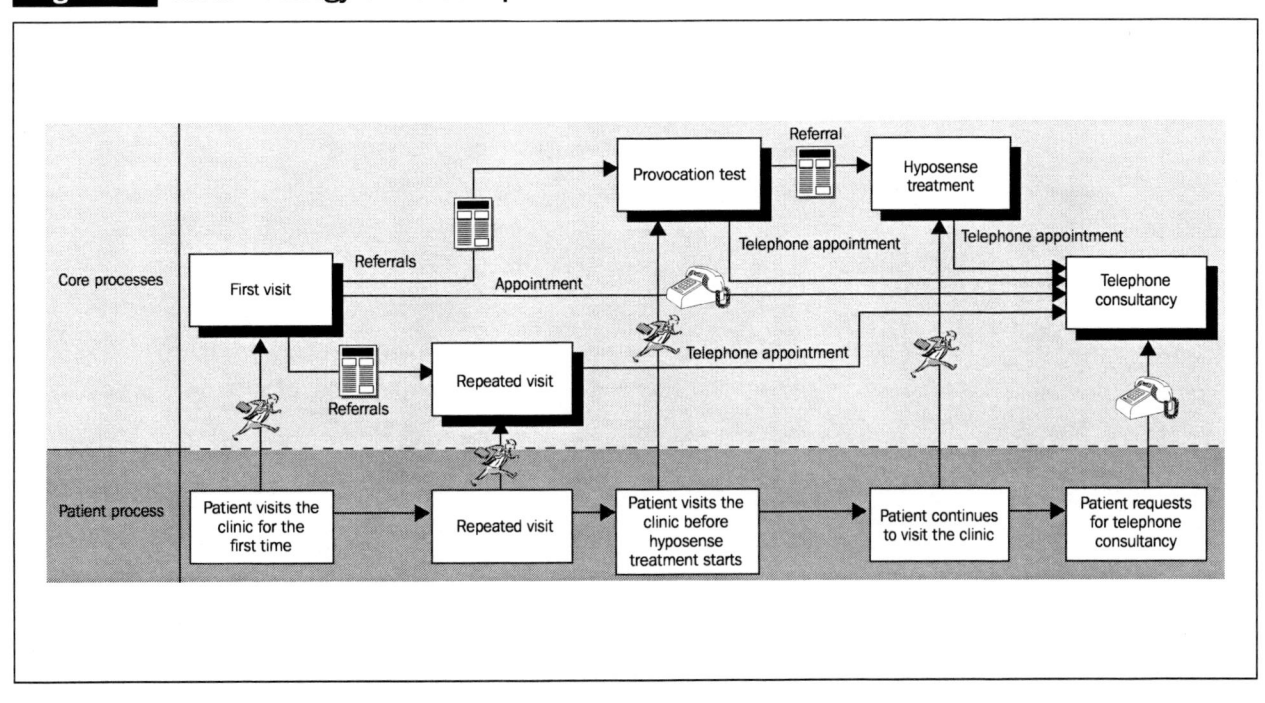

Results

Examples of improvements include the following:

- Since recommendations to allergy patients are often similar, the doctors found themselves repeating the same advice to many patients. The process changes resulted in a more effective information system, consisting of relevant videos and brochures handed out to the patient after visits. In turn, doctors and nurses were able to spend more time on value-adding activities and less time and resources on repeating information to the patients.

- The administrative costs of a patient visit were $55. In order to reduce these costs, as many tests as possible were performed on the first visit (instead of doing a number of visits and one test at each visit). The follow-ups for these visits are now done over the telephone, at a reduced cost of $6 per follow-up. This has also been welcomed by the patients, who prefer not to make unnecessary visits to the hospital.

- By calculating the costs of different services offered by the allergy clinic, it was possible to evaluate trade-offs between the different tests performed. For instance, the blood tests used to determine what type of allergy the patient suffered from had been regarded as an inexpensive method. The analysis proved the opposite. In addition, the patient had to wait for the results of the blood test, which was sent off for a diagnosis. By changing the method to dot tests, the time for this activity was reduced and delays for patients shortened.

- Another problem that was identified was that the journal system for patient notes was too inflexible and this was replaced with a computerised documentation system in 1998.

- A problem that will take slightly longer to resolve is a radical change in the organisational structure to capture substantial savings in facilities and administrative activities.

The immediate ideas for improvement represented a saving of approximately 10% of total costs. The longer-term planned savings will amount to 30% of total costs when fully implemented.

Conclusion

Dr Ulf Hallgarde concluded that in order to succeed and reach the targets set in organisations, it is of utmost importance that the right kind of information tools are used. In this new scenario, previous measurement systems based on traditional measurement techniques do not give enough relevant information. Using the approach of process-based performance measurement, costs can be allocated to a hospital's services more appropriately and at the same time process-based information can be obtained. It is a tool for both management and staff and can be used for managing change more effectively.

CASE STUDY
ABT and benchmarking at Metropolitan Housing Trust[6]

Background

Metropolitan Housing Trust (MHT) operates out of four regions, three in London and one in the Midlands. Senior management wanted to look at the relevance and cost effectiveness to MHT of activity-based techniques by undertaking an exercise to look at the administrative processes from receipt of a maintenance fault notification to the payment of the invoice, referred to for this exercise as the 'reactive repair process'.

A new housing-specific software package had been installed by MHT about a year prior to this project being undertaken. This software was designed to enable properties to be viewed on-line while calls from tenants were in progress. A methodology for using the new system was agreed and all regions were trained. The objectives of the ABT exercise were agreed as follows:

Activity/process-based techniques

- Map the 'reactive repair process' (RRP) and identify any differences between regions.
- Cost the activities within the process.
- Examine quantitative and qualitative performance measures for the process.
- Hold workshops to discuss analyses and identify improvements and best practice.
- Review external influences and support activities.
- Benchmark the process with another housing association, Northern Counties, based in Manchester, which uses the same software package. (This objective was added during the project to enable a better understanding of the problems being experienced with IT performance.)

ABC

A member of staff built an ABC model using a spreadsheet package, determining the costs of the activities within the process, see Fig. 5.29, RRP activity costs, for each region, see Fig. 5.30, RRP – regional activity costs per order, and for costs per order and stock unit, see Fig. 5.31, Average costs for repairs and maintenance administration. This information made MHT aware that the administration of each reactive repair order was costing about £50, which, when multiplied by the number of average repairs per year per stock unit, equalled about six weeks' rent. This useful ABC data was available to inform and influence the future operational management of the process.

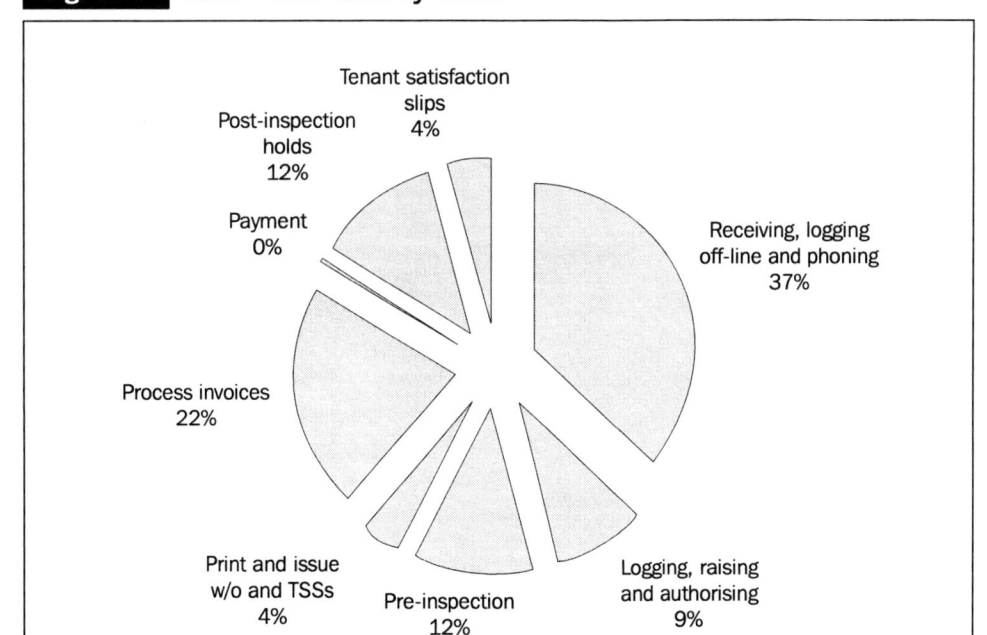

Fig. 5.29 MHT – RRP activity costs

Activity	%
Receiving, logging off-line and phoning	37%
Logging, raising and authorising	9%
Pre-inspection	12%
Print and issue w/o and TSSs	4%
Process invoices	22%
Payment	0%
Post-inspection holds	12%
Tenant satisfaction slips	4%

107

Transforming the Finance Function

Fig. 5.30 MHT – RRP regional activity costs per order

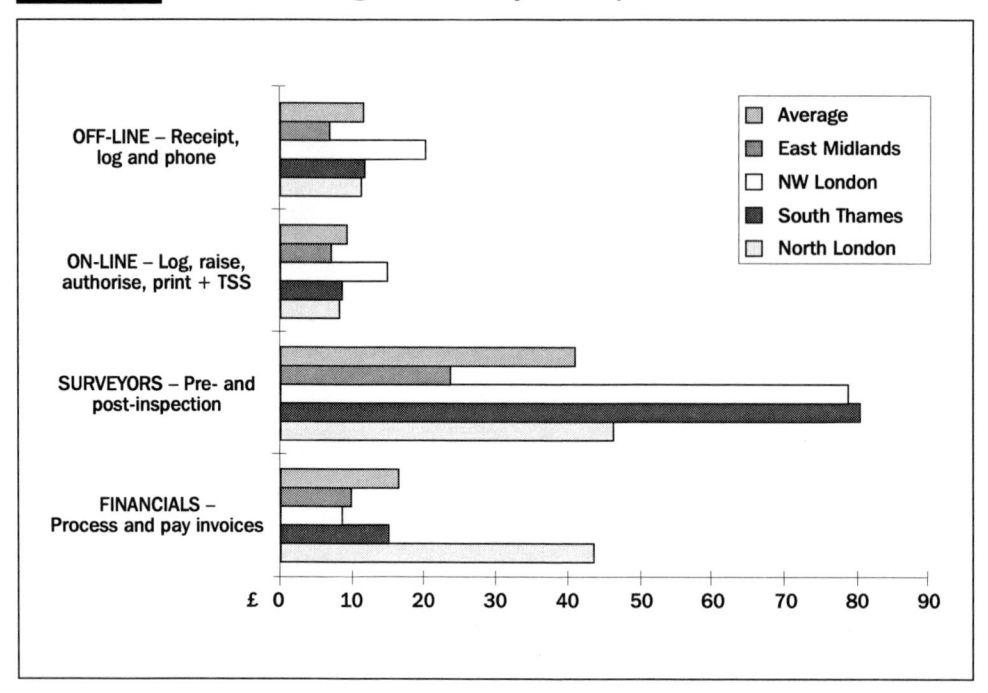

[Bar chart showing costs in £ for OFF-LINE – Receipt, log and phone; ON-LINE – Log, raise, authorise, print + TSS; SURVEYORS – Pre- and post-inspection; FINANCIALS – Process and pay invoices. Legend: Average, East Midlands, NW London, South Thames, North London.]

Fig. 5.31 MHT – Average costs for repairs and maintenance administration

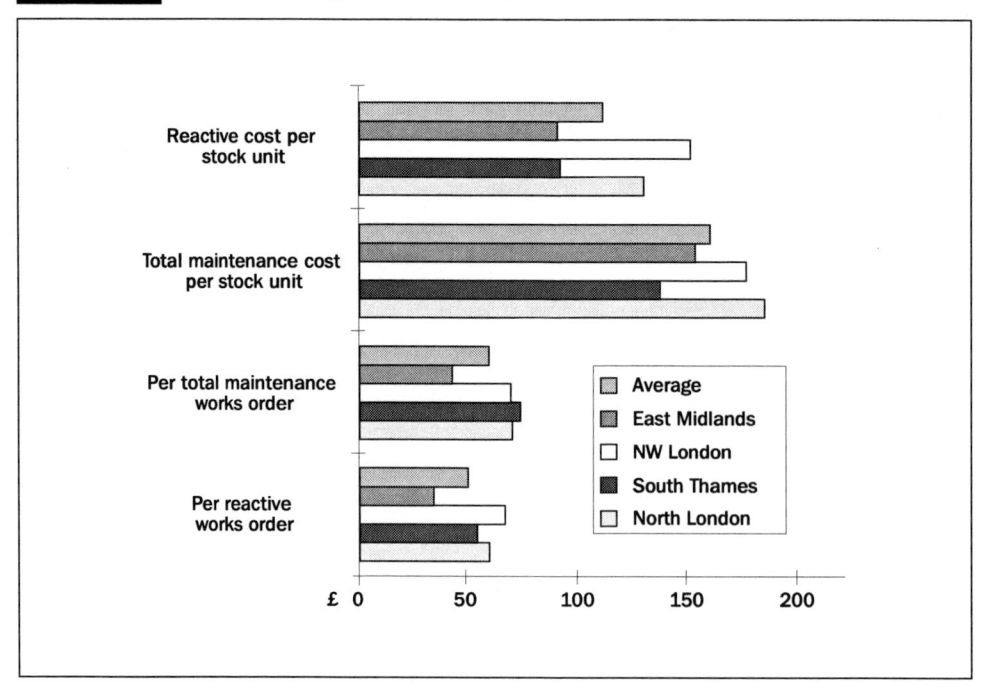

[Bar chart showing costs in £ for Reactive cost per stock unit; Total maintenance cost per stock unit; Per total maintenance works order; Per reactive works order. Legend: Average, East Midlands, NW London, South Thames, North London.]

BPR and benchmarking

The mapping of the processes in each region revealed, not unusually, a number of different practices, which proved beneficial input to the best-practice workshop. However, the one main common problem that all regions were experiencing was the failure to be able to operate on-line when tenants phoned in. It was as a result of this that the decision was taken to benchmark with another housing association, which also used the software package, with the aim of identifying the cause of the problem. A one-day benchmark visit was organised and a report prepared for both parties, which compared:

- general information about the size, geography etc. of the organisations
- maps of the 'reactive repair processes' of both organisations
- the repairs organisational structures and practices
- IT hardware, software and practices.

From the ABC, BPR and benchmarking information, the main influences on cost, i.e. cost drivers, were identified as well as the potential savings if all of the possible changes were put into place; see Fig. 5.32, RRP cost drivers.

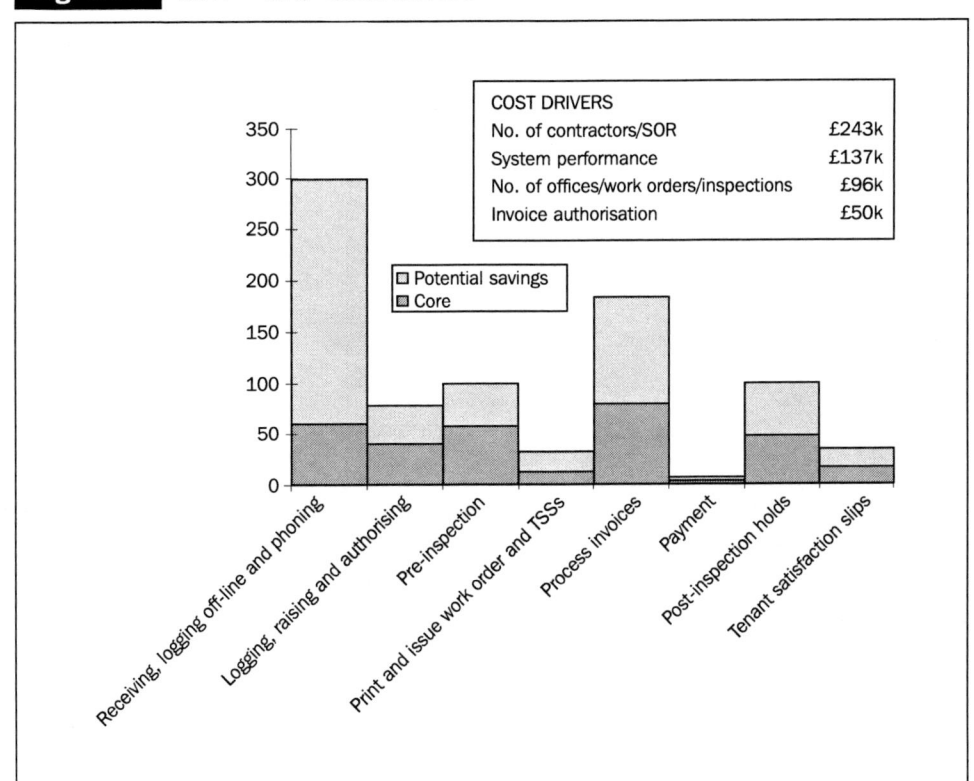

Fig. 5.32 MHT – RRP cost drivers

[Bar chart showing cost drivers with Potential savings and Core categories across activities: Receiving, logging off-line and phoning; Logging, raising and authorising; Pre-inspection; Print and issue work order and TSSs; Process invoices; Payment; Post-inspection holds; Tenant satisfaction slips]

COST DRIVERS
No. of contractors/SOR   £243k
System performance   £137k
No. of offices/work orders/inspections   £96k
Invoice authorisation   £50k

Balanced performance measurement

However, to stress the importance of not just looking at cost information in isolation, a series of balanced performance measures needed to be examined as well as taking account of the obvious social considerations of such an organisation. These included the following:

Cost measures

- Per call received
- Per works order raised
- Per inspection carried out

- Per invoice processed
- Per payment made
- Per repair carried out
- Per stock unit.

Time measures

- Time taken to answer phone calls
- Time taken to carry out inspections
- Time taken to carry out repairs
- Time taken to pay contractors
- Time taken to process invoices
- Time taken to set up new contractors
- Time taken by system to process fault.

Quality measures

- Tenant satisfaction
- % of inspections carried out
- % of inspections that proved unsatisfactory
- % completed within priority levels
- % of errors made on payments
- Number of repairs per stock unit.

Activity-based budgeting

Because this was a pilot project, information needed to be collected from all of the support processes and decisions taken on how the costs should be allocated to the 'reactive repair process', which had been ring-fenced for the exercise. These included costs from all the head office departments and some regional overhead costs. The traditional costing/budgeting system allocated central overheads to regions based on the number of housing units or on staff numbers. These central costs were then added to the regional overhead costs and incorporated as a percentage on-cost into the estimate of time spent on each housing type made by all direct employees.

The ABC/ABB methodology took the average cost of each repair and multiplied it by the number of repairs that actually took place in each housing type, scheme, region, patch. This information was readily available in the housing software; see Fig. 5.33, Repairs and maintenance budget – traditional versus ABC. Equally, if applied across all of MHT's processes then these differences would become more marked. Other processes would include voids, arrears, applicants on waiting lists, allocations and tenancy management. Each of these processes would show a different pattern in different housing types and areas, significant information when housing associations are bidding to take over other properties.

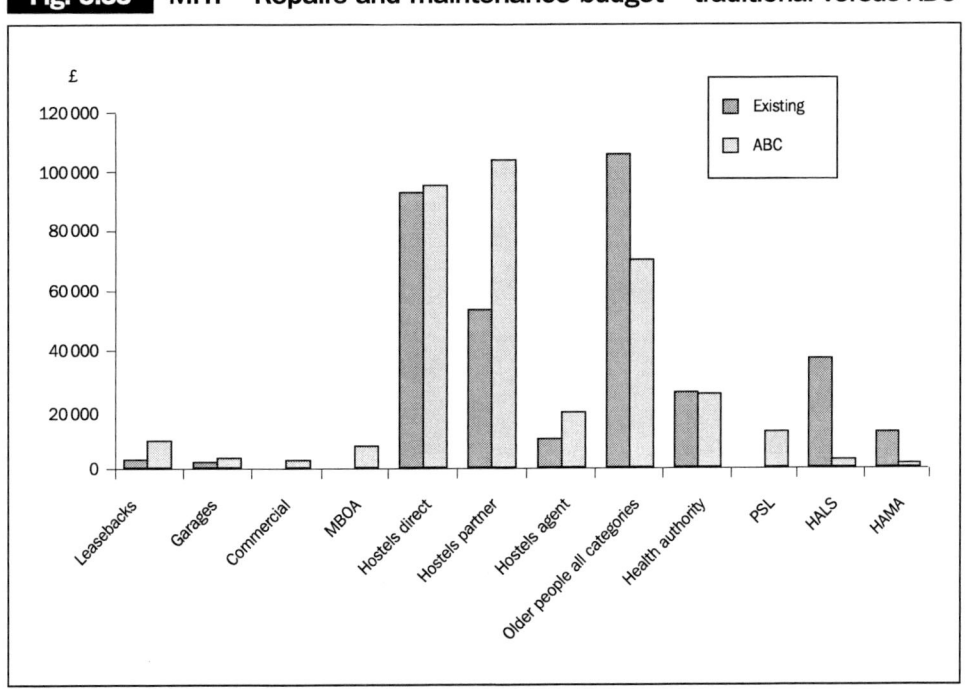

Fig. 5.33 MHT – Repairs and maintenance budget – traditional versus ABC

Conclusion

All of the information and analyses were input into the best-practice workshop for consideration, including:

- external benchmark data
- costing data
- regional analyses
- ideas for improvements, identified from all involved in the process. These included suggestions relating to those departments that interfaced with the process, such as finance and IT.

Attending the workshop were staff and management from the processes in each region and representatives from the interfacing departments, enabling all issues to be discussed, including the external benchmark data. The exercise concluded with a presentation to the senior management team. The main benefits of the exercise were identified as:

- Allowing complexity of maintaining provision to be costed and informing future housing strategy.
- Mapping of processes and procedures allowing best practice to be ascertained and maintained.
- Examination of activity costs by region, allowing more informed operational decision making.
- Assignment of budgets and performance measures to activities, allowing alternative service levels to be evaluated and performance monitored.

6

Benchmarking

- 6.1 Introduction 115
- 6.2 Types of benchmarking 115
- 6.3 Data-gathering methods 117
- 6.4 Phases of the benchmarking process 118
- 6.5 The Benchmarking Code of Conduct 120
- 6.6 Benefits of benchmarking 121
- 6.7 Case study – Tower Hamlets benchmarking 121

6.1 INTRODUCTION

Benchmarking is a tool used to establish processes, costs and performance indicators and compare them against similar organisations, with the aim of identifying and progressing towards 'best practice and best value' through continuous improvement. The importance of ensuring 'true comparability' cannot be stressed strongly enough. It is unlikely that any two products or services will be identical; the key is to identify all of the relevant performance measures, ensuring that the level of service is clearly demonstrated. In this way similar services can be compared, with differences clearly understood.

No two organisations carrying out the same services will necessarily agree on the 'best' level of service to be provided in terms of quality, time and cost at all stages in the process. However, by making comparisons they each learn about the other's costs, methods, procedures, values and judgements. At the end of the process, providers will need to justify the 'value' in the service they are providing and it will be up to customers to decide what level of service they are willing to pay for. Benchmarking can be facilitated by utilising the activity-based techniques described in Chapter 5, particularly the definition and prioritisation of service levels, and the balanced scorecard techniques discussed in Chapter 4.

6.2 TYPES OF BENCHMARKING

Internal

Depending on the type and size of organisation, there is often opportunity to benchmark services internally. This can be made possible because there are several operational units performing the same tasks or because there are numerous subsidiaries/divisions/business units all having their own support functions, including, for example, finance, personnel, training, purchasing, facilities management and payroll. Internal benchmarking, wherever possible, should precede external benchmarking.

External databases

There are now a vast number of external databases, provided mainly by firms of consultants, which make industry, functional, process and other specific comparisons. These are variable in nature and degrees of usefulness. The features to look out for in particular are the following:

- How many organisations are taking part?
- Over what period have the comparisons been made? – Beware of any over more than a two-year period.
- Are they divided into organisation size, industry sector etc.?
- What information is analysed and at what level? Be wary of those that deal at a superficial level and are unable to identify important differences in processes.
- What data is fed back and how often is it updated?
- Is access offered to other benchmark organisations?
- What does it cost?

One such database in the finance function is run by PricewaterhouseCoopers and is called the Global Benchmarks Alliance. It is reasonably priced, has many organisations participating, gives extensive feedback and offers contact with other benchmark organisations. However, it does operate at a high level of process.

Collaborative

Collaborative benchmarking falls into two categories.

In the sector

Again, large numbers of collaborative initiatives are now taking place, and numbers will grow considerably with the advent of 'Best Value' in the public sector, where benchmarking is a condition of the philosophy. These also occur in the private sector, providing that the exchange of information is carefully controlled, often by a third party. One example, which has been under way for a number of years, is that of the London Boroughs Process Benchmarking facilitated by Tower Hamlets and detailed in the case study at the end of this chapter.

Outside the sector

Collaboration does not have to take place within the same industry sector, especially where competitive pressures make it impossible. The support processes discussed above in internal benchmarking lend themselves to benchmarking across a wide range of organisations within the public and private sectors. Equally, benchmarking partners can be identified who share similar operational problems but are in different business sectors. For example:

- The British Airports Authority, Wembley Stadium and Ascot Racecourse all share the problems that come with managing large numbers of people and cars.
- McDonald's, banks and the Post Office all share the problems associated with customers queuing for service.

Competitive

Benchmarking in competitive situations is obviously more difficult. Sometimes information can be found in the public domain (discussed later), or a more unusual approach may be called for. A well-publicised example is Xerox, which:

- runs a competitive analysis laboratory to test and analyse competitors' products, testing after-sales service by calling out engineers and measuring their performance
- bought ten Canon personal copiers when they were first introduced and gave them to its customers to analyse and test their reactions
- studied Japanese inventory methods and as a result reduced the number of vendors from 5000 to 300
- compared itself to Kodak, IBM and Bell. One metric it used in comparisons was the median time from concept to product, for example.

6.3 DATA-GATHERING METHODS

Data-gathering methods for benchmarking will vary in terms of cost, amount and accuracy of the data collected and must be driven by the purpose of the benchmarking. They include:

- clearing houses, exchange groups and benchmarking clubs, already discussed above
- consultant and academic research, frequently carried out for publication in conjunction with sponsors. For example, CIMA Research Foundation is sponsoring a project by University of Leeds, comparing 500 UK implementations of the balanced scorecard
- reverse engineering, as discussed above in the Xerox example
- company visits, which if well planned can achieve a great deal; or can quickly become industrial tourism if not
- questionnaires
- mail or telephone surveys
- internal sources, which include:
  - sales and technical representatives
  - buying officers and suppliers
  - delivery drivers
  - quotes
  - surveys

- customer and factory visits
- competitive analysis
- library databases
- public domain sources, which include:
  - trade publications and shows
  - user groups
  - analysts' reports
  - annual reports
  - patent records
  - research papers
  - newspapers, newsletters
  - buyers' guides
  - government information
  - focus groups
  - World Wide Web.

6.4 PHASES OF THE BENCHMARKING PROCESS

Selecting and prioritising benchmarking projects

While wishing to benchmark everything eventually, it is advisable to select those processes that are likely to yield the most benefit and prioritise them for action first.

Organising benchmarking teams

When selecting a project team to conduct the benchmarking project, always involve people who are knowledgeable about the individual processes in addition to permanent members of the benchmarking team. Skills to consider in selection should include:

- functional/process knowledge
- credibility and respect
- communication skills
- teamwork skills
- interest/motivation
- project-management skills.

It is worth remembering that this benchmarking team will be representing the company externally and should project its culture and image.

Documenting own processes and measures

Before attempting to benchmark externally, it is essential that the company clearly documents its own process using process-mapping techniques and identifies a balanced set of performance indicators, including time, quality and costs. Both techniques were discussed in the last chapter on ABT.

Researching and identifying benchmarking partners

The selection of benchmarking partners for each process will be driven by the project objectives, but needs to be undertaken as early as possible in the process, as there can be a long leadtime.

Analysing benchmarking data and choosing enablers

Analysis of the data collected is crucial to the success of the project, as is the use of tried and tested tools such as:

- data stratification using the fishbone diagram for root cause analysis
- Z chart, which illustrates graphically the gap between the historical trend and the planned future trend
- force field analysis, which demonstrates the impact of helping and hindering forces
- process enablers hierarchy, which shows the path from goal to new practice via the enabler.

These are important in communicating the results in the most effective way possible to aid the success of the project.

Implementing benchmarking study recommendations

Once the desired practice has been agreed through a process of consultation, clear plans of implementation need to be drawn up with responsibilities identified.

Review benchmarks regularly

It is necessary to continue to monitor progress to ensure that gains against benchmarked partners are maintained. Although initial studies may reveal the organisation to be competitive, it needs to be remembered that benchmarking partners and competitors could improve disproportionately. Recalibration should take place at least once a year.

6.5 THE BENCHMARKING CODE OF CONDUCT

This code has been reproduced from *Implementing Benchmarking*, published by the Society of Management Accountants of Canada.[1]

Principles

- Legality – beware implied restraint of trade or price fixing.
- Exchange – willing to provide same level of information.
- Confidentiality – between benchmarking partners.
- Use – use only for purpose agreed.
- First-party contact – obtain mutual agreement on any hand-off.
- Preparation – demonstrate commitment by adequate preparation at each step.

Benchmarking etiquette and ethics

- Establish ground rules up-front.
- Do not ask for sensitive data.
- Use an ethical third party for competitive data.
- Treat information as internal and privileged.
- Do not:
  - disparage a competitor's business to a third party
  - limit competition or gain business through the relationship
  - misrepresent oneself as working for another employer.
- Emphasis on openness and trust.

Benchmarking exchange protocol

- Abide by the Benchmarking Code of Conduct.
- Follow the benchmarking process.
- Determine what to benchmark and complete self-assessment.
- Develop a questionnaire and interview guide.

- Have the authority to share information.
- Work through a specified host and agree a meeting schedule.
- Follow good practice guidelines in face-to-face site visits:
  - provide meeting agenda in advance
  - be professional, honest, courteous and prompt
  - introduce all attendees and explain why they are present
  - adhere to agenda
  - do not use own 'jargon'
  - do not share proprietary information without prior approval
  - offer to set up a reciprocal visit
  - conclude meetings and visits on schedule.

6.6 BENEFITS OF BENCHMARKING

Once an organisation has measured its own performance and made improvements through internal discussion, the next logical step is to make comparisons with similar external organisations, particularly those considered to be utilising 'best practice' and 'best value'. Some benefits of the technique include that it:

- provides a better understanding of exactly where the organisation stands compared with best practice
- focuses attention on those areas needing improvement
- helps to cure tendencies toward self-satisfaction
- encourages innovation
- forces change
- facilitates the demonstration of 'best value'.

CASE STUDY

Tower Hamlets benchmarking[2]

Background
Following a change in political parties taking control of the London Borough of Tower Hamlets in 1994, the Council found itself needing to consolidate seven neighbourhoods that had been decentralised since 1986, operating with mini Town Halls and policy agendas, back into one corporate unit. To facilitate this process, Tower Hamlets had to undertake benchmarking between the neighbourhoods' council processes and decided to invite the other 32 London Boroughs to participate in the project, which Tower Hamlets was offering to resource.

After research examining benchmarking initiatives elsewhere, both in the private and public sectors, Tower Hamlets London Borough Council found a tool that combines attention to current performance with preparation for a probable future. This tool is process benchmarking. In respect to current performance, process benchmarking identifies good practice to improve quality and/or value. Comparisons, as well as being odious, have been notoriously difficult to undertake successfully. Service providers can find a multitude of reasons for contesting that any given comparison has not been conducted on a like-for-like basis. Generally, the common denominator used to assess performance has been cost. There is justification for the view that this mechanism alone does not adequately reflect comparative quality, value and political priorities.

All local authority services, which are offered on a regular basis, operate via a process. Detailed mapping of processes and comparison of the time/effort involved in reaching various milestones can indicate which process is the most efficient and effective. Process analysis does not attempt a like-for-like contrast; rather, it is concerned with a like-for-best comparison. It does not judge whether the process is operated well or whether it is appropriate to the needs of the community. It does, however, find a 'best' way of organising a service. Just as the medium was the message, the process is now the priority.

Methodology

The first phase of the Tower Hamlets benchmarking exercise involved 25 of the 32 London Borough Councils and covered 28 different activities. These ranged from high-volume, repetitive administrative tasks, such as benefit processing and development control, to operations incorporating a long chain of different professionals, such as identifying and satisfying the need for an adaptation to a property to allow continued occupation by a disabled person. A further category of study involved emerging services, such as responding to racial harassment where there is, as yet, an absence of accepted professional practice. See Fig. 6.1, Phase 1 List of activities and published reports.

Fig. 6.1 Tower Hamlets – Phase 1 List of activities and published reports

1	Council Tax Collection*
2	Payments
3	Compulsory Competitive Tendering
4	Housing Benefit Application Processing
5	Purchasing
6	Aids and Adaptations*
7	Access to the Under 8s Service*
8	Social Work Caseload Management System
9	Electoral Registration*
10	Members Support
11	Education Statementing
12	Adult Education Enrolment
13	Student Awards*

> 14 Youth Service Management and Contract Administration
> 15 Former Tenants' Arrears*
> 16 Housing Allocations
> 17 Homelessness to Section 64 Determination*
> 18 Development Control
> 19 Building Control
> 20 Markets Administration*
> 21 Parking Control Penalty Ticket Processing
> 22 Sundry Debt Collection*
> 23 Contract Monitoring
> 24 Racial Harassment
> 25 Community Safety (focusing particularly on domestic violence)
> 26 Noise Nuisance Enforcement*
> 27 Access to Domiciliary Care
> 28 Staff Performance Appraisal
>
> *** denotes published study**

The Tower Hamlets approach began with the secondment of three officers to research benchmarking literature and devise a specific local authority methodology. The method developed involves careful selection of subjects for study, eliminating those that are too circumscribed by statutory procedures to yield substantial scope for process improvement, and obtaining an overview of the chosen activities by interviewing service managers. This leads to the production of a management and performance data questionnaire for circulation to the participating authorities.

Returned questionnaires are assessed on:

- the range of the service provided: that is, whether, in addition to the core elements of the service, activities such as an advice function are carried out
- the level of the service provided: that is, the maximum number of service events per 1000 head of relevant population
- the 'quality' of the service: that is, the mechanism for quality assurance, the accuracy, the adherence to statutory timescales, the internal performance targets and so on.

The services represented by the returned questionnaires are ranked by this assessment routine and the staffing input of those in the upper quartile is then assessed. In other words, the better services are assessed by their cost in terms of staff and that with the lowest staff cost is assumed to have the 'best' processes.

While the questionnaires are completed and assessed, a detailed map of the processes used by Tower Hamlets is drawn up. A similar exercise is then undertaken with the 'best' practice authority. The maps are compared at a benchmarking club meeting involving staff of all the participating authorities, where constructive criticism of the 'best' practice can identify improvements.

A benchmarking report details the 'best' practice identified and recommends the adoption of appropriate improvements. These are quantified and fed into the budget process, where they result in cost reductions, and into the performance-monitoring system, where new performance targets are required.

Results

The first study, about electoral registration, has found sufficient ideas for improvement to give a slightly improved outcome with a reduction of about 50% in staffing. The study of housing benefits processing resulted in a potential saving of £1mn as a result of the following process changes identified:

- centralise the processing of claims
- IT allows local access for queries
- DIP further streamlines processing
- separate public and private claimants
- patchwork systems should be used
- pressure for remote-access terminals.

Similarly, council tax collection yielded ten possible process changes, with a potential saving of £0.5mn from the following:

- send bills as soon as possible
- delay benefit bills until correct
- billing runs twice a week
- encourage direct debit
- work closely with housing benefit staff
- council tax and housing benefits work alongside one another
- repercussions accompany reminders
- fax signatures on summons forms
- discounts simple to apply for
- monitor discounts through sharing information, e.g. parking control
- centralise council tax, incorporate with NNDR.

Conclusions

Problems found from the project include:

- taken longer than anticipated
- resource problems
- developing the methodology
- waiting/idle times
- confidentiality
- performance information

- names
- ownership.

Benchmarking has been defined by the Audit Commission as

> *the process of comparing procedure and performance levels between and within organisations, in order to identify what improvements are possible, how they might be achieved and how much benefit might be delivered.*

Since the project began, the Labour Government has been elected and has adopted the Best Value initiative, which incorporates benchmarking with the following identified characteristics:

- continuous process of measuring services against others for improvement
- identifying and sharing good practice
- focus on proving 'Best Value'
- commitment to learning from others.

The second phase of the benchmarking project is now under way and has extended the club to outside of London, to include the private sector and non-council processes, such as payroll, personnel and catering. Completed reports are available for purchase from Tower Hamlets for a modest fee to cover production costs.

7

Information management

- 7.1 Introduction 129
- 7.2 Defining the business requirement 129
- 7.3 Formulating a company-wide information strategy 130
- 7.4 Evaluating enterprise-wide software 135
- 7.5 Activity/process/value-based software 137
- 7.6 Case study – ABM systems design at Anglian Water 143
- 7.7 Case study – Data warehousing at Nationwide 148

7.1 INTRODUCTION

In the twenty-first century, the role of the information manager will be pivotal within the organisation. The challenge is to replace the myriad unconnected 'legacy' systems with an 'enterprise-wide' system that can deliver that information the company needs to ensure that it continues to add value year on year. Many organisations are now taking steps to identify all knowledge and information so that it can be recorded, managed, retained and used by everybody within the company. However, care must be taken to ensure that the end result is not 'information overload'. The key is intelligently to identify and filter the useful information and utilise such tools as alerts, exceptions, rules, traffic lights and trend analysis, to present and highlight only those areas needing attention.

Companies today are typically spending tens of millions on large-scale system changes. Many, driven in haste by the need to replace old equipment to beat the Millennium bug and EMU requirements, have failed to take the necessary steps to ensure that they have properly thought through the massive investments. The all-too-frequent failure of IT to deliver on business goals means that in future the crucially important role of information management is more likely than ever to form part of the newly transformed finance function.

7.2 DEFINING THE BUSINESS REQUIREMENT

Traditionally, companies have had scores of independent IT systems, often dependent on, and driven by, individual functions, built up over decades. They usually consist of a raft of different technologies, making integration very difficult and expensive or sometimes even impossible. The 1990s became the decade when companies came to realise the importance of breaking down their functional boundaries and viewing their organisations through streamlined processes. With this realisation, there is not just an appreciation of the need for a process-oriented, enterprise-wide decision-support system, but an urgent demand for its implementation, to enable companies to maintain their competitive advantage. In the modern organisation, these processes will extend far beyond old company and geographic boundaries to link their IT systems with those of their suppliers, partners and customers worldwide.

The days are over when managers produced their own set of business information and time at meetings was wasted, arguing over whose figures were correct. No longer is it acceptable to take management decisions relying on 'gut feel', or to spend time 'firefighting' problems rather than eliminating the causes. Technology can now provide easy, real-time access to decision-support information that combines quantitative and qualitative, financial and non-financial data, from internal and external sources.

Main areas of input to an information system will include:

- data from companies' functional systems, such as accounting and operations
- specific external data on such areas as competitors, customers and benchmark data
- general relevant external information on the economy and the stock markets
- the organisational objectives with links to other sources of information to show how these are being met, for example balanced scorecard and budgets.

The primary role for a company's information system[1] is to provide an integrated understanding of the financial and operational position of the company in a dynamic business environment and should have the following characteristics:

- be flexible enough to change as the business does
- support the company's strategy
- provide multiple views of the same data
- provide a balanced scorecard of operational and financial performance measures
- support a process/activity view of the business, in addition to a functional view
- provide for the fast collection and dissemination of data
- utilise exceptions, alerts, rules, trend analysis and other such tools to guard against information overload.

7.3 FORMULATING A COMPANY-WIDE INFORMATION STRATEGY

Set up a project team

The information manager needs to start the process by setting up and leading a project team of colleagues, representative of all parts of the organisation.

Analyse existing company, supplier and customer systems

This includes systems local to individual departments, some of which may be PC and some manually based. Look also outside the organisation to possible links into the systems of suppliers and customers. These days the use of electronic commerce and electronic data interchange (EDI), working in partnership with suppliers and customers, often removes the need for paper and duplicate keying of data as well as speeding up such processes. Analyse the key features of these systems, including:

- inputs
- outputs
- frequency of use
- purposes
- interfaces with other systems
- technical requirements.

Understand the latest technological options available

Enterprise systems

These include enterprise resource planning (ERP), such as SAP, BAAN, Peoplesoft and Oracle. ERP is software architecture that allows the exchange of information between all functions within the organisation, e.g. manufacturing, finance, procurement and human resources. It is based on client/server technology, which means that users access information from a central database via personal computers, and it is usually portable across platforms. ERP is covered in detail in Section 7.4.

Company-wide desktop personal tools

For example Microsoft Office and Lotus SMARTSuite products, including such applications as wordprocessing, spreadsheets, databases, mapping tools, project management, shared diaries, organisers, internal mail, compression software, Web browsers and presentational tools.

Business intelligence tools

Data warehousing

Data warehousing[2] allows companies to build, maintain and manage large amounts of data and query them at will. Data entering the warehouse from multiple sources are placed in a common format and then 'mined' for important information. The database software itself operates in a client/server architecture, usually needing very powerful servers. Features of data warehouses include:

- transactional-level database, usually a relational database
- the data warehouse holds a copy of data from other systems
- used in conjunction with ERP and other packaged software to avoid degradation through excessive querying on the live system

- its purpose is to optimise enquiries rather than data entry
- it is time variant, i.e. date-stamped historical data
- non-volatile data (static)
- often consisting of one or more data marts – a subset of the data warehouse or standalone covering, say, one function
- it is organised by subject or entity not application
- it can feed a multidimensional database, i.e. OLAP.

On-line analytical processing (OLAP) and decision-support systems (DSS)

OLAP servers, such as Essbase and Microsoft SQL, transfer the data to a separate multidimensional database for accounts using a spreadsheet link, like Visual Basic. OLAP occurs in many forms with greatly varying features and functionality, offering different advantages and disadvantages for both IT and end users. These include:

- cost
- level of detail
- data capacity
- speed of operation
- types, e.g. Desktop OLAP (DOLAP).

The terms decision-support systems, enterprise information systems (EIS) and management information systems (MIS) appear interchangeable and refer to end-user information-delivery systems that come in all shapes and sizes, offering simply managed queries or more complex drilling and simulation. These tools often incorporate OLAP. Most of the DSS tools could be used to access data directly from source applications, but the data warehouse provides the ideal foundation for integrating the data and taking it off-line, and as such is becoming increasingly popular as part of modern IT architecture.

Electronic commerce (e-commerce)

Electronic commerce refers to Internet, extranet and intranet access and electronic data interchange. The Internet is a powerful tool, likened by Jeremy Rasmussen[3] to a Swiss Army knife, with multiple functionality. It can provide, among other things:

- communication via e-mail
- a quick, convenient and reliable method of transmitting documents
- an opportunity for companies to promote their products and services via a Web page

- access to data on other organisations and learning worldwide
- an opportunity to do business with other companies, such as placing orders and receiving software upgrades. This could lead to the transfer of routine tasks to suppliers and customers, which would access the company systems directly
- speed and ease of communication
- bulletin boards, used for such things as frequently asked questions and technical support
- security issues are raised by allowing outsiders to use your internal systems and must be addressed.

To use the Internet, companies require a Web browser, such as Netscape or Explorer, an e-mail system and appropriate software.[4]

An extranet deals with business-to-business customers and suppliers and allows services that are charged for, like published materials, to be accessed via the Internet on payment of a fee. It is comparable to 'pay-per-view' television.

An intranet is a mini-Internet – a network of computers set up to be closed to the outside world, allowing access to traditionally 'difficult-to-access' data to those within the company. The intranet browser allows occasional users of packages to access them without the need for package-specific training. It can run the same application types as the Internet, including e-mail and the World Wide Web. With animated instructions on how to sell a product or assemble it, pictures of all staff available and voice memos concerning customers and suppliers, the technology has many attractions, including support for hyperlinks. Hyperlinks enable links from one place in a document to another, or indeed to another document that may be on the same computer, a computer in another department, location or even in another country. So successful are these systems that companies now have to use strict codes of conduct and 'filtering' systems to ensure that only priority information is received and read.

Collaborative computing

Workflow systems

Workflow systems can be designed to deliver specified data periodically to selected people. It can remove the need for paper, automatically route electronic documents and enforce procedures written into a process, used widely for such things as state-of-the-art purchase order-processing systems.

Document management

Document management is a standardised approach to the indexing and management of documents entering the company in whatever form, for example paper, computer systems, Internet, microfiche, fax and e-mail, utilising such techniques as document imaging. Having compiled a comprehensive database of information, it can be queried at will via the desktop, saving considerable time and space and providing a necessary back-up for paper records.

Computer and telephone integration (CTI)

The use of CTI technology is revolutionising systems, with telephones linked directly into ERP and other computer software and voicemail products, for example routing consumer calls into the right part of the company customer services, via customers pressing numbers on their digital telephone.

Groupware

Groupware packages allow groups to work together, using shared access to programs and data, even though they may be geographically dispersed. Examples of such products are Lotus Notes, e-mail, computer diary scheduling and videoconferencing.

Analyse 'future' business needs

Although it is not the intention when setting out, often under pressure of time constraints far too many IT implementation teams simply end up replacing legacy systems with new ones, which operate in exactly the same way as the old ones. It is essential to reengineer processes and design in new high-level management techniques that allow the organisation to continually add value. Examples explained in this book include:

- value-based management
- process/activity-based techniques
- balanced business scorecard
- integrated performance-management systems
- decision-support or enterprise information systems
- improved and standardised company-wide processes
- benchmarking
- business process reengineering
- priority-based budgeting.

Consult independent experts

These may be specialists and/or potential outsourcers/partners. Remember that this is one of the most important decisions that the organisation will make, not just in terms of an IT investment strategy costing tens of millions but in making an essential contribution to the company's future ability to compete successfully.

Prepare the business case

Compile a detailed and compelling business case, evaluating all the benefits, costs and risks of all the elements of the proposed implementation project. The finance function, now transformed, will evaluate this as an essential 'investment' in the company's future – not, as it might have done in the past, as a 'cost'.

Consult widely

While time is of the essence in moving towards new technological advantage, remember that the new transformed finance function no longer prescribes what information the business needs but facilitates the provision of relevant information for operational managers. It is they who will be using it and therefore they who can offer constructive thought on the design. It is, therefore, strongly advisable to win support from all parts of the enterprise before proceeding with implementation. This will lessen the pain later.

Continuous improvement

Once the system is installed, it is important that a culture of continuous review and improvement is adopted. It is recommended that, at a minimum, an annual audit should be undertaken.

7.4 EVALUATING ENTERPRISE-WIDE SOFTWARE

Introduction

Enterprise resource planning[5] is fast becoming the accepted solution for larger organisations, as they seek to gain corporate advantage from the automation and integration of the separate parts of their businesses, in addition to solving problems connected with the Year 2000 bug and the introduction of the euro. In the last year of the old millennium, the new challenge for ERP is to break into the middle-range company market, where budgets are tighter and long (typically 18 months) system-implementation cycles are unacceptable. In medium-sized companies, the ERP vendors, which include SAP, Peoplesoft, BAAN and Oracle, are moving towards dealing via value-added resellers, which are offering a more streamlined packaged approach via the use of templates and implementation methodologies.

Advantages of ERP

Advantages of the ERP suites of application software modules include the following:

- integrated common database-management system, giving obvious advantages for maintenance and end-user training
- reduction of redundant data
- ERP application software has advantages over bespoke software in that it is able to take advantage of upgrades and a large user base
- increased efficiency through the ability to drill down to source transactions
- facilitation of OLAP and data warehousing
- ability to handle dual-currency requirements
- Year 2000 enabled.

Problems encountered

Problems encountered in installing ERP systems include the following:

- sometimes implementations can be very time consuming, often measured in years
- implementations can be costly, with estimates of costs varying from three times software price from BAAN to ten times from SAP
- estimate overruns are known to occur
- there may be a failure to reengineer processes prior to implementation
- the complexity of such systems requires considerable amounts of consultancy
- tweaking and tuning of the standard package can prove expensive
- scope creep may occur, with companies adding functionality during implementation
- on-going requirement for support and services
- failure to manage expectations of what it can deliver
- underresourcing the implementation
- high levels of user training required
- inflexible to change
- poor access to data for analytical purposes.

Development of ERP systems

ERP systems, according to Butler Group's *Enterprise Resource Planning* report,[6] are able to meet only about 80% of business needs, although they continue to develop at a pace, with Oracle, for example, being one of the first to offer a Web-enabled version of its application suite. Data warehousing and greater flexibility in reporting are becoming important issues, with the Gartner Group's Dataquest report, *The European Software Market in 1997: Application Packages Lead the Way*,[7] seeing business intelligence software sales grow by 26% in that year. Peoplesoft has released Enterprise Performance Management that can be used with rival ERP packages to tackle this demand; while Baan's Enterprise Decision Manager automatically exports into a data warehouse for use with Cognos tools; and SAP is providing more hooks into its environment so other suppliers' products can get at SAP data.

The Dataquest report explains that the key IT decision going back 20 years was the choice of hardware vendor. Ten years ago it was about database-management systems (DBMS); now it is the choosing of a business application package that has become the key from which other IT decisions flow. The report focuses on 35 significant ERP software vendors and claims that total European sales of application packages in 1997 was $1.9bn, with German-based SAP as the clear market leader with 35% of sales.

7.5 ACTIVITY/PROCESS/VALUE-BASED SOFTWARE

Introduction

Organisations have recognised the need to link strategy to operational performance through identifying those drivers that create value. Figure 2.2, Integrated performance management (p.26), illustrates the necessity of linking any value-based management initiative, in Chapter 3, to strategy with a balanced scorecard, in Chapter 4, and underpinning it with detailed activity-based management information, in Chapter 5, that drills down through the organisation to ensure that all decision making is properly informed.

Earlier in the chapter, the need to define the business requirements clearly was spelt out and this includes these decision-support systems. Having established the need for process/activity-based information, this should be designed into the heart of the IT systems, not treated as a 'bolt-on extra'. As we have seen, ERP solutions are based on processes, but at the time of going to press, they are still generally lacking in adequate ABC/M modules. However, most have accepted the demand from their customers for these systems and are in the stages of development of such modules. For example, SAP has formed an alliance with ABC Technologies to produce a SAP ABC/M module based on OROS for SAP R/3.

Full integration with enterprise-wide systems needs to be the ultimate goal, but a client/server-based 'best-of-breed' ABM package may be the solution in the short to medium term. The specification and development of the VBM, ABM, BSC analysis and links to source data and front-end systems are time-consuming processes and often best carried out on one of the purpose-built packages, which are designed to input and output data from other systems.

Development of activity-based packages

Traditionally, ABT analysis (covered in Chapter 5) was either carried out:

- at head office and used as a corporate modelling tool in such areas as pricing decisions, product/customer/sector profitability, transfer pricing, budgeting and planning, overhead allocations, cost-reduction initiatives, *ad hoc* decision making, regulatory accounts, activity and unit costing; or
- within individual departments, processes and units and in areas such as budgeting, performance measurement, costing, value analysis, benchmarking, management and cost reduction.

Evidence of how it was used in the early 1990s is found in a CIMA Research Study published in 1995,[8] where Friedman and Lyne investigated 11 organisations that had been working with ABT over at least three years. They found that while most began using ABT for one purpose only, often costing or performance-improvement initiatives, they had gone on to use an average of three ABT over time, following the success of their initial application, including for budgeting and regular monitoring.

Following the initial development phase, ABT are now more commonly used as multiuser, all-encompassing decision-support systems. Specialist vendors produce linked modules for process mapping, activity-based costing, customer profitability, activity-based management (ABM), activity-based budgeting, performance measurement and balanced scorecards, in addition to link engines to manipulate data between external systems and report-writing tools. These modules are linked to a common database, which holds the central activity analysis around which all the other techniques are based.

Design considerations

Consideration needs to be given to how the multiuser system will function, as it could:

- be updated and produced centrally and then made available to specified users in total or in part

- be updated and produced locally and then consolidated at the centre in detail or in summary
- have several users, each producing their own unique information for different purposes and different audiences.

Decisions need to be made about how information will be distributed to the end users – paper reports should be a thing of the past. Most organisations will expect information to be accessed on screen via networks and selected information to be dispersed to an even wider audience via the corporate intranet. Will the system incorporate all relevant information into one system, for example qualitative measures alongside quantitative, operational and financial, utilisation and simulation data; and if so, is this specialist package to be used as the information-delivery tool or will the data be downloaded into an enterprise information system? Access rights need to be considered and appropriate licences negotiated – different levels of user will include those who administer and build the models; those who have responsibility for inputting data and monthly running of models; and those who wish to view the results. Finally, thought needs to be given to what sort of output is required, for example graphical, tabular with ability to 'slice and dice' and interactive, allowing 'what if' scenarios to be modelled.

Most packages can now cope with at least two currencies and are Year 2000 compliant. It is essential that technical IT specialists are involved in the selection of the package, since it needs to be a coherent part of the overall IT strategy. If choosing client/server technology, then it is likely that the selection of the database needs to be compatible. Hardware and network configurations and usage will have to be carefully considered as well as the details of the methodology of running and links needed to other systems/data.

Before looking at the purpose-built software package suites, evaluate whether your business needs can be met either by a module for your existing packaged software or by a package already in use within the organisation, such as an OLAP, spreadsheet or EIS tool. Does this existing tool:

- have the necessary functionality for your business needs?
- allow ease of use (e.g. Windows based and/or menu driven)?
- make change of ownership of the models easy? Difficulties can sometimes be encountered when spreadsheet models are transferred from the builder to another person.
- demonstrate the necessary robustness? It is essential that accounting data flowing into the system can be verified and validated at all stages in the process, if credibility of the data is to be maintained.
- enable models to be built speedily, outweighing the advantages of a purpose-built package?

Checklists of features and functionality of purpose-built packages

Reporting

- Does the package have extensive reports built in, like QPR[9] CostControl?
- Does it link dynamically to Excel for reporting purposes, like Hyper[10] ABC, (recently renamed Metify)?
- Does it allow purpose-built reports to be created within the software, like OROS?[11]
- Does it have purpose-built links to an EIS tool?
- How good are its graphical capabilities?
- Does it allow periods to be compared for trend analysis?

Modularity

- Is the package modular, allowing the purchase of just the relevant parts, like ABC Technologies' OROS suite, which allows you to purchase any part of the suite on its own, with all parts being individually priced (e.g. Easy ABC module at about a quarter of the total price)?
- Does the same software vendor provide complementary packages, such as balanced scorecards and business process mapping, and to what degree are they integrated? Examples of these types of vendors would be Sapling Corporation,[12] QPR and Prodacapo.[13] Others have strong links with other vendors providing such functionality (e.g. OROS with Panoramic Business Views and Hyper, now renamed Metify, with CorVu).
- Does the package have three, four, five or six dimensions? For example, OROS has three and performs customer profitability not through an extra dimension but through reporting; Hyper (now Metify) has four dimensions (resources, activity, product and customer); QPR has five dimensions, allowing individual cost elements to be grouped into resources; and Prodacapo has six, incorporating a process module as part of the analysis flow.

Technology

- Is it full client/server architecture, allowing you to select any database?
- Is it 32 bit technology?
- Is it fat or thin client?
- What specification of hardware does it run on (e.g. Windows, NT)?

- Does it permit models to be merged, in part and in full?
- Is it suitable to link to other in-house packages?
- Is it suitable for use as an information delivery system or better suited as a calculation tool only?

Tailoring

- Can the language used in the package be customised to suit specific corporate jargon (e.g. QPR)?
- Can reports be built within the package (e.g. OROS)?
- Are the vendors amenable/able to develop and make modifications to meet your requirements?

Basic calculation features

- Is it self-balancing, does it perform validation checks and reconciliations?
- Does it perform continual reiterations of allocations (e.g. Hyper ABC, now Metify)?
- Can it perform chain allocations?
- What costing methodology does it use (they vary from package to package)?
- Does it allow hierarchies to be built in all dimensions?
- Can allocations be made from any part of the hierarchy?
- Does it allow allocations to be made at a high level and to drip down to lower levels?
- Does it show unit costs at all levels in the hierarchy?
- Does it permit random collection of activities, not otherwise appearing together in the hierarchy; very useful for benchmarking and process analysis?

Budgeting and simulation features

- Can it do resource and activity utilisation and capacity calculations?
- Does it allow 'what if' simulations to be performed on, for example, the product mix, back calculating to show implications on resources and activities?
- Can fixed and variable indicators and multipliers be applied to resources, allowing, for example, labour to be fixed for 36 hours, then move into time-and-a-half for a further ten hours?

Other functionality

- Does it permit additional measures, financial, numerical and qualitative, to be contained in the same package?
- Does it permit value-added statements to be produced, incorporating assets, cost of capital and income into models?
- Is it designed for ABC or ABM or both?

Prices

- Single-user V/ABC/M packages cost between £10 000 and £20 000.
- Some provide a cut-down version suitable for pilot purposes at a few hundred pounds.
- Process mapping tools that link into the ABC/M tools vary from £1000 to £6000 for fully functioning standalone BPR tools, and those featuring IDEF methodology.
- Multiuser systems are negotiable and will vary with the type and number of licences required.
- Maintenance should include normal upgrades and is usually around 15–20% of the purchase price, inclusive of hot-line assistance.

Good-practice reminders

- Insist on seeing and talking with at least one appropriate reference site.
- Take a copy on evaluation for a period (usually time expired) prior to purchase.
- Ask for an outline model of your own company to be demonstrated, making it easier to compare the different features and functionality of the packages.
- Ensure that you understand when a demonstration switches between packages.
- Involve your corporate IT department.
- Test downloading and uploading data from existing systems.
- If you use consultants, ensure that they are independent of software vendors, or be aware if they are not.
- Your own staff should always carry out the implementation, ensuring that the company retains ownership of models after the consultant leaves.
- Consultants' expertise is best used at the system design and specification stages, when most value can be added, for experience on overall planning and approach and in training, directing and overseeing roles during implementation and roll-out.

Implementation planning

- Coding system design (will vary to suit software selected).
- Activity dictionary design (standardise wherever possible).
- Training of model builders (should include some of company's own staff).
- Building of models in conjunction with end users.
- Testing of models and reporting.
- Automate downloading and uploading links with other systems.
- Design intranet links.
- Training of system operators.
- Training and awareness roll-out programme for system users.

CASE STUDY
ABM systems design at Anglian Water[14]

Background

Anglian Water Services is that part of the Anglian Water Group that runs the Regulated Water and Waste Water businesses. It is geographically the largest of the ten regional water services companies of England and Wales, with a region stretching from the Humber to the Thames and to Oxfordshire in the West. AWS employs in the region of 5000 people and has an annual turnover of approximately £700mn.

Anglian Water Services decided in 1997 to upgrade its three-year-old, centrally operated ABC system based on Microsoft Access to the QPR activity/process-based suite of tools. The existing system had analysed all budget centres into activities and ran through actual data on a quarterly basis, producing statements that balanced back to the accounting information. This system meant that activity analysis was discrete to each budget centre and limited in how it could be developed by Access's functionality.

The solution

A network of QPR models was designed as its replacement, with detailed models for each business unit/territory, replacing the hundreds of budget centre statements produced via Access. As you can see in Fig. 7.1, Anglian Water user network, the design allowed for the individual models to be merged providing consolidated information at various stages, culminating in a summary version that could be used for corporate purposes, including a regulatory model. Figure 7.2, Billing and collection process (micro), shows the process as it appears within the customer services department and Fig. 7.3, Billing and collection process (macro), shows the same process at corporate level once it has been merged with other departments, with activities being added from networks and finance and planning departments.

Transforming the Finance Function

Fig. 7.1 AW – User network

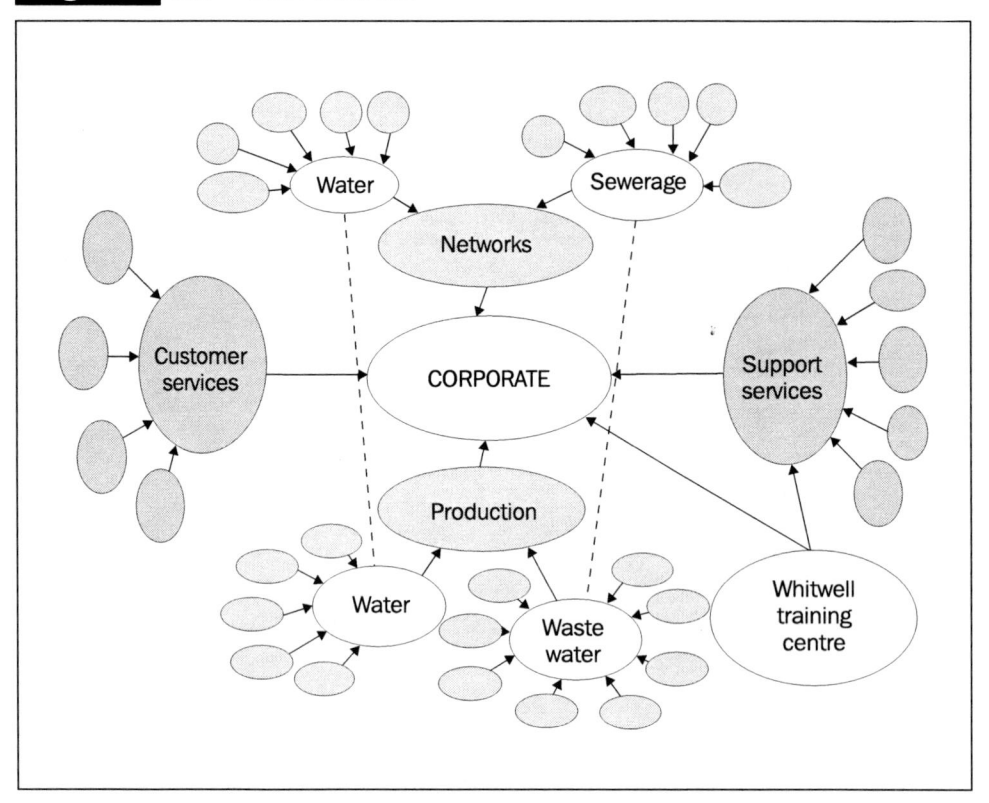

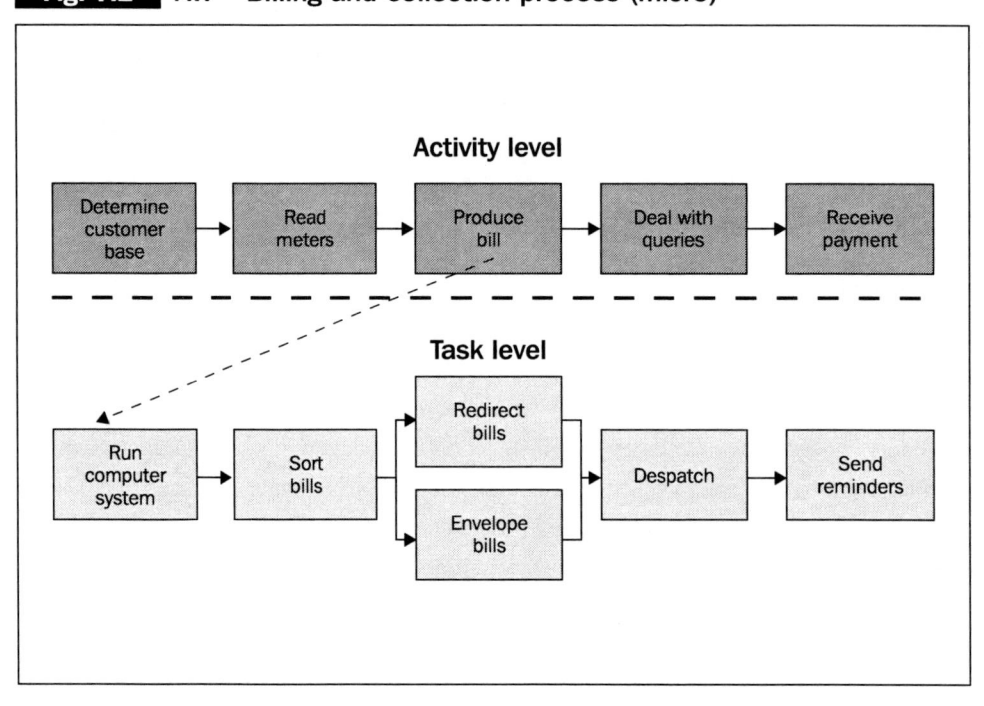

Fig. 7.2 AW – Billing and collection process (micro)

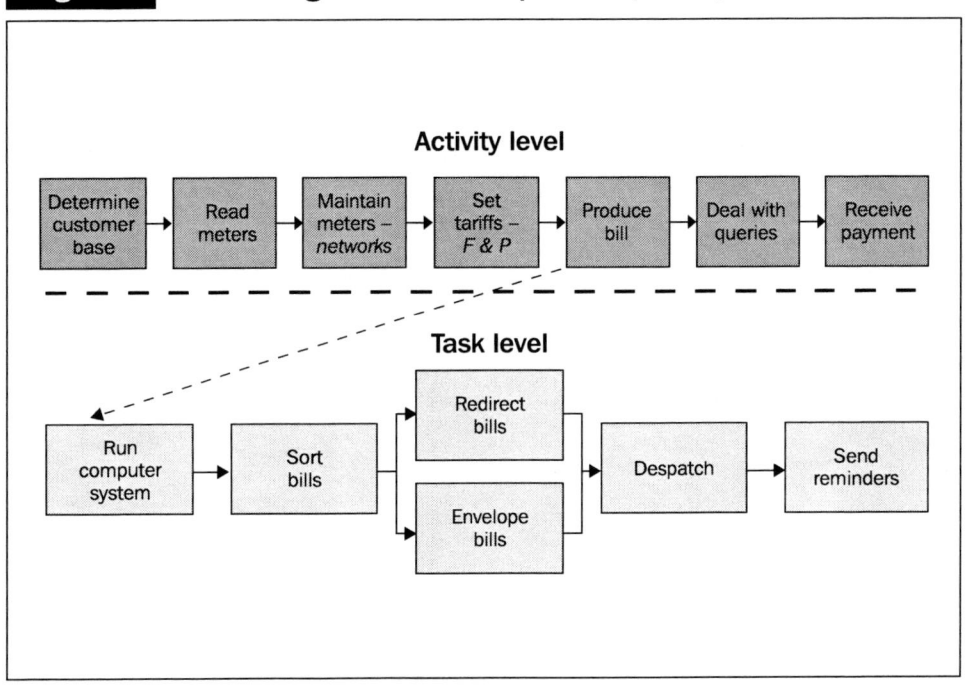

Fig. 7.3 AW – Billing and collection process (macro)

Activity level

Determine customer base → Read meters → Maintain meters – networks → Set tariffs – F & P → Produce bill → Deal with queries → Receive payment

Task level

Run computer system → Sort bills → Redirect bills / Envelope bills → Despatch → Send reminders

The system is designed so that each of the 40 micro models is owned and run every month by the business unit management accountants/performance managers, who have responsibility for incorporating operational performance as well as financial. Once run, the models are then made available on the computer network and are accessible by specified managers and staff, who can manipulate the data in this QPR suite of interactive tools. Plans are in place to post limited information on to the Anglian Water intranet, using QPR CostControl and the interlinking mapping tool, Process Guide. For example, the production drill-down, geographic, operational computer system ARTS 2000, illustrated in Fig. 7.4, ARTS 2000, which all production staff are accustomed to using, has been copied by the mapping tool, which displays cost and output information instead of operational data, as seen in Fig. 7.5, Process guide.

This new, advanced activity-based management system was built in QPR to provide value-adding features and functionality in an interactive tool capable of being used as the end-user information delivery system. As you can see from Fig. 7.6, Anglian Water QPR system, it was designed to download data from the then accounting system, Millennium, and to enable it to be converted to receive a download from the planned ERP system, SAP R/3. Information is also obtained from numerous other operational systems, depending on the specific models, for example, the production model data coming from the ARTS 2000 telemetry system, the training model data coming from the bookings database.

Fig. 7.4 AW – ARTS 2000

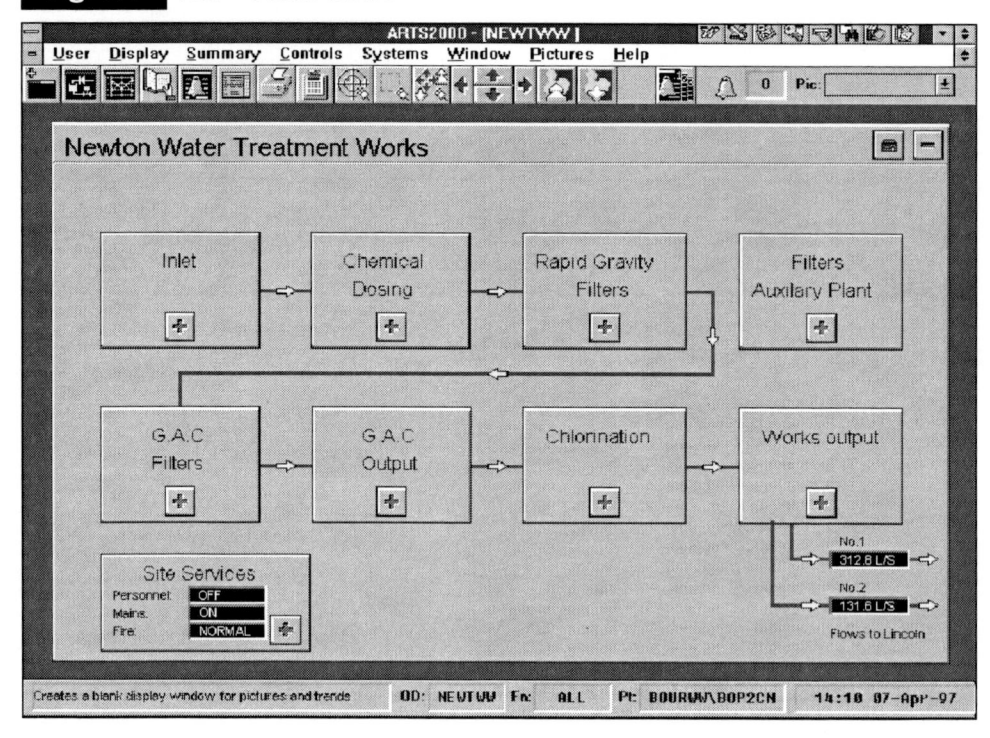

Fig. 7.5 AW – Process guide

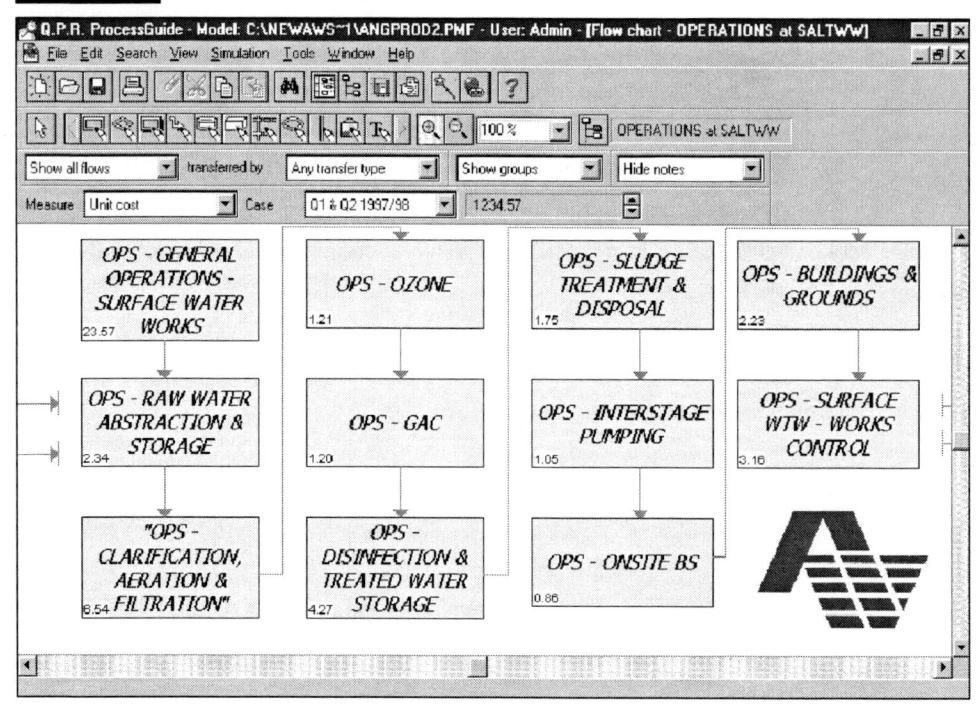

Fig. 7.6 AW – QPR system

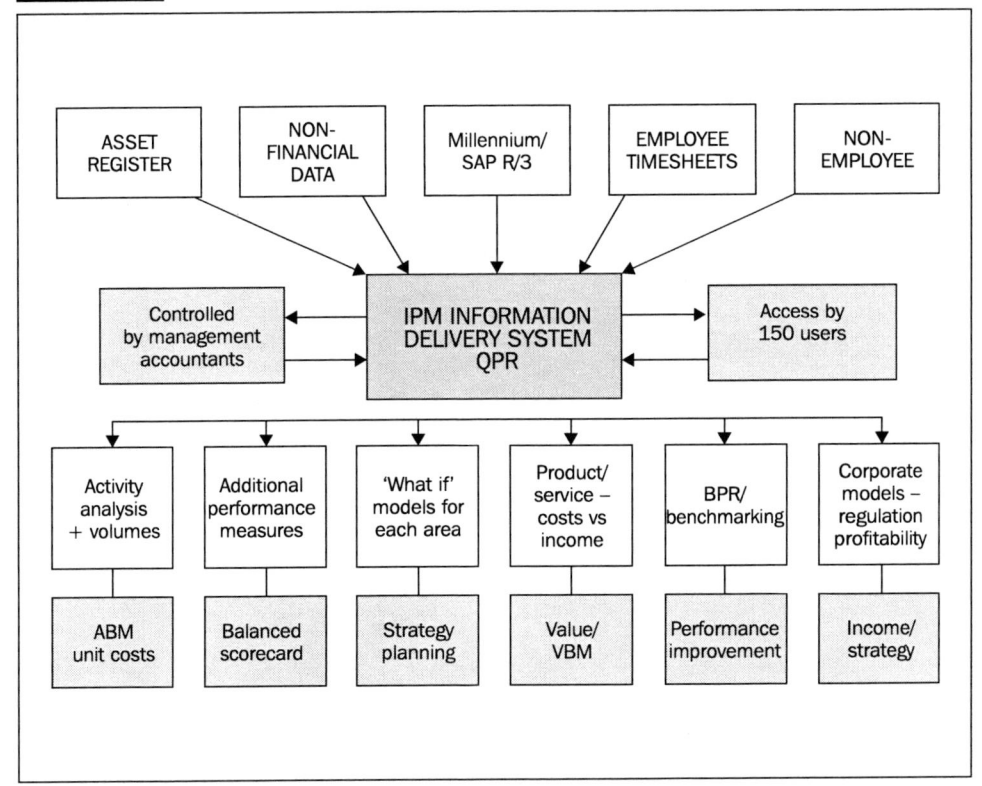

[Diagram: Inputs — ASSET REGISTER, NON-FINANCIAL DATA, Millennium/SAP R/3, EMPLOYEE TIMESHEETS, NON-EMPLOYEE — feed into IPM INFORMATION DELIVERY SYSTEM QPR (Controlled by management accountants; Access by 150 users). Outputs: Activity analysis + volumes (ABM unit costs); Additional performance measures (Balanced scorecard); 'What if' models for each area (Strategy planning); Product/service – costs vs income (Value/VBM); BPR/benchmarking (Performance improvement); Corporate models – regulation profitability (Income/strategy).]

System uses (see Fig. 7.6)

- Outputs from the QPR system provide hierarchical activity analysis and unit costs at all levels.

- Product and service costing, compared to income, customer (including internal customers via service-level agreements) and market/sector analysis, also incorporating income.

- The tool allows for asset and income data to be incorporated to provide value-based management statements, which drill down to the detailed activity-based management information held in the models.

- A module provides for additional metrics to be incorporated against activities; these can be additional quantitative measures/drivers or qualitative information – this will enable a drill-down from the corporate balanced scorecard, once complete.

- The QPR suite of tools also provides the basis for performance-improvement techniques, discussed in previous chapters, to be applied, e.g. business process reengineering and benchmarking. Considerable opportunities for internal benchmarking are available within the operational areas.

- Finally, in selecting the software, the ability to create a budget model – with fixed, variable and semi-variable indicators on resources that allows for 'what if' simulations to be evaluated – was considered an essential tool in the armoury of the new generation of value-enhancing manager. An example of this feature can be seen in Fig. 7.7, QPR efficiency analysis, which graphically illustrates the impact on resource and activity utilisation.

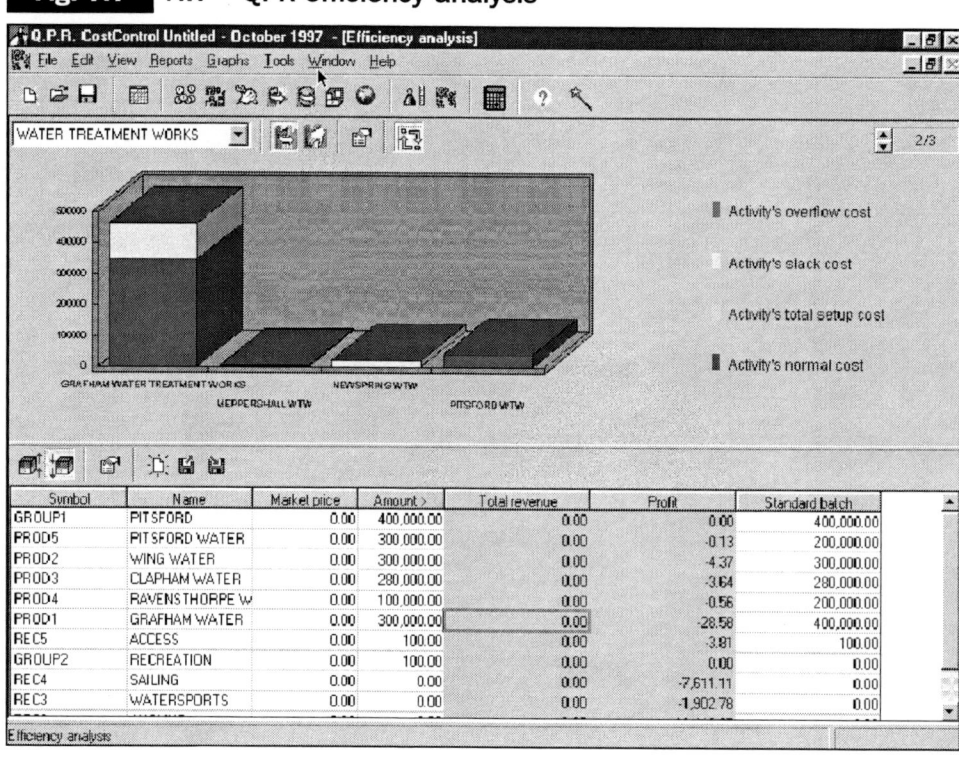

Fig. 7.7 AW – QPR efficiency analysis

CASE STUDY

Data warehousing at Nationwide[15]

Background

Nationwide Life and Nationwide Unit Trust Managers were formed as the regulated financial services subsidiaries of Nationwide Building Society. They began trading in January 1996, offering good-value products to customers introduced through the society's branch network. Development of the systems and processes took over two years, from a greenfield site in Swindon. A substantial part of the operation was outsourced to third parties.

It was obvious that implementation of a management reporting function faced a number of challenges. As requirements specification was taking place while the full management team was still being recruited, requirements were changing and the systems architecture was still developing, an adaptive approach was essential. With around a dozen production systems being developed, a client/server data-warehousing approach was chosen for the provision of management information. Although this was a high-risk approach relative to the traditional method of report production from production systems, the advantages far outweighed the downside. Those advantages are:

- ability to produce *ad hoc* reports
- local control of reporting
- low development costs
- flexibility of reporting

- ability to analyse data across diverse systems
- ability to produce operational reporting.

The specification

The system was developed around a high-specification central server, with distributed report access available from around 50 local client PCs using a graphical query tool. This allowed access to pre-defined reports where the user chose report parameters and provided the ability to produce *ad hoc* queries with 'super user' training – no reports are produced centrally for paper distribution to these users. Furthermore, the system allows different data views to different categories of user.

The system was built from the bottom upwards – including tackling the issues of data integrity, quality, consistency and control across different platforms. This approach to data-warehouse development permits the system to be used as the basis of an executive information system. Data warehousing permits analysis of the complete lifecycle of a product sale, from initial customer contact to post-sale events.

The data warehouse approach represents an ideal solution in a multiplatform systems environment, allowing consolidation of atomic-level business data from diverse systems on to a central relational database. Such an implementation requires less analysis of data, but carried a greater overhead in future development of the system, which can largely be carried out locally by the system administrator.

Management reporting solution

Delivery of a system was a small (but key) part of the development of the management reporting solution. This involved addressing cultural and educational issues around implementation of a solution, addressing data and information ownership, development of critical success factors and key performance indicators and a monitoring basis for all business areas.

An integrated balanced business scorecard approach was adopted for management reporting, aligning the corporate vision with guiding principles and a balanced business plan. The emphasis was not on just the traditional financial measures but also on non-financial business measures.

The objective was to divide company reporting to monitor performance against the corporate vision and values (customer perspective, organisation development, sales performance and operational performance). These are the business determinants that deliver financial performance, the ultimate consequence of corporate success. Although traditional monthly management accounts have tended to focus on financial measures alone, they have not monitored the 'levers' that drive corporate performance.

The board information pack is a largely graphical balanced scorecard of mainly non-financial measures, providing information and detailed analysis of results. This includes a section on organisational development, measuring a number of human resources performance measures:

- organisation culture
- staff competency

- staff satisfaction
- absence and staff turnover against workloads
- costs of staff development against productivity improvements.

Benchmark data is used to measure performance against the industry.

The customer perspective covers the following areas:

- customer satisfaction
- customer complaints
- policy turnaround
- persistence.

Transformation of the finance function

With a high level of automation of reporting, the management accounting function can devote resource to providing value-added support to the business, as opposed to the traditional view of the finance function as a group of 'beancounters' producing historical financial information. This transformation of management accounting needs to be implemented in a number of ways:

- development of a vision for the finance function
- establishment of guiding principles
- alignment of objectives with corporate goals
- measurement of team performance, including customer satisfaction
- benchmarking against best practice
- measurement of productivity
- application of quality processes and standards.

Traditionally, the management accounting function has measured performance of the operation, but has rarely had the confidence to measure its own performance. The result of such a focus has been to stifle continuous improvement and limit the influence of finance within the organisation. The alternative is to establish metrics to monitor performance, measuring performance and implementing a development plan to improve the service provided by finance.

The measurement of finance performance exposes the function to the same disciplines that operational areas of the company have. Priorities of the finance function can be easily established through consultation with its customer areas: what are the key corporate objectives and how can finance help the company achieve these?

Conclusion

Corporate priorities can be ranked in terms of both short- and long-term importance to establish a comprehensive strategic plan for the organisation, resulting in an action plan for future development. A formal monitoring framework will allow progress reporting against the action plan.

It is important to manage resource to minimise the part of that resource dedicated to operational activities and increase the amount of time available to perform value-added tasks. This involves managing the balance between 'urgent' and 'important' – investment in the latter produces significantly greater returns.

In conclusion, management reporting has developed into a proactive commercial management function, committed to adding maximum value to the business through the implementation of leading-edge solutions to business problems. The emphasis has moved from reporting historical financial statistics to analysing the full range of business determinants and influencing corporate strategy.

Part 3

Transformation of the finance function

- 8 How to plan and implement the necessary changes   155

- 9 Outsourcing and shared service centres   173

- 10 The finance function as facilitator of change, adding company-wide value   193

8

How to plan and implement the necessary changes

- 8.1 Introduction   157
- 8.2 Establishing the transformation project   158
- 8.3 Analysis of the present finance function activities   159
- 8.4 Develop the vision for the future of the finance function   162
- 8.5 Create the change strategy   166
- 8.6 Align staff skills and competencies   166
- 8.7 Implement the transformation   169
- 8.8 Monitor success and results of implementation   170
- 8.9 Case studies – Worldwide excellence in finance   170

8.1 INTRODUCTION

In Part 1, why the finance function needs to change was analysed and in Part 2, the value-adding tools and techniques that need to be deployed company wide in order to effect the necessary performance improvement, performance management and information management were explained. In Part 3, Transformation of the finance function, the focus is on the practical issues involved in making the necessary transformation to enable the finance function to facilitate the transformation of the rest of the organisation to adding value.

Figure 2.1, Transformation of the finance function (p.19), illustrates the change that must take place over the next five years, not only converting half of the function's activities to 'value-adding', decision-support activities, but also reducing costs significantly overall. As John Fisher, a US consultant, commented:[1]

> *The accounting back office must be relocated to the front lines. And finance executives must shed their mundane record-keeping tasks and develop the skills necessary to provide high-level information for company wide consumption. Specifically, they must:*
>
> - *develop a marketing orientation*
> - *develop a product orientation*
> - *know the business's core competencies*
> - *provide a higher level of financial analysis*
> - *offer strategic planning, budgeting and control leadership.*

The change will come and it must not be taken for granted that the finance function will be allowed automatically to take on this new value-adding company-wide role. There will be other disciplines which believe that they are equally well qualified for this broader role that encompasses as much non-financial as financial content. Susan Jee, Head of Finance for the Magnox Business Group of British Nuclear Fuels,[2] has been quoted as warning:

> *We have to earn the right to be taken seriously by the business generally. We have to prove that we can provide more than just the numbers while recognising that these numbers are still of critical importance. It is arrogant for us to believe that if we find the time to look over a new business proposal we will automatically add value. People within the business have been doing this very well without us for a long time.*

In this chapter, the generic process that needs to be undertaken is detailed, from analysis of the present finance function activities, developing future vision for finance, assessing current staff skills and competencies, creating strategy for change, and implementing changes to monitor actions and results. This is followed by three brief case studies, which demonstrate worldwide examples of transformed finance functions in action.

8.2 ESTABLISHING THE TRANSFORMATION PROJECT

Put together a business case

The senior management team needs to be committed to this project, which, although focusing primarily on the finance function, will encroach on the whole of the rest of the business at various stages of the project. Whatever the organisation, private or public sector, the case for change is compelling and is laid out in Part 1 and 2 of this book – from cost reduction to realignment to the needs of the ever-changing business to Best Value.

Appoint a steering group

A steering group should be formed comprising the finance director, the project manager, the consultant (if used), the head of IT and, ideally, at least three other senior managers from within the business, including the chief executive. This group needs to agree the objectives, timescales, resources and methodology of the project and review its progress regularly.

Appoint a project team

Because of the obvious sensitivity of the nature of the investigation and the inherent barriers to change from within finance itself, care must be taken in choosing the 'best' people to carry out the investigation. The success of the operation will depend largely on the team selected. It is worth considering who within the finance function is capable of carrying out this analysis in a constructive, sensitive and unbiased manner. Consider whether the team can be supplemented by staff from other departments who are trained in carrying out this kind of analysis, and indeed whether you need to include outsiders, possibly consultants who can take an impartial view and have knowledge of the running of other organisations' finance functions. Whatever the eventual make-up, the project team must be able to address strategic, operational and technological issues. It is probable that some members of the team will change as the project progresses.

Identify customers and suppliers of the finance function to consult

Although not full-time members of the project team, representatives of the internal suppliers to and customers of the finance function need to be identified and some of their time earmarked for the project. Without their views the analysis will be worthless. Be sure to get a wide range of opinions – critics as well as fans.

Identification of benchmarking partners

The identification of appropriate finance function 'benchmarks' will be invaluable as the transformation process progresses. The methodologies that can be used were discussed in detail in Chapter 6. Identifying two or three partners who wish to benchmark directly and who are willing to exchange information freely would be the ideal scenario.

Set up communication media

It is important to communicate objectives, timescales, progress and other news about the project on an on-going basis, both to the finance function and company wide.

8.3 ANALYSIS OF THE PRESENT FINANCE FUNCTION ACTIVITIES

Introduction

Once the project is properly established, the first stage in the transformation must be an analysis of what the finance function currently does. Utilising some of the value-adding tools and techniques described in Chapter 5, a systematic analysis of the activities performed must be undertaken. Stages in such an investigation would include the following.

Documentation of the finance activities and processes

Methodology

Even if these are already documented, it will be necessary to carry out a detailed activity analysis update of all the activities undertaken by the finance function. It will be necessary to understand all attributes of the activities/processes, including:

- activity flows
- inputs
- outputs
- consumption of resources
- objectives and responsibilities
- unit costs
- subprocesses and processes that they form part of
- suppliers
- customers
- performance measures
- critical success factors
- core, diversionary or support
- ideas for improvements to processes
- service-level agreements or customer requirements
- levels of service being delivered
- constraints
- process maps.

Finance process map example

Figure 8.1, Sales invoicing process, is a real example of a finance function process that has been documented not only in finance but throughout the business, where it can be seen that considerable activity took place, both in operational and support areas. The process map shows that invoices are raised manually and then typed on a wordprocessor by the operational teams where direct contact with the customers takes place; the processing is then carried out in finance, transferring the information on to Oracle Financials. Out-of-pocket (OOP) expenses are added to customer invoices, resulting in an expensive process of mainly manual collection and analysis of OOP.

It is also necessary to note that this example service company had about 500 customers, a high proportion of whom have a minimum fee charge of £2000 per annum, with the process being applied to all customers in the same way. Until the process analysis was carried out, the organisation had no appreciation of the total true cost of the process, which was approximately £1000 a customer. It is not difficult once presented with this information to find ways of simplifying the process and reducing costs, including possibilities for:

- inputting invoices directly into Oracle
- transferring minimum-charge customers on to a fixed fee inclusive of OOP, rendering this expensive process unnecessary in these cases; invoices needed to be raised and paid only once a year
- automating the collection of OOP data through use of the operational systems, which not only reduced considerable manual effort in the support, finance and operational areas, but provided improved customer billing information and considerably reduced the number of queries being raised
- removing duplication of maintenance of customer information
- eventual plans to automate the process fully.

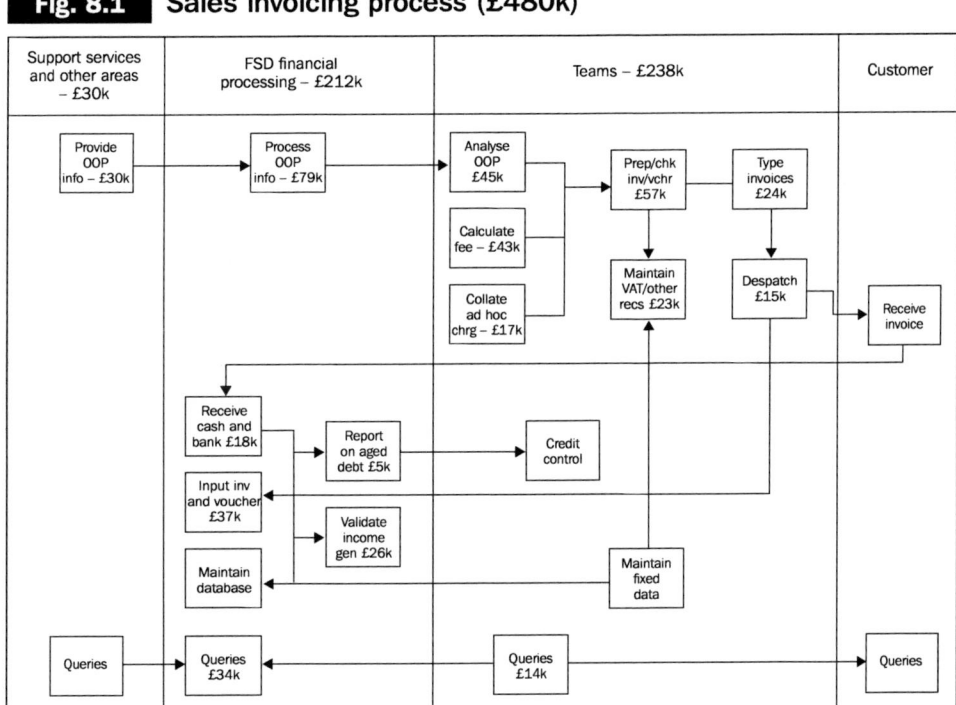

Fig. 8.1 Sales invoicing process (£480k)

Support services and other areas – £30k	FSD financial processing – £212k	Teams – £238k	Customer
Provide OOP info – £30k	Process OOP info – £79k	Analyse OOP £45k → Prep/chk inv/vchr £57k → Type invoices £24k	
		Calculate fee – £43k	
		Collate ad hoc chrg – £17k → Maintain VAT/other recs £23k → Despatch £15k	Receive invoice
	Receive cash and bank £18k → Report on aged debt £5k →	Credit control	
	Input inv and voucher £37k ← Validate income gen £26k		
	Maintain database	Maintain fixed data	
Queries	Queries £34k	Queries £14k	Queries

Validate the data collected

Once analysed, the data collected needs to be verified with the staff to ensure that it is correct and amendments made as necessary.

8.4 DEVELOP THE VISION FOR THE FUTURE OF THE FINANCE FUNCTION

Introduction

Once the present finance function activities are fully understood, it is time to start collecting comparable information on best practices in finance and building the future vision, in consultation with colleagues throughout the business.

Collect benchmark data

In addition to a complete picture of what finance is currently doing, it is necessary at this point to collect benchmark and best-practice data from other organisations. The aim of this exercise is to compare all aspects of finance activities, both quantitative and qualitative, against what is regarded as best practice and to measure where the gaps exist and how efficiency and effectiveness can be improved. As discussed in Chapter 6, the ideal situation would enable discussion to take place between the partners to understand fully the reasons for the differences.

Some organisations find self-assessment against one of the quality frameworks (*see* Section 4.6) to be a beneficial measure of necessary quality improvements. One such company is Sun Life Assurance, which is quoted[2] as measuring itself against the EFQM criteria and finding that

> *the results highlighted the fact that finance was not customer focused, didn't really understand processes and was weak in areas of people strategies and leadership*

explained Keith Brassington, Business Improvement Manager.

Hold brainstorming sessions throughout the organisation

The analyses collected on the current finance activities and the best-practice finance data, together with the senior management team's view on the requirements of the business from the finance function, are presented for discussion both by the finance function itself and by its customers and suppliers throughout the business. Figure 2.1, Transformation of the finance function (p.19), gives a good indication of the likely outline change that will be needed at this stage. Process simplification and rationalisation will not on their own deliver the radical change needed.

Parts 1 and 2 of this book have concentrated on the need and direction that change must take. That view is confirmed by Christine Gattenio[3] of the Hackett Group, who outlines how finance professionals from the traditional finance function are perceived by their peers as:

- hard workers
- historical reporters
- data manipulators
- transaction processors
- reactors and followers
- corporate cops.

Compare this to the role that they can be expected to play in the new transformed finance function:

- focus on better information
- provide insightful direction
- be concerned with planning for the future
- help build relationships
- become change agents
- take a global perspective
- reduce costs.

EDS's finance function's own vision, mission and value statements and key goals are typical of those organisations leading the way:[2]

> *Vision:*
> *To create a world-class financial team.*
>
> *Mission:*
> *To provide global financial leadership and expertise to EDS.*
>
> *Value statement:*
> *The controller organisation will enable EDS to achieve its vision by providing leadership with a broad and unique business perspective and relevant information through efficient business processes.*
>
> *Goals:*
> - *Develop business leaders*
> - *Drive strategy formulation and decision making*
> - *Provide actionable information.*

Define and agree the transformed finance function specification

Once the process has reached this stage, a clear vision should have emerged through consensus throughout the company. The specification that is then drawn up must spell out how the transformed finance function is going to deliver added value.

What services is finance going to deliver in future?

- Operational services, possibly outsourced or a shared service centre approach.
- Facilitators of company-wide value-based management.
- Facilitators of company-wide performance management.
- Facilitators of company-wide performance improvement.
- Facilitators of company-wide information management.
- Strategic and operational decision support.
- Facilitators of company-wide risk management.
- Financing and stewardship services.

What efficiencies need to be achieved in delivering services?

- BPR applied to all processes.
- Specifics as identified.
- Benchmark gaps.
- Continuous improvement culture.
- Flexible and responsive.
- Eliminate 'diversionary' activities.
- Customer focus.
- Service orientation.

What technological advances will be harnessed to effect that delivery?

(*See* Chapter 7 on Information management.)

- Enterprise-wide systems.
- Desktop personal tools.
- Business intelligence tools.
- E-commerce.
- Collaborative computing.
- Decision-support tools.

What combination of competencies and skills are required?

(*See* Section 8.5 below.)

- Business consultants.
- Business analysts.
- Technical specialists.
- Job and person specifications.
- Training and development programmes.

What organisation structure will be appropriate?

(*See* Chapter 9.)

- Outsourcing.
- Shared service centres.
- Devolved to business units.
- Centralised.
- Non-financial staff incorporated.
- Customer focused.
- Service oriented.
- Clearly defined accountability, authority and responsibility lines.

What control and measurement of the finance function will be maintained?

(*See* Part 2.)

- Qualitative.
- Quantitative.
- Customer satisfaction.
- EFQM.
- Balanced scorecard (weighted).
- Integrated performance management.
- Linked to compensation.
- Service-level agreements monitoring.
- Continuous benchmarking.

8.5 CREATE THE CHANGE STRATEGY

It will be necessary to prepare a detailed plan at this stage, setting out the following.

Project plan

Depending on the radical nature of the changes that have been agreed, it could take up to two years to complete the transformation fully, particularly if the changes involve the implementation of IT solutions such as ERP and EIS or the setting up of a global shared service centre. It will be possible to schedule other changes during that period and a detailed project plan, clearly showing interdependencies, will need to be drawn up without delay. If too many ideas were forthcoming from the visioning exercise, then it may be necessary to prioritise and phase the improvements and changes at this point. Do not underestimate the resources required to make the changes successfully.

Business case

Once the detailed plan has been produced and fully costed, it needs to be incorporated into a business case to gain official board approval. This should be a formality at this stage, as all the SMT members will have been involved in the discussions to formulate the new strategy. The end vision should be so compelling, both in terms of reduced costs and improved services, that no opposition should emerge.

8.6 ALIGN STAFF SKILLS AND COMPETENCIES

Introduction

According to Price Waterhouse's *CFO 2000* survey,[4] by far the biggest barrier to improving finance's role is the current level of competencies among finance staff. CIMA Research on *Changing Work Patterns*[5] discovered that accountants in business rank current and future required skills and knowledge in order of importance as:

- business acumen/commercial awareness
- interpersonal/communication skills
- managing people

- strategic thinking (second in future analysis)
- information technology
- management accountancy (traditional).

These are very different to the technical skills of traditional finance function personnel.

Assess existing staff for new posts

The company human resources (HR) specialists will be involved in this process, which may consist of the following steps.

Draw up job and people specifications

The first step is to draw up job and people specifications to match the transformed finance function specification. These will be in line with those described by SMAC in *Redesigning the Finance Function*,[6] falling into three categories.

Business consultants

Business consultants are usually a core of shared-service corporate staff, who specialise in specific processes, models or initiatives, providing advice and support to the business units. They typically perform the following tasks:

- global economic and business monitoring
- continuous improvement
- benchmarking
- new ventures
- strategic analysis
- process redesign.

Business analysts

Business analysts are generally operating from within the business units as the financial specialist on the management team. In addition to the traditional roles of the business unit financial controller or management accountant of scorekeeping and traditional budgetary control, the analysts are at the sharp end of delivering the new decision-support and value-adding roles discussed in detail in Part 2, Value-adding tools and techniques. Their job roles include:

- project leader
- information provider
- business partner

- analyst
- performance measurement
- business unit reporting
- competitor analysis.

Technical specialists

Technical specialists are experts in finance and accounting, who provide the traditional transaction-processing, financing and stewardship activities, using the new systems with improved reporting and control services at much reduced costs. These professionals are often located centrally and are far fewer in number than in the traditional finance function. Their roles include all of the traditional tasks:

- information systems
- general ledger
- audit
- tax
- legal
- compliance
- accounts receivable
- accounts payable
- treasury.

These new dynamic finance professionals will become leaders of multidisciplined teams engaged in strategic and tactical planning, taking equal responsibility for the future success of the company.

Compare requirements with existing staff profiles

- Compare the requirements established to the current staff skills and competencies profiles.
- Identify any matches, near matches and mismatches and draw up plans, without delay, for slotting existing personnel into jobs.
- Consider if any staff from other departments might be suitable for the business analyst or consultant roles and raise internal job advertisements.
- If a downsizing is resulting from, for example, setting up an SSC in another country, then great skill needs to be exercised to keep those staff who will become redundant until the transfer is complete, possibly utilising termination bonuses. In some cases it will be crucial to keep key staff and their retention needs to be treated as a priority.

- Assess whether new staff, with different skills, need to be recruited from outside the company and begin the process of recruitment.

Draw up staff training and development plans

Begin to arrange the necessary additional training and development that will be required for staff. All staff will undoubtedly require customer-focus training, even if they are going to fulfil one of the technical roles for which they are a good skills match. Many will need more extensive new skills training and support, particularly in creative problem solving, communication skills, business and commercial understanding and company-wide value-adding skills.

Communicate

Communicate the results of the exercise as quickly and as sensitively as possible. Undue delay in this process causes anxiety, demotivation and uncertainty and can result in the best staff departing.

8.7 IMPLEMENT THE TRANSFORMATION

- Successful implementation will require considerable efforts, not just in terms of good project planning but in effective leadership, company-wide communication, project selling and management of the change process. This will take time, so be sure to build it into your plans.

- Transition planning must be rigorous to ensure that customers do not suffer unduly during the changes. It is often prudent to make changes and minor improvements in existing systems immediately to gain the support of the customer and ease the transition.

- Take care to agree service-level agreements and project plans with every customer individually, getting each business unit's 'buy-in' to the transformation. If new costing and decision-support systems are being built, remember that finance is facilitating this process for the operational managers and not the other way around.

- Ensure that all staff, particularly finance staff, are communicated with regularly during the implementation process. This must include progress reviews of training and development programmes.

8.8 MONITOR SUCCESS AND RESULTS OF IMPLEMENTATION

- The success of the implementation against plan should be monitored regularly by the steering group. This will include monitoring of timescales, resource utilisation, expenditure, staff retention and recruitment.

- Once complete, each stage of the project must then be monitored against the set objectives to ensure that they are being met in full, including customer satisfaction and culture changes.

- Continue to monitor staff requirements for additional training, development and support.

- Continue to benchmark against 'best practice' and 'best value' to ensure that the company maintains upper-quartile performance.

- Regularly review SLAs with customers.

- Produce a balanced scorecard monthly for SMT to monitor progress.

- Link compensation to performance and achievement of corporate objectives.

- Communicate success company wide.

CASE STUDIES
WORLDWIDE EXCELLENCE IN FINANCE

Adidas-Salomon[7]
In five years the German footwear and apparel manufacturer Adidas-Salomon has pulled back from bankruptcy, gone public and seen its stock price triple. Once a classic case of mismanagement, the company is striving to become a decentralised, virtual enterprise with multicultural management. Robert Louis-Dreyfus, who took over as CEO in 1993, launched a company-wide campaign to reduce its cycle times, increase on-time delivery, manage seasonal inventory and respond quickly to changes in consumer tastes.

The CFO, Australian Dean Hawkins, set about establishing closer relationships between his department and operating areas. The tenets of the company's formal finance mission statement stress that the finance function's primary duty is to support the decision-making process of senior management and operating divisions. He made it his main goal to demonstrate to business heads that finance could do more than manage the books. Mr Hawkins said:

> *I want to effect this change through trust-building measures, trust-building measures result when members of the finance function provide value-added analysis before it is requested. Ideally, the finance function is not to be viewed as a necessary evil but rather as a partner.*

The drive to 'add value at every point where the work of finance touches the rest of the business' runs like a *leitmotif* through Mr Hawkins' strategy. In his short tenure as CFO he has effectively 'changed the status quo of what was previously acceptable for the CFO to do'. He has employed the 'right mix' of people (including new recruits who do not have accounting backgrounds), improved analysis, and fostered better understanding, more trust and fewer political agendas.

Dell Computer[7]

Dell Computer Corporation boosted its return on invested capital from 37% in 1995 to 186% in 1998, due to a single-minded focus on financial and operating discipline, says Tom Meredith, CFO. The company combines a clear understanding of its business model, a company-wide determination to boost return on invested capital, a fierce appetite for information and a rigorous analysis of both financial and operating performance. At Dell, say Tom Meredith and Michael Dell, chairman and CEO, financial understanding is not the province of the finance department only but permeates the atmosphere.

The thrust of the changes was as follows:

- **Finding a common data model**, which was a global financial initiative to develop a common architecture, system and practice.

- **Balancing liquidity, profitability and growth**, reducing inventories down to seven days, by reducing the numbers of suppliers.

- **Changing focus and behaviour**, by educating employees about the increasing emphasis on ROCE – which included tying a significant portion of employee compensation to that measure.

- **Creating value for customers profitably.**

- **Maintaining a focus on people development.** In addition to reinvigorating finance's recruiting and development efforts, Mr Meredith now spends more of his own time educating financial managers. 'I don't believe finance is a support function,' he says. 'We are either integral partners or we are rented units.' The quest to improve the finance team's knowledge is never ending. 'If I have a real heartache,' says Mr Meredith, 'it is that we're not yet able to spend more time analysing, and a whole lot less time compiling, information. We're starting to move from information to knowledge. Eventually, I hope we'll move from knowledge to wisdom.'

SmithKline Beecham[8]

Hugh Collum, Executive Vice-President and CFO of SmithKline Beecham, says:

> *Accountants could go the way of coal miners! A mighty industry that once employed three-quarters of a million and helped bring down a government today employs fewer than SmithKline Beecham. I believe that accountants in industry could go the same way if they do not realise the fundamental changes they need to make.*

SmithKline Beecham's R&D division has been transforming its finance function from scorekeeper to business partner by focusing on the following:

- **Streamlining transaction processing.** It has moved from the individual businesses to company and country-wide shared service centres.
- **Establishing decision-support tools and processes.** Finance has built up a team with skills to support decisions.
- **Developing skills and technologies.**
- **Building the finance discipline.** A central team maintains the finance discipline within R&D. Its role includes the continual development of processes, tools and systems, adopting best practice wherever possible.

9

Outsourcing and shared service centres

- 9.1 Outsourcing 175
- 9.2 Shared service centres (SSC) 181
- 9.3 Case study – Outsourced shared services at the BBC 186

9.1 OUTSOURCING

Introduction

Outsourcing is the transferring of internal business functions or processes, together with any associated assets, to an external supplier or service provider, who offers a defined service for a specified period of time, at an agreed set of rates. Organisations are recognising that many of their non-core activities and processes can be operated more efficiently by an outside company that specialises in added-value outsourcing. Facilities management describes the management of existing property and equipment, for example in IT, the installation and operation of hardware, systems software, communications and the transfer of operators and systems IT staff. However, the transfer of the development of applications systems and the applications staff would normally constitute added value and be defined as outsourcing.

It is not unusual for organisations to part or selectively source a function, retaining significant parts in-house. The public sector, driven by Compulsory Competitive Tendering legislation imposed by the government, is one of the main outsourcers. Examples include the Passport Agency, outsourced to Siemens; Bromley Borough Revenues and Exchequer Services, outsourced to Capita; and DTI Accounting Services, outsourced to CSL.

IT outsourcing

Historically, service functions such as security, cleaning, catering and payroll have been outsourced, but over the last 15 years information technology has become the main target for outsourcing. The rationale was that IT was not part of the core business and that it would be good business sense to transfer its running to an organisation for which it was a core activity. Eastman Kodak is thought to be the first company to have outsourced its IT in this way. Research carried out by Andersen Consulting, commissioned by Harris Research, revealed that 90% of the organisations it interviewed had discussed outsourcing, 70% at board level.[1]

Main reasons for outsourcing

- Poor in-house computer systems that were inefficient and ineffective.
- Reduction in costs, better value and improved quality of service.
- Greater flexibility.
- Access to expertise at a time of impending system changes.

- Focus on core activities at a time of major change and intense competition.
- The need for relocation or other space constraints.

Reasons for rejecting outsourcing

- Concern about loss of control.
- Lack of identifiable benefits.
- Decision that IT is strategic to the business.
- Effect of outsourcing on staff morale.
- What to do with existing IT personnel.
- Contract difficulties.
- Large-scale business change.
- Not the right time.

Risks in outsourcing

- Hidden costs of contract.
- Credibility of vendor claims.
- Irreversibility of contract.
- Lack of expertise in managing contracts.
- Loss of control over operations.
- New IT expertise from vendor fails to materialise.
- Loss of control over strategic use of IT.

Main problems experienced during outsourcing

- Defining service levels.
- Managing the contract and its details.
- Getting different contractors and vendors to work together.
- Vendor's lack of flexibility.
- Vendor's lack of responsiveness.

Lessons learnt from experience

Preparation

- Detailed strategy and objectives for outsourcing.
- Clearly defined requirements specification and invitation to tender (ITT) process.
- Thoroughly vet vendors for claims and culture.
- More sensitive treatment of staff.
- Detailed financial and quantitative evaluation.

Contractual

- Tighter contract terms.
- More detailed, comprehensive service-level agreements.
- Anticipate 'hidden' costs.
- Inclusion of penalty clauses.

Contract management

- Active management of supplier.
- Regular reviews of performance.
- Clear agreements on multivendor situations.
- Build flexibility into contract.
- Ensure sufficient in-house staff dedicated to IT.
- Ensure that staff vendor quality is maintained.

Finance function outsourcing

Outsourcing of the finance function is a more recent occurrence. According to J. Brian Heywood,[2] the first three major private-sector clients to outsource a significant part of the finance function were BP Exploration (in 1991), Conoco, and Sears, all three of which outsourced to Andersen Consulting. A survey carried out by Manchester Business School in 1997 among 400 small, medium and large organisations found that over 50% were outsourcing some aspects of the finance function.

Those finance function processes commonly being outsourced are the low-value-adding, transaction-processing activities, such as:

- primary data capture and checks
- transaction processing

- information and reporting preparation
- control systems
- function management.

A survey of the top 1000 companies carried out by Walker International[3] research found that payroll was outsourced in 20% of those companies and accounted for 50% of all accounting services outsourced, followed by asset management, tax advice, internal audit and accounts payable.

Steps in outsourcing finance

Gather basic information

- Possible options for outsourcing, e.g. purchase ledger only or whole accounting function.
- Number of people that will need to be transferred, their roles and locations.
- Quantitative information on number of cost centres, number of transactions in ledgers, details of reporting process.
- Maps of existing processes and services being outsourced.
- Management and location of each part of the process.
- Details of related IT, telecommunications and other shared services.
- Information to be provided to potential outsourcers:
    - background details of the organisation
    - reasons that outsourcing is being considered
    - objectives of outsourcing
    - other alternatives being considered
    - anticipated contract length
    - any joint-venture possibilities.

Begin dialogue with providers

- Hold discussions with potential outsourcers utilising basic information.
- Select a short list of three or four possible providers based on culture, reference sites and credibility.

Prepare the invitation to tender

- General company details.
- Levels of confidentiality required.

- Background to decision to outsource, including strategy, objectives, extent of outsourcing, current projects.
- The processes to be outsourced with details on each, including:
  - objective of process
  - transaction details, volumes per year
  - process maps, staffing details
  - current working practices
  - strengths and weaknesses of current process
  - features/changes required from any new outsourced system.
- Timing of ITT and contract.
- IT strategy as it affects outsourcing.
- Details of staff to be transferred.
- Transitional arrangements.
- Details and format required in outsourcer proposal.

Provide assistance to outsourcers during bid process

- The more assistance you provide, the better match the proposal is likely to be.
- Ensure a level playing field for all bidders, providing the same support to all.

Evaluate bids

- Test suppliers through conventional contracts first, if possible.
- Always check out reference sites and take care to ensure that there is a 'culture fit'.
- Look for innovative risk/reward-sharing proposals that give both sides of the partnership incentives to make it work cost effectively.
- Are the staff to be transferred to be treated equitably? Will staff have enhanced career prospects with the outsourcer?

Decision

- Ensure that the contract allows for flexibility, change and development over the length of the contract.
- Set up a balanced scorecard to monitor performance.
- Build in regular meetings of senior management on both sides of the partnership.

Potential benefits from outsourcing finance

- Reduced operating costs through reengineering, introducing best practice and the economies of scale available to the provider.
- Avoidance of one-off costs associated with new equipment and systems.
- Greater control and predictability of expenditure.
- Significant improvement in service, resulting from enforceable service-level agreements.
- Increased flexibility arising from the provider's ability to reallocate staff between different contracts and service centres.
- The possibility of lower capital costs if the involvement in a shared service centre is acceptable.
- Frees resources to focus on core financial value-adding services.

Potential risks of failure in outsourcing finance

James Creelman[4] claims that the potential risks of failure are:

- loss of control over the decision-making process
- selection made on lowest-cost basis alone
- failure to consider the longer-term requirements
- failure to incorporate continuous improvement into service-level agreements
- difficulty in harmonising the objectives of the two parties
- lack of flexibility to allow for inevitable changes in assumptions made at start of contract
- tendency to try to 'get the better of' the other party, usually favouring the supplier
- undermanagement of the contract, due to lack of appreciation of amount of work involved or loss of staff who were familiar with the contract negotiations (sometimes due to their transfer to the outsourcer!)
- inadequacy of communication channels
- poor management of people issues.

Outsourcing partnerships

In the last couple of years, outsourcing deals appear to have moved into a second generation. Matthew May[5] explains that no longer is the emphasis on highly prescriptive contracts, but instead on risk sharing, partnerships and joint ventures. Michael Beebe, President of CSC's chemical, oil and gas group, is quoted as saying:

> *In the past, companies would ask how much of a contract would be value-added services, but never made any buying decisions on that. Now they are making decisions on the basis of what added value can be provided.*

Some examples of the new deals being struck include:

- Caixa Catalunya, Spain's third largest savings bank, has signed a seven-year deal with Andersen Consulting, which has set up a 50–50 joint venture between the bank and the outsourcing firm.
- In 1997, DuPont entered into a ten-year deal with CSC, which includes CSC selling IT products and services outsourced from DuPont to other chemical firms and splitting the profits between them.
- In 1998, Elf Oil, the UK marketing arm of Elf Aquitaine, outsourced its financial accounting staff to PricewaterhouseCoopers, although it chose to keep the staff located on the company's premises. The contract provides that any savings and improvements in existing business processes will be split 50–50 between the parties.
- In 1996, Swiss Bank Corporation (SBC) agreed a deal with Perot Systems, a US IT outsourcer, lasting 25 years with an equity swap arrangement. SBC gave Perot a 40% stake in its systems and development unit, Systor; in return, SBC had an option to acquire up to 25% of Perot.

All of these deals recognise the shortcomings of earlier outsourcing arrangements and, through various different innovative contracts, have tried to overcome them. In particular, the inevitable conflict of interests and lack of incentive to save money and add value inherent in the old-style deals are being addressed. The British Institute of Facilities Management (BIFM) is seeking not only to raise standards but to set a benchmark – widely recognised accreditation – against which providers can be judged.[6] It has engaged Aimita to devise an accreditation programme for its 200 corporate members based on EFQM.

9.2 SHARED SERVICE CENTRES (SSC)

Introduction

As Europe becomes more homogeneous through the convergence of fiscal, legal and tax regulations and the introduction of the single currency, it is harder to justify the higher costs of maintaining duplicate infrastructure within each country of operation for international, pan-European or global companies.

Shared services are a type of 'internal outsourcing', the focus being to provide non-core services to individual business units, but often they are set up and run in conjunction with an external outsourcing partner. Shared service centres can contain one or several support processes, from high-volume, transaction-based processes like purchase order processing to specialist services like legal. Cost savings achieved through utilising SSCs are quoted as high as 50% in the USA and 30–40% in Europe.

Research conducted by PricewaterhouseCoopers in 1998[7] indicates that when you strip most business processes down to their basics, about 70% of these processes are generic. The processes are operated differently in different countries, mostly because of history, tradition and culture. John Barnsley, PwC Global Leader of business process outsourcing, said:

> *It is possible to reduce processes to common elements which enable those processes to be carried out in the same way, very efficiently, for different companies and in different countries, and even to concentrate them in one country. In fact, a key factor in business process outsourcing is that you can arrive at a common, generic process to deal with many different local processes and then decide on the single location where this will be handled. Technology and telecommunications have made this possible.*

For example, it was recently announced that BMW and Rover would centralise procurement in one European location to reduce costs.

Costs are not the only factor. When PwC was setting up a shared service centre in Europe in cooperation with BP and Mobil, Rotterdam was chosen because of its ability to provide the necessary multilingual staff, which, on this occasion, gave the Netherlands comparative and competitive advantage. Another important consideration in Europe is the potential tax savings that can be achieved. Some countries, like Belgium and the Netherlands, have introduced specific tax regimes to encourage SSCs being located in their countries. Equally, other factors must be considered including relocation of staff, process reengineering, legal implications, IT and individual country statutory requirements. For example, in Sweden it is a criminal offence not to hold computerised accounting records on a computer physically located in Sweden.

Checklist of technical considerations in establishing an SSC[8]

Which processes are best suited to be incorporated within an SSC?

With the move to profit-accountable business units, with ever greater autonomy, it is more important than ever to ensure that support functions are as efficient as possible. The difficulties involved in negotiating the sale of centralised services to profit-oriented business units are great. If they find through benchmarking and market testing that the services are not provided as efficiently as can be bought in from outside, what do you do? Generally speaking, ground rules are introduced to protect in-house services, at least in the short term. However, it is incumbent on all support functions to ensure that in the medium term they provide the most customer-oriented, appropriate, flexible, effective and cost-efficient services, which can compete with outside providers.

So considerable soul searching is needed in radically examining all support activities, including those that are partly or completely contained within the individual business units, such as some HR and finance activities. When considering which processes to install in an SSC, the obvious first choices would be the high-volume, transaction-based processes, like purchase ledger. Such activities are generic and yield obvious synergies when centralised. Other support services fitting this category include:

- purchase order processing
- sales order processing
- information consolidation
- general ledger accounting
- management accounting
- foreign currency exchanges
- treasury operations.

However, further investigation will reveal that the SSC concept is also suited to the provision of specialist services, like legal. Quite often business units, depending on their size, cannot justify employing in-house expertise for these services and find that a centralised specialist unit, which has full corporate knowledge, is the ideal solution. Other specialist services that fit into this category include:

- human resources
- logistics
- property management
- taxation
- IT.

How can accounting and legal differences be catered for?

Unfortunately, despite the progress towards the European Union's aim of a single market, considerable differences still exist in terms of accounting and legal requirements in the different member countries. There is no single set of European Accounting Standards and the method of regulation is peculiar to each country.

For example, in Germany and France the government regulates accounting standards, but both have recently passed laws permitting group accounts to be prepared according to International Accounting Standards (IASC) rules. In Italy, accounts must be notarised and all pre-printed documents prepared by state-authorised printers; such problems with documents can be overcome by the use of document imaging.

Other difficulties include the need to standardise on a chart of accounts when each country has its own set of accounting and reporting practices, for example France's 'Plan Compatable', which requires a pre-defined set of codes. The problem of common codes has been experienced for years by head office consolidation teams trying to consolidate information, and as a result software is available that can convert each country's codes into a common chart of accounts.

Group taxation opportunities and problems created by the location of SSC

The key driver for opportunities in terms of taxation is the methods chosen to charge business units for the services provided by the SSC. This is, of course, first and foremost a commercial decision, but the method needs to be agreeable to individual country tax authorities. Europe operates an arbitration convention to obtain corresponding adjustments to iron out any difficulties caused by differing tax treatments due to inter-country transfer pricing. The principle of arm's-length negotiation should be adopted and documented to avoid problems.

Some tax considerations to be taken into account when deciding in which country to locate the SSC are:

- variable corporation tax rates, which are over 40% in France and Germany
- methods of calculating profits eligible for taxation, e.g. capital allowances, financing costs, intangible asset treatments
- utilisation of tax losses
- transfer of goodwill
- tax incentives offered by different countries, such as the Netherlands
- commission structures, which could be beneficial, meaning that sales are made from the central unit, which pays commission to local sales offices as agents, providing the opportunity to earn more profit in a low-tax regime
- VAT and other indirect taxes
- document compliance.

How can the challenges to IT be overcome?

Recent developments in IT, including the introduction of enterprise-wide software discussed in Chapter 7, and in telecommunications have provided three essential capabilities in:

- managing language requirements; these can be handled on-screen by ERP software and calls from different countries can be diverted via telecommunications, but generally staff with the necessary language skills will need to be employed
- improving accessibility of information via enterprise-wide networks and other technological advances, which avoids the need to duplicate information
- dealing with diverse processing requirements, such as multiple currencies; different VAT treatments are handled well by ERP solutions.

Phases in implementation of shared service centres

Depending on the results of the analysis, Price Waterhouse suggests[9] that it may be appropriate to phase in the implementation of a global SSC by first progressing through one or more of the following stages:

- simplification
- standardisation
- centres of excellence
- national SSC
- regional SSC
- global SSC
- outsourcing.

The lifecycle of an SSC project will include the following phases.

Making the business case

- Understand financial issues.
- Understand non-financial issues.
- Communicate the business case and get 'buy-in' from senior management and staff.
- Demonstrate added value to shareholders and stakeholders.

Determine methodology

- Analyse best practices.
- Consider options.
- Develop ground rules and service-level agreements.
- Make each business unit's agreement personal and unique.

Implementation

- Calculate the impact of changes on staff morale and corporate culture.
- Plan well in advance for the people issues, ensuring that key staff are retained.
- Develop and get 'buy-in' to transitional and implementation plans.
- Retrain as necessary to provide a service-oriented, standardised approach.
- Develop and agree a balanced scorecard of performance measures.
- Align reward to performance.

Service provision

- Deliver operational services to business units in line with SLAs.
- Continue to improve services and performance and reduce costs/prices over time.
- Benchmark performance externally.
- Identify new services that could be incorporated into the SSC.
- Rigorously review processes, customer satisfaction and progress regularly to ensure that benefits identified in the business plan are realised.

CASE STUDY
Outsourced shared services at the BBC[10]

Background

The British Broadcasting Corporation (BBC) receives around £2.8 bn of licence fee funding annually (linked to RPI) and earns around £400 mn from its commercial activities. It operates in a competitive environment, which has major cost implications and a sophisticated internal market where programme makers have choice on source and supply. The challenges facing the BBC include:

- Convergence of telecoms, media and computing.
- Flat licence fee income.
- Moves into new businesses.

- Introduction of digital terrestrial channels.
- Expansion of commercial activities.
- Non-strategic asset sales (e.g. transmission).
- Re-organisations on a regular basis.

The changes faced and the diverse nature of its operations result in a number of specific financial management issues across the BBC including:

- Separate requirements of the several businesses within BBC.
- Range of different financial processes, supported by different (and incompatible) financial systems.
- Difficulty of obtaining timely and appropriate financial information.
- Key finance functions devolved to organisational layers.
- Financial processing activity occurs at many sites and involves a large number of staff.
- Finance people perceived merely as 'score-keepers'.

The BBC's requirements

The BBC's business imperatives are:

- To reduce substantially the processing and administrative costs of the BBC.
- To improve the quality (including accuracy, relevance and timeliness) of information delivered to programme makers and line managers.
- To modernise the approach to information management, and the systems and services that support it.

The objectives of what the BBC calls the APOLLO Campaign, are to streamline and standardise finance and business systems and processes across the corporation, based on SAP R/3, and to create and manage a shared service centre for all financial transaction processing and finance system support. The implementation of the integrated and common financial, administrative, purchasing, personnel and business information system throughout the BBC is based on standard SAP/R3 software for up to 30,000 users.

When the BBC decided to introduce SAP, it chose to outsource rather than go it alone. Finance Director John Smith explains:

> *We thought it would be better value for licence payers to have a joint venture to achieve all this. We needed expertise to make the changes, and we recognised that we had only limited capability in-house.*

In February 1997, the BBC awarded the contract to EDS and Pricewaterhouse Coopers for a ten-year period and they formed Media Accounting Services Limited (MedAS) to deliver the contract, structured as shown in Figure 9.1, Overview of the arrangements.

Fig. 9.1 Overview of the arrangements

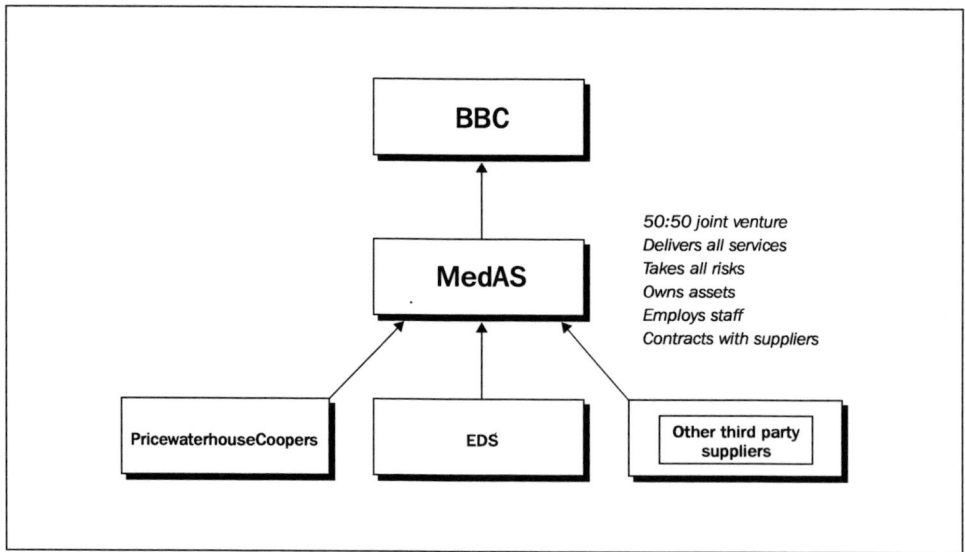

Diagram: BBC at top, MedAS below (50:50 joint venture, Delivers all services, Takes all risks, Owns assets, Employs staff, Contracts with suppliers), with PricewaterhouseCoopers, EDS, and Other third party suppliers feeding into MedAS.

During the contracting process the BBC applied the EU procurement process, which resulted in four bidders being short-listed. Contractual negotiations were undertaken with MedAS, who it can be seen from Figure 9.2, MedAS can deliver all components of finance and IT services, with the entire process from OJEC notice to signed agreement taking around 18 months. Other key features of the contract include:

- 10 year duration
- Fixed charges regime
- Significant consulting effort for transformation work
- Creation of an IT & finance shared services operation with contractual & enforceable SLAs
- TUPE arrangements apply

Fig. 9.2 BBC – MedAS can deliver all components of finance and IT services

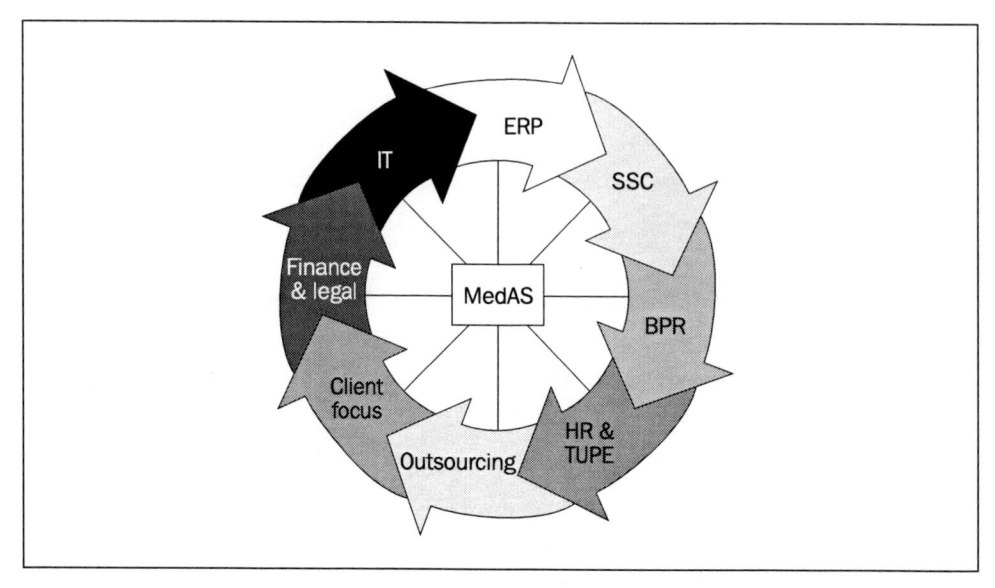

Circular diagram with MedAS at centre surrounded by: IT, ERP, SSC, BPR, HR & TUPE, Outsourcing, Client focus, Finance & legal.

Finance IT staff and contractors and a range of legacy systems were transferred to the new company on 1 March 1997 with the priority of continuing to operate and maintain financial systems. MedAS then commenced reengineering the BBC's 18 financial processes, followed by the transfer of a further 400 finance staff on 1 March 1998 together with a range of financial processing activities and provision of services to the BBC. The implementation of the reengineered processes with SAP R/3 software will start later in 1999.

Why Outsource Finance and IT Services

It can be seen from Figure 9.3, There are a variety of service delivery models.

Fig. 9.3 BBC – There are a variety of service delivery models

Client → More services outsourced →				
All build and operational services delivered by internal resouces	Most build and operational services delivered by internal resources	All operational services provided by internal resouces	Some operational services provided by internal resources	Strategic services retained by BBC
No services	Some specialised IS/IT services (e.g. SAP) provided by contractor(s)	Turnkey facility is built by the contractor(s)	Turnkey facility is built and operated by contractor(s)	Turnkey facility is built and operated by contractor(s)
← Less services outsourced				Third party supplier

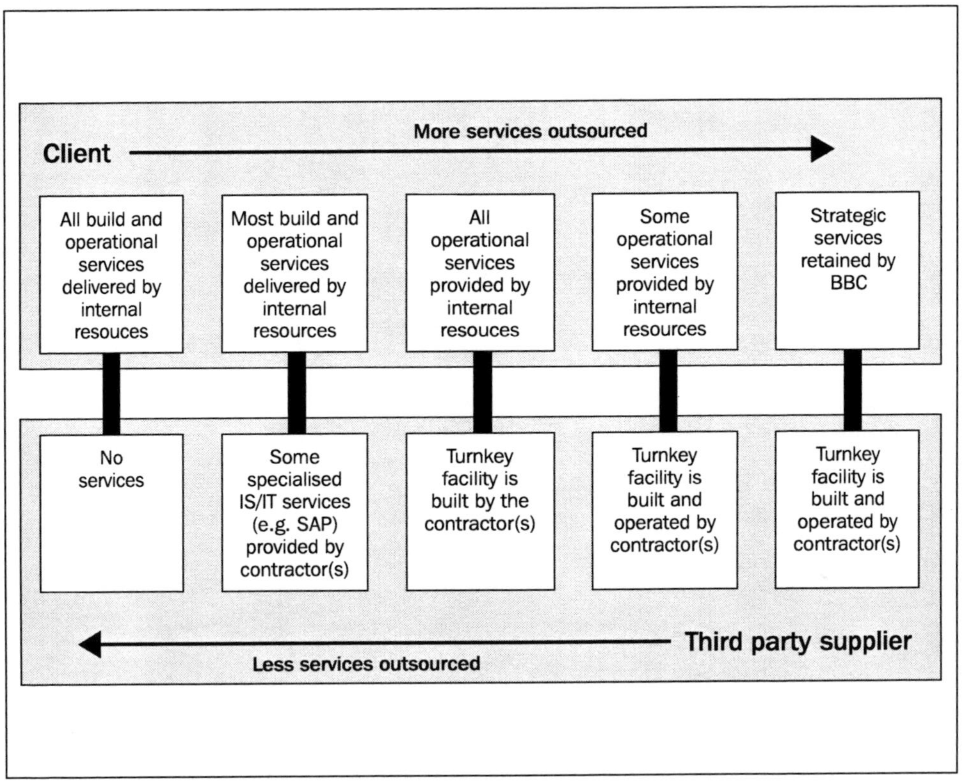

Issues to be addressed when considering outsourcing should include:

- Pricing/funding arrangements (e.g. cost-benefit, fixed charge profile, funding requirements).
- Willingness to take risks (e.g. project and service delivery, financing, benefits realisation).
- Internal capabilities and past performance (e.g. demonstrated ability to deliver projects and services).
- Diversity, complexity and vested interests (e.g. the diversity/power of the business units).
- Partner(s) capabilities and experience (e.g. able to deliver the requirements).
- Service flexibility (e.g. ability to change services to meet new requirements).

Figure 9.4, Examples of in-house v outsourced service delivery, contrasts some of the main differences in the two methodologies, whilst Figure 9.5, Outsourcing service delivery models, shows the three main contractor model alternatives. Some of the conditions where outsourcing could be appropriate are:

Fig. 9.4 BBC – Examples of in-house v outsourced service delivery

In-house	Outsourced
self-funded	external funding
cost budgets	fixed charges regime
retain all risks	transferred risk
internal SLAs	enforceable SLAs
cost centre focus	profit focus
non-core activity	core competencies
single-customer focus	multiple customers
internal culture	refreshed culture

Fig. 9.5 BBC – Outsouring service delivery models

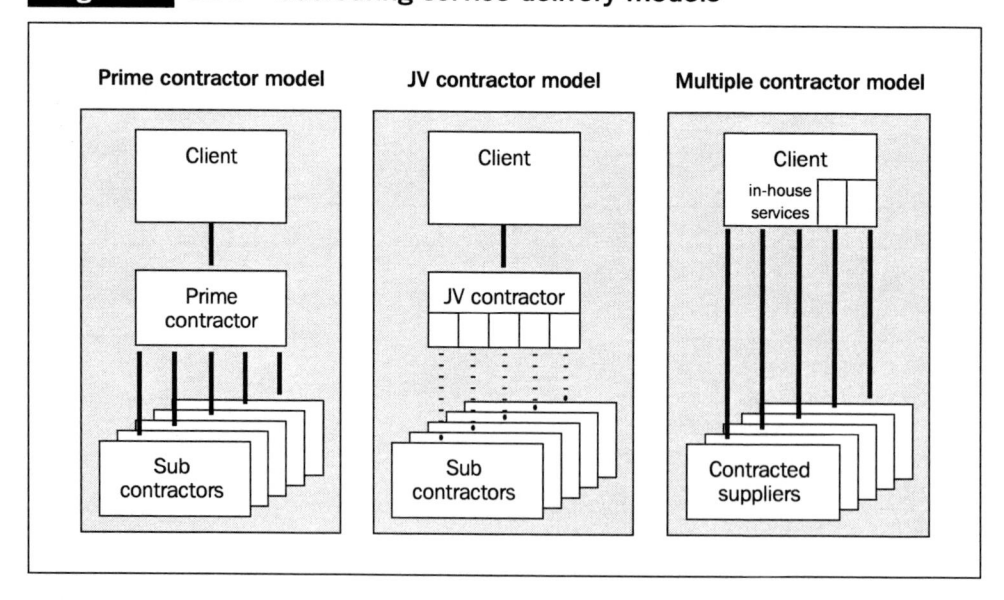

- Sufficient scale of operation.
- Significant service transformation requirements and organisation concerned with the risks.
- Service integration requirement (eg from merger and acquisition activity).
- Business requirements are for guaranteed and lower cost profile.
- Changes to regulatory or statutory requirements.

Benefits accruing from outsourcing finance and IT services may include:

- Fixed price regime with guaranteed price for the services outsourced, and inclusive of funding arrangements.
- Services delivered by organisations whose core competencies, and management are directly focused on these services (core v non-core).
- Transfer of key risks (finance, service, project, benefits realisation) to external organisations.
- External service providers can apply functional and industry best practice.
- There may be improved opportunities for staff (cost reduction focus v multi-client growth focus).
- Internal organisation blockages, which affect existing services, can be removed or minimised through use of an outsourcing contract.
- External service providers are in a better position to provide flexible service arrangements (e.g. price arrangements, service components).

Considerations and conclusion

For outsourcing arrangements to be successful they require considerable commitment from both sides and are unlikely to happen without:

- client sponsorship throughout
- changes in approach and procedures requiring training and change management support
- leadership and input to transformation work (resources, decision-making, prioritisation)
- ongoing management of finance and IT across the client organisation.

Figure 9.6, Outsourcing contracts can be complex, illustrates some of the areas that need to be dealt with and why it takes a long time to negotiate – 18 months in the case of the BBC.

Fig. 9.6 BBC – Outsourcing contracts can be complex

Scope of services	BBC responsibilities
Services performance obligations	Financial guarantees and deposits
Term of contract	Warranties and indemnities
Fee and payment arrangements	Monitoring and control procedures
Roles and responsibilities	Dispute arrangements
Assets and intellectual property	Termination arrangements
Liabilities	Confidentiality and publicity
Staffing issues	Contractual variation procedures
Premises and location	General contractual clauses
Transition arrangements and timing	Arrangements for next contract

. . . and can take a considerable amount of time to finalise.

Figure 9.7, Different (and conflicting) agendas exist within an organisation, gives some indication of the differences that can occur, all of which needed to be carefully managed. Other considerations include:

- Executive sponsorship is required for the outsourcing arrangements to be successful.
- Although the contract is important, a partnership approach must be adopted with compromises being made from time to time.
- The customer-supplier interface needs to be clarified and implemented as a priority.
- Expectations need to be managed about the pace of service improvement following a TUPE transfer.

Fig. 9.7 BBC – Different (and conflicting) agendas exist within an organisation

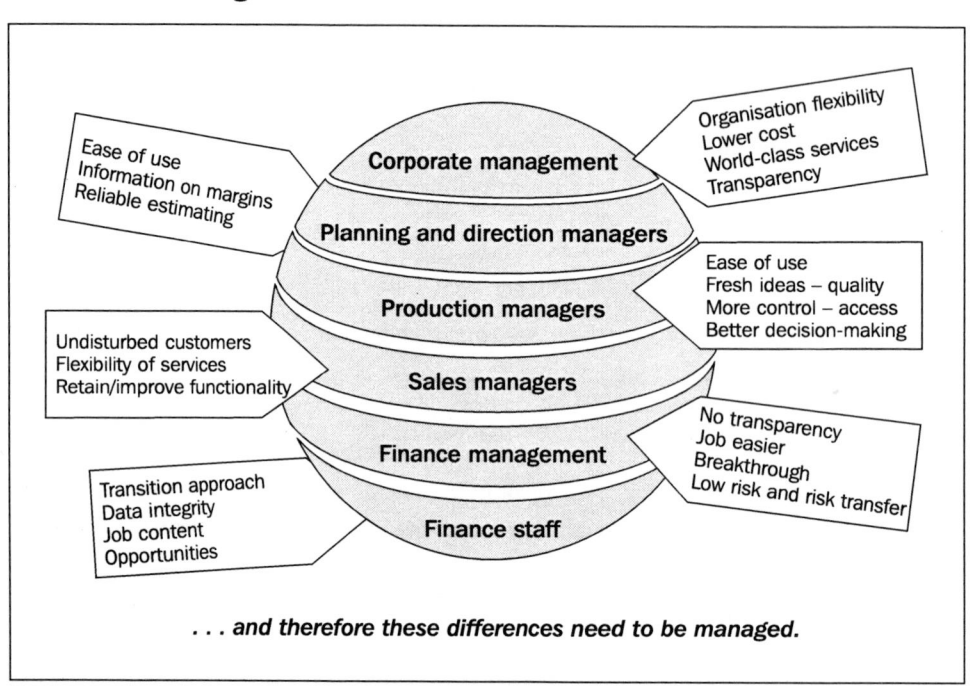

Corporate management
- Ease of use
- Information on margins
- Reliable estimating
- Organisation flexibility
- Lower cost
- World-class services
- Transparency

Planning and direction managers

Production managers
- Ease of use
- Fresh ideas – quality
- More control – access
- Better decision-making

Sales managers
- Undisturbed customers
- Flexibility of services
- Retain/improve functionality

Finance management
- No transparency
- Job easier
- Breakthrough
- Low risk and risk transfer

Finance staff
- Transition approach
- Data integrity
- Job content
- Opportunities

... and therefore these differences need to be managed.

John Smith believes the BBC's outsourcing contract lays the foundation for the BBC's aim of greater business efficiency and improved financial information into the digital age.

> *The BBC is pleased to have reached this position and looks forward to a successful partnership with MedAS. There is a significant task still ahead of us, but the result will be the best possible finance systems for the BBC and its staff, and substantial savings will be ploughed back into programmes and services for licence payers.*

10

The finance function as the facilitator of change, adding company-wide value

- 10.1 Introduction 195
- 10.2 Achieving successful change 195
- 10.3 How not to do it 197
- 10.4 Case study – Company-wide ABC and BPR at ABB 198

10.1 INTRODUCTION

The transformed finance function has a key role to play in facilitating performance improvement and necessary change company wide. It is its role to ensure that finances are used as efficiently and effectively as possible throughout the whole business and to drive the implementation of value-adding tools and techniques. Wilson and Chua's[1] definition of management accounting:

> *encompassing techniques and processes that are intended to provide financial and non-financial information to people within an organisation to make better decisions and thereby achieve organisational control and enhance organisational effectiveness*

emphasises this role. Equally, the ultimate test of a successful management accounting system is whether or not it motivates and assists managers in achieving organisational control and enhancing organisational effectiveness.

While finance no longer owns the information it provides within the business, it has clear roles to fulfil with regard to it:

- To train, to ensure understanding of all the value-adding tools and techniques throughout the business.
- To collect, analyse and present information. This must include design and implementation of models and enterprise-wide information systems.
- To act as a catalyst for change and improvement, facilitating cross-functional workshops and panels.
- To assist in assessing improvement ideas and proposals coming out of these processes. The financial perspective is essential.
- To assist in planning, budgeting, performance measurement and monitoring.
- To validate all information. This is an audit role that finance is best qualified to carry out.

10.2 ACHIEVING SUCCESSFUL CHANGE

ABC and BPR have received much bad press, with high failure rates reported. Like all the techniques and tools explained in this book, their success depends entirely on how they are implemented. Far too many of these initiatives were regarded as mechanical exercises, often undertaken by engineers or accountants with little or no regard for the human component. The success of change using BPR and other techniques will be dependent on successfully involving staff at all levels, gaining their 'buy-in' and commitment, selling them the benefits, allaying their fears about job losses that may result, to gain their trust and cooperation. Such involvement, commitment and support are needed as much from middle and senior management as from the staff performing the work. Far too many traditional managers see change and new ideas as threats to their security and, even worse, as personal criticism of their existing systems. All of these problems need to be understood and dealt with when making any of the changes discussed in this book. It was Machiavelli who said:

> *Change is difficult – those who stand to lose will resist, while those who stand to gain don't know it yet.*

Figure 10.1, The impact of change, shows the normal negative reaction of those who are subjected to change. The speed at which people move from shock to acceptance will vary considerably from person to person. Nick Obolensky, in his book *Practical Business Re-engineering*,[2] says that resistance is a natural occurrence. To overcome it, one must motivate changes in people's behaviour. There are several techniques that can be used to do this:

- Bring resistance to the surface and continually gauge readiness for change.
- Create and maintain dissatisfaction of the status quo.
- Generate new training for new skills.
- Allow participation in planning and implementing change.
- Reward required behaviour and results in the transition and future states.
- Provide time for people to disengage from the current state.
- Use pilots and reposition the remainder.
- Burn bridges and build ambassadors.
- Actively manage in/out-placement in a firm, clear and sympathetic way.

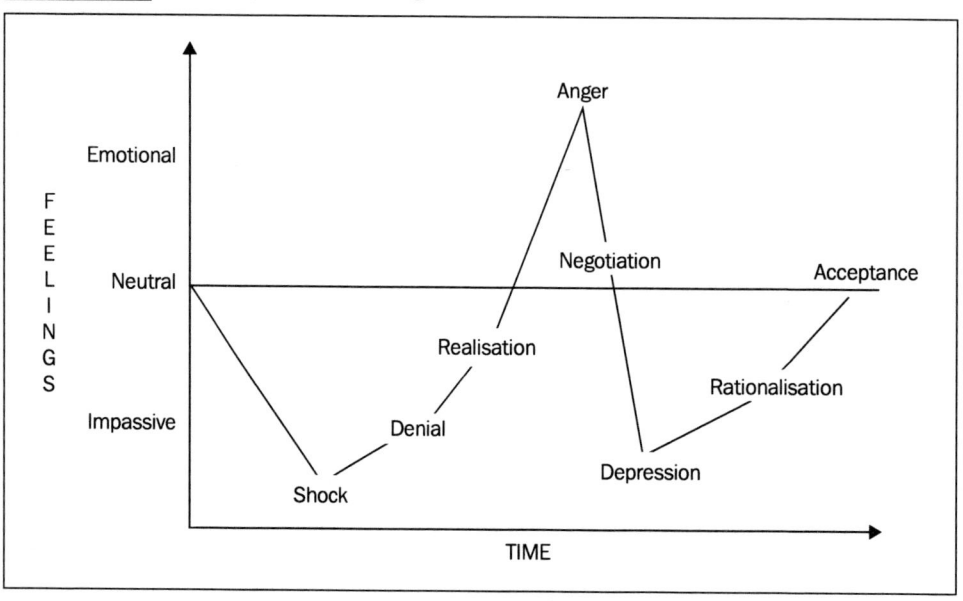

Fig. 10.1 The impact of change

10.3 HOW NOT TO DO IT

Figure 10.2, The boat race, is a humorous reminder and warning about the way in which projects need to be undertaken effectively with the right leadership.

Fig. 10.2 The boat race

MEMORANDUM

To: Whom it may concern

From: Management, Chicago

Date: May 1999

Subject: **ANNUAL BOAT RACE**, Lake Michigan Marina

Company A and Company B decided to have a competitive boat race on Lake Michigan. Both teams practised hard and long to reach their peak performance. On the big day they were as ready as they could be.

RESULT: Company A won by a mile.

Afterwards, Company B's team was very discouraged by the loss and morale sagged. Corporate management decided that a reason for the crushing defeat had to be found. Subsequently, a task force comprised of key executives, called the ANALYSIS OF SUPERVISORY SYSTEMS for EXECUTIVES and SUBORDINATES (A.S.S.E.S.), was formed to investigate the problem and recommended the appropriate corrective action.

THE A.S.S.E.S.' CONCLUSION
The facts indicated that both teams had nine people involved in the contest, however the distribution of duties differed considerably. Company A's team had eight people rowing and one steering, whereas Company B had eight people steering and one person rowing. The task force concluded that it was obvious that the loss was due to poor rowing staff performance.

THE A.S.S.E.S.' RECOMMENDATION
To prevent this from happening next year, the person rowing the boat should work harder to be a premier performer during the next evaluation period. To reach this goal, the steerers should delegate authority and give the staff rower empowerment to do better. The rower should be placed on progressive discipline.

> **RESULT OF THE NEXT YEAR'S RACE:** Company A won by two miles.
>
> Company B's management laid off the rower for poor performance, sold the paddles, cancelled all capital investment for new equipment, halted development of new canoes and distributed money saved as a bonus to senior executives for the risks they had taken.

CASE STUDY

Company-wide ABC and BPR at ABB[3]

Background

Asea Brown Boveri (ABB) is a global $30bn engineering and technology group serving customers in electrical power generation, transmission and distribution; automation; oil gas and petrochemicals; industrial products and contracting; and financial services. The group employs 200 000 people in over 100 countries.

True to its tradition of innovation and leadership, ABB launched a company-wide activity-based costing project in 1996. 'The decision to go for ABC represented a corporate concern and priority to, at the end of the day, further our competitiveness in an increasingly global and competitive marketplace,' says Volker Hevler, Vice-President and Project Manager ABC Group based at ABB headquarters in Zurich, Switzerland. The decision taken was to implement activity-based costing as ABB's common costing method throughout the world by the end of 2000. 'We set our sights very high from the start – ABC must cover the entire group and include full management buy-in and commitment. It is not sufficient to use ABC in your current cost accounting system or to use it as a parallel tool. Rather you must do it by the book and progressively,' explains Volker Hevler.

One reason behind this decision was the recognition that there had been a significant change in the make-up of product costs during the preceding three decades. Indirect costs are now a larger proportion of the whole and there is a need to find a better way of assigning those costs than purely by percentage allocation. This can be clearly seen in Fig. 10.3, The development of product cost structure, with Fig. 10.4, Improvement potential, showing the scope for potential improvement.

In fact, ABB's declared objectives are fourfold:

- To cost and price products better by assigning many more indirect costs to products and services than can be achieved with traditional cost accounting.
- To enable better management with thorough analyses and insights into activities and processes.
- To use ABC as a tool for change management in the organisation and its processes.
- To facilitate strategic decision making based on relevant cost calculations.

Fig. 10.3   ABB – The development of product cost structure

Cost type \ Year	1960	1967	1977	1987	1990
Overhead costs	34%	50%	62%	68%	70%
Wages (direct)	28%	16%	14%	10%	6%
Material costs	38%	34%	24%	22%	24%

Fig. 10.4   ABB – Improvement potential

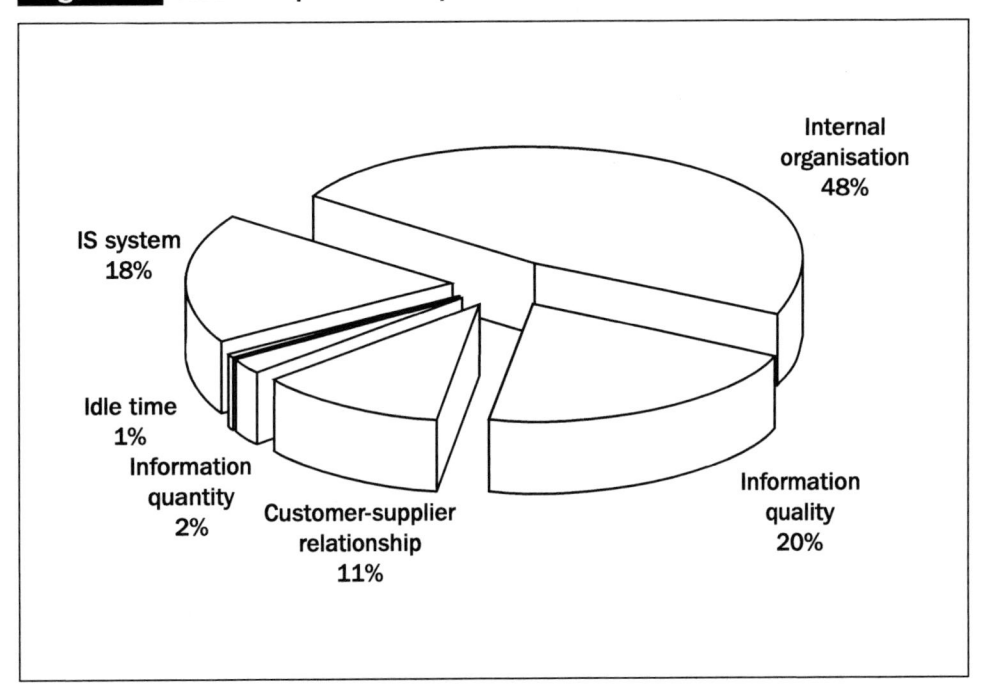

- Internal organisation 48%
- Information quality 20%
- IS system 18%
- Customer-supplier relationship 11%
- Information quantity 2%
- Idle time 1%

The analysis is aided by the use of a software tool from Prodacapo, a Swedish software house chosen by ABB to provide a standard solution worldwide.

Although the project is defined and driven by Volker Hevler's Central Project Group, the execution and implementation are the responsibility of country management. Local projects in the operating companies are led by experienced certified facilitators. The manager of ABC projects in the UK Region is Andy Daniels, FCA and he is responsible for 29 projects running in 18 units and is assisted by ten trained facilitators.

One of the benefits of a standard methodology is the ability to offer cross-border support. This has been demonstrated recently by teams from the UK successfully working on projects in both the USA and Turkey. This not only overcomes resource problems but creates the opportunity to share experiences.

Methodology

ABB has split the ABC project into two clearly defined phases:

- **Stage 1** involves the analysis of processes and activities in the business followed by optimisation of those processes; in addition, data is gathered about cost drivers, business volumes and resources.
- **Stage 2** uses the data from Stage 1 and seeks to develop an integrated cost accounting solution, which will result in the regular reporting of financial performance using ABC as the base.

Stage 1, which has been the main area of focus up to now in the UK, involves interviews with all members of staff to ascertain the type of work done. This creates a detailed picture of the business when combined with the relevant financial information and enables selection of the key processes that will offer the greatest opportunity for improvement.

These processes are mapped in detail in two forms: 'as is' – how the work is actually done now – and 'should be' – the optimised way of performing the work. In order to move from the 'as is' situation to the 'should be', an action plan must be developed and implemented.

This key step involves the creation of cross-functional teams who actually work in the process and experience the day-to-day problems. This also serves as a good teambuilding and learning experience.

UK case study of Company A

'Experiences of Stage 1 projects in the UK have been generally favourable,' explains Andy, 'with many good examples of employee-driven change. However, not all projects are a success and there are lessons to be learned from both the successes and the "non-successes", where the results could be better with improved focus.'

One of ABB's success stories in the UK is Company A. This company is involved in the management of large-value projects and the subsequent provision of spares. Created by the merger of two divisions following an acquisition, there were a number of cultural differences to overcome, as well as the inefficiencies of duplication.

From the first meeting, management recognised the benefits that could come from the project and made a firm commitment to ensure success. This positive message was sent throughout the company and helped to overcome the sceptics.

The initial analysis identified that 3 out of 17 processes accounted for over 50% of the indirect cost base – clearly, these were the areas on which to focus. Teams were set up to map the processes, ensuring that the make-up was representative not only cross-functionally but also cross-business unit.

The outcome was a common set of recommendations for change, which were presented to management. It was clear from these recommendations and the initial analysis that there were significant opportunities for savings. However, there was still a degree of scepticism that anything would be done with this information, previous initiatives having suffered from poor follow-up.

Management's response to this was to appoint a coordinator with responsibility for ensuring that the opportunities became reality. A team structure was put in place to ensure continuity with the mapping teams and also to involve as many people as possible, as illustrated in Fig. 10.5, Working team structures. Each of the five teams was tasked with looking at one of the key improvement areas – setting targets and timescales that were acceptable to both staff and management. The role of management became one of support rather than execution: making time (a scarce resource) available for more team meetings.

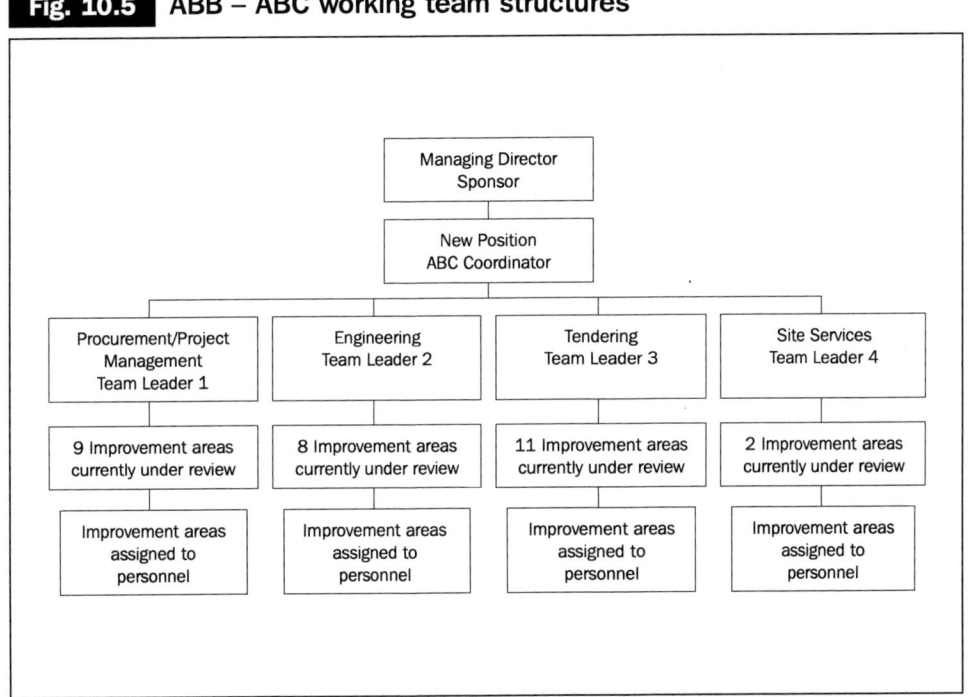

Fig. 10.5 ABB – ABC working team structures

```
                    Managing Director
                        Sponsor
                           |
                     New Position
                    ABC Coordinator
    _____|_____
    |              |              |              |
Procurement/   Engineering    Tendering     Site Services
Project        Team Leader 2  Team Leader 3 Team Leader 4
Management
Team Leader 1
    |              |              |              |
9 Improvement  8 Improvement  11 Improvement 2 Improvement
areas          areas          areas          areas
currently      currently      currently      currently
under review   under review   under review   under review
    |              |              |              |
Improvement    Improvement    Improvement    Improvement
areas          areas          areas          areas
assigned to    assigned to    assigned to    assigned to
personnel      personnel      personnel      personnel
```

The real test of any project is whether the changes bring results, especially in the area of customer relationships. For this company, the proof came when it applied its new optimised tendering process to a customer enquiry that it had no real prospect of winning, all previous bids to this customer having produced no orders. Resource was assigned to follow the new process and the bid was submitted. Despite not being the lowest price, the contract was awarded to ABB on the strength of the quality of the bid. Clearly, the challenge is now to replicate this success.

Internally, the project has brought about change in a number of ways. Previously two engineering departments worked separately with different standards, mainly for historical reasons ('We're different'). The experience gained from working together during the process-mapping sessions demonstrated that the differences were more perception than reality. There is now one engineering department working to common standards.

One common failing of 'improvement' initiatives is that they are not coordinated with the overall business plan, leading to confusion and frustration. Company A has sought to overcome this by putting in place a link between the business plan, the improvement plans and individuals' objectives. This link is created through the improvement teams and an appraisal scheme, which in turn is the basis for the training plan, as seen in Fig. 10.6, Linking the plans.

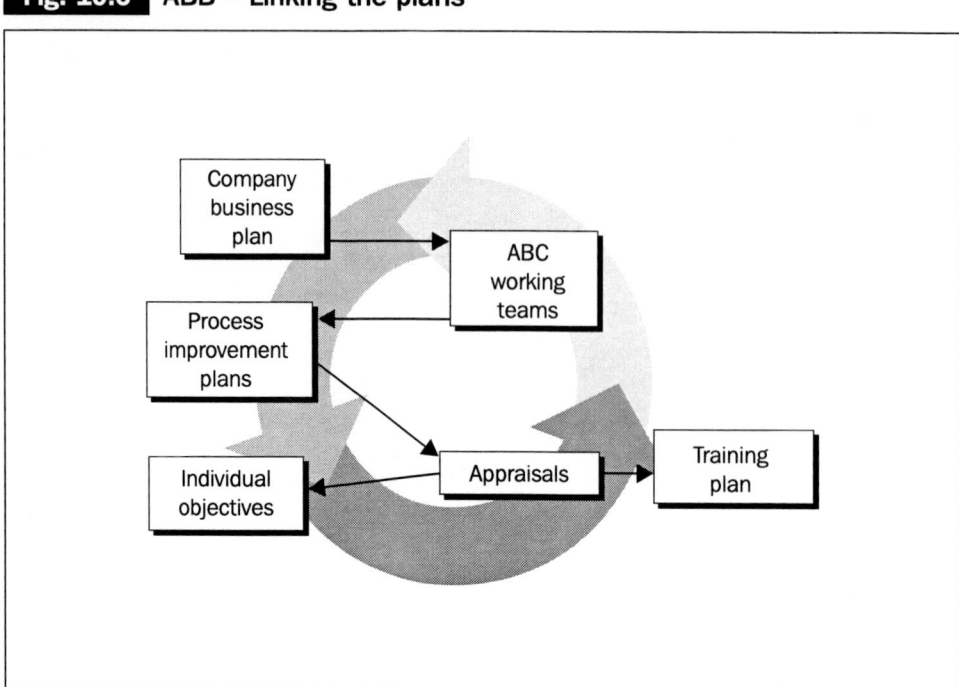

Fig. 10.6 ABB – Linking the plans

Conclusions

What has all this to do with activity-based costing? A good question, to which there is a clear answer.

It is essential that to gain the maximum benefit from the new measurements that ABC will bring, you must first change the way in which you work and manage the business. Simply implementing a new costing system will not improve your business. Likewise, only optimising your processes without on-going, meaningful measurements will not bring about lasting change and real business improvement.

Finally, without the active support of senior management, the chances of success are reduced considerably.

Part 4

Executive summary

PART 1 WHY THE FINANCE FUNCTION NEEDS TO CHANGE

1 Problems with the traditional finance function

1 Over the last 15 years companies have faced unprecedented change and this has inevitably placed new demands on the finance function.

2 It is no longer acceptable to spend 84% of resources on transactional processing and control activities utilising outdated financial computer systems that focus efforts on processing and spreadsheets.

3 The traditional finance function's insular approach, concentrating on its financial, control and statutory obligations, has lost sight of the need to produce relevant, timely and meaningful information for business.

4 Traditional costing methods developed in the 1960s lead to inaccuracy when applied to modern-day companies' cost structures and are inappropriate and misleading.

5 Traditional budgetary control processes with no clear links between strategy, operations, resource allocation and performance, leading to arbitrary 'across-the-board' cuts, are endangering the long-term health of businesses.

6 Traditional performance management systems are based on backward-looking financial measures and are unable to give a balanced view of overall company health.

7 Traditional 'top-down control cycle' organisational cultures stifle innovation and are not conducive to maximising shareholder value. Finance functions are lagging behind in switching to the 'bottom-up empowerment cycle' organisational culture.

8 In the public sector, legislation over the last 15 years has meant considerable change to financing and culture. Resource accounting and budgeting, Continuity and Change and Best Value require the adoption of very different tools and techniques.

2 The need for transformation of the finance function

9 The challenge for the finance function is to become more cost effective, value adding, embedded within the business processes, customer focused and service oriented, adding company-wide value, reacting quickly when responding to ever-changing needs.

10 The impact of technology has resulted in not only the automation of processes but also access to data; the breaking down of boundaries between finance and other functions; and new possibilities utilising web-enabled systems. All are impacting on the methods and structure of the traditional finance function.

11 Costs of the finance function will need to fall by one-third on average, with transaction-processing costs falling by two-thirds using modern enterprise resource planning, web-enabled systems and 50% of the activities in the transformed finance function switched to decision support and adding value company wide (*see* Fig. 2.1, p.19).

12 Finance professionals, who have traditionally been content spending their time on processing and technical issues, will need to be realigned and retrained to sell and deliver value-adding services out in the business.

13 New methods of planning, measuring and controlling the company must replace traditional budgeting. Resource allocation needs to be linked to company strategy and priorities and performance benchmarked against comparable organisations, both internally and externally.

14 It is essential to introduce a balanced set of performance measures along the lines of Kaplan and Norton's balanced scorecard, examining all relevant business perspectives, including customer, learning and innovation, internal business and financial, in addition to external influences such as competition and the environment.

15 The finance function needs to take control of the organisation's integrated information and performance management strategy, becoming company-wide information facilitator.

16 Best Value will replace CCT in 2000, requiring local authorities to demonstrate to the community and stakeholders that service provision provides value for money, by utilising value-adding techniques.

PART 2 VALUE-ADDING TOOLS AND TECHNIQUES

3 Value-based management

17 Research carried out by Price Waterhouse in 1997 revealed that CFOs worldwide placed maximising shareholder value as their number one priority.

18 A gulf has opened up between profit used by the company as a measure and cash-generation used by investors to judge company performance. Adoption

of common measures based on cash was first put forward by Rappaport in 1986, based on seven value drivers.

19 Following Rappaport, a number of different shareholder value calculation models have been developed falling into three main categories: economic value added, cashflow return on investment and cash value added.

20 Shareholder value analysis needs not only to drive strategic decision making but to become embedded in the behaviour of all levels in the organisation, integrating the various management processes including remuneration.

21 In organisations adopting VBM, the creation of autonomous strategic business units, trading with each other, utilising service-level agreements and inter-SBU charging, is now becoming the norm. This encourages the behaviour of a third-party supplier eager to please its customers.

22 The requirement to develop comprehensive company-wide processes and policies for identifying, understanding, assessing and mitigating risk, which give assurances that controls are in place to assess significant risk and highlight strategic opportunity, is fundamental to maximising shareholder value.

23 The case study of VBM at British Aerospace explains how the success of the pilot projects carried out at Regional Aircraft is now being mirrored across the whole company. VBM is a priority action for BAe in helping to deliver long-term sustainable growth in value for its customers, employees and shareholders.

4 Balanced scorecard

24 The balanced scorecard shows how to link the corporate vision to critical success factors or outcomes and key performance indicators, representing all perspectives of the business. This compels the senior management team to operate as a unified team, balancing competing objectives to achieve the optimum result for the company as a whole.

25 By weighting the different measures within the BSC the technique enables scores to vary according to importance, within the overall vision and achievement of specified outcomes.

26 The ten commandments of balanced scorecard implementation, researched by KPMG in Europe in 1996, lays out the dos and don'ts to be followed for success. This is advice that would hold good for any project.

27 Research sponsored by CIMA in the UK in 1999 lists key learning points for any managers involved in BSC implementation and design.

28 Because of the focus and detail of the quality frameworks (such as EFQM and Baldrige), there is considerable merit in linking this detail to both balanced scorecards and activity-based management accounting systems. This is particularly pertinent to Best Value.

29 In the case study at Eurotunnel, the BSC was used to transform the company from tunnel builder to commercial train operator. Its four perspectives are financial targets; the performance of the railway; customer satisfaction; and staff satisfaction.

30 In the Manchester Housing case study, the information strategy utilising Business Objects and the intranet was used to bring together information contained in disparate systems and provide a corporate traffic light BSC, utilising alerts, exceptions and trends, for the DMT. In addition, it replaced the service plan with a tree of measures, drilling down beneath the BSC to service the information needs of all employees.

5 Activity/process-based techniques

31 Activity/process-based techniques are now widely used and fall into three main categories: costing, performance improvement and performance management. Over the last five years, ABT have stopped being used as one-off techniques and have become a company-wide, all-embracing, advanced planning, monitoring and control system.

32 All ABT involve analysing the business to gain a greater knowledge of what activities it performs and how those activities relate to one another to form processes. This analysis forms the central database for all ABT. The level of information collected will depend on the objective and the ABT being used.

33 ABC is now generally accepted as the most appropriate method of costing company products and services. The main difference between ABC and traditional costing is that instead of collecting overhead costs into one or more central pools to be allocated arbitrarily to all products and services, it first allocates resources to activities, prior to allocating activity costs to products and services based on actual usage.

34 The fourth dimension of the ABC model provides customer/market/sector profitability, by multiplying product and service costs and revenues by the volumes of sales to each customer and attaching any customer or market-driven costs directly.

35 Early activity-based cost management performance-improvement initiatives based on functional responsibilities have now given way to business process redesign or reengineering, focusing on processes and constraint removal, not departments and functions.

36 The need for one integrated performance management system that links strategy via the BSC to a detailed model of the organisation, incorporating objectives and balanced measures of time, quality and cost cascaded down to each level of activity and process throughout the organisation, is now well understood (see Fig. 2.2, p.26).

37 Activity-based management accounting is a series of ABT including activity-based budgeting; the need to cascade objectives down the organisation through processes and activities; the setting of balanced performance measures and targets; the ability to evaluate alternate service levels and prioritise them, i.e. priority-based budgeting; and activity-based reporting, including earned value analysis, where time recording is not required.

38 The Lund University Hospital case study demonstrates how the organisation overcame both financial and quality problems by utilising process-based performance measurement. Dr Hallgarde said:

> *It is possible to achieve continuous improvements by measuring process-based measures like activity cost, leadtime or quality. The focus is on the processes of the organisation and not on departmental costs or specific expenditures.*

39 The Metropolitan Housing Trust case study utilised many ABT in its reactive repair process, calculating the cost of administering each order at £50; benchmarking the process with another organisation utilising the same software; establishing best practice for its four regions; identifying potential cost savings and performance measures; and comparing ABB against its traditional budgeting.

6 Benchmarking

40 Benchmarking is a tool used to establish processes, costs and performance indicators and compare them against other similar organisations, with the aim of identifying and progressing towards best practice and best value through continuous improvement. Care must be taken to ensure true comparability.

41 Types of benchmarking include internal; external databases; collaborative, within and outside the sector; and competitive. When benchmarking outside the organisation, the accepted code of conduct should be followed.

42 Methods of gathering data vary in terms of cost, accuracy and amount of data collected and must be driven by the purpose of the project. Methods

include clubs; research; reverse engineering; company visits; surveys; questionnaires; internal and public domain sources.

43 Phases of the benchmarking process include selection and prioritisation of processes; forming project teams; documenting processes; researching and identifying partners; analysing data collected; determining best practice; implementation; and review.

44 Once an organisation has measured its own performance and taken steps to improve, the next logical step is to make comparisons with outside organisations to demonstrate efficiency and effectiveness. The benefits of benchmarking include its ability to focus attention on areas needing improvement, driving innovation and change where necessary.

45 The London Borough of Tower Hamlets case study explains the process benchmarking project that it has been running for the last five years, involving 25 London boroughs and 28 different council processes in the first phase. The second phase has been extended outside of London and the public sector and covers non-council processes common to most organisations.

7 Information management

46 The role of information manager is pivotal within the organisation. The challenge is to replace the myriad unconnected legacy systems with an enterprise-wide system that can deliver the information that the company needs to ensure that it continues to add value year on year.

47 Great care must be taken to define the business requirement for the company's information system, to provide an integrated understanding of the financial and operational position of the company in a dynamic business environment. Its success is not important merely to ensure value for money but to maintain the company's competitive position.

48 When formulating the company-wide information strategy, the following steps need to be taken: set up a project team; analyse existing company, supplier and customer systems; understand the latest technological options, such as ERP, middleware, web-enabled, data warehousing, decision-support systems, (DSS) e-commerce and collaborative computing; analyse future business needs; and gain consensus from the whole organisation for the recommended solution.

49 ERP is fast becoming the accepted solution for larger organisations, as they seek to gain corporate advantage from the automation and integration of the separate parts of the business, in addition to solving problems connected with the Year 2000 bug and introduction of the euro.

50 Activity/process-based analysis is now fundamental to the way organisations are managed and should be an integral part of the design of any enterprise-wide system, not treated as a 'bolt-on' extra. While the eventual ideal scenario would be to utilise a module of the ERP suite for V/ABM, they are often not yet as advanced as required and not suitable for the initial development phase.

51 Checklists of features and functionality of the purpose-built packages for V/ABM, BSC, ABB and BPR include reporting, modularity, technology, tailoring, basic calculation features, budgeting and simulation features, and prices.

52 The Anglian Water case study examines the company's design methodology, using QPR software, building detailed business unit models and merging them to form a consolidated, less detailed corporate model. The software was selected because of its suitability to be used as an end-user information delivery system, with 'what if' simulation capabilities.

53 The Nationwide case study explains how a data warehousing solution was applied to the set-up of a new operation at a greenfield site in Swindon. Delivery of the system was a small but key part of the development of the management reporting solution. It involved addressing cultural and educational issues around implementation, addressing data and information ownership, development of CSFs and KPIs and a monitoring basis for all business areas.

PART 3 TRANSFORMATION OF THE FINANCE FUNCTION

8 How to plan and implement the necessary changes

54 In the words of John Fisher in *CFO Magazine*:

> *The accounting back office must be relocated to the front lines. And finance executives must shed their mundane record-keeping tasks and develop the skills necessary to provide high-level information for company-wide consumption.*

55 In the words of Susan Jee of Magnox:

> *We have to earn the right to be taken seriously by the business generally. We have to prove that we can provide more than just the numbers while recognising that these numbers are still of critical importance.*

These new jobs within business units, which replace traditional financial positions, can just as easily be filled by non-financial staff, as the financial content is now less than half the new role.

56 Steps in the transformation project include putting together the business case; appointing a steering group and project team; identifying customers and suppliers to the finance function to consult; identifying benchmarking partners; setting up communication media; analysing the present function activities and processes; developing the vision for the future of the finance function; creating the change strategy; aligning staff skills and competencies; implementing; monitoring and communicating results.

57 Case studies illustrate worldwide leading-edge examples: Adidas-Salomon affected change through trust-building measures, which result from when members of the finance function provide value-added analysis before it is requested. Dell Computer combines a clear understanding of its business model, a company-wide determination to boost return on invested capital, a fierce appetite for information and a rigorous analysis of both financial and operating performance.

58 Hugh Collum, Executive Vice-President and CFO of SmithKline Beecham, is quoted by KPMG as saying:

> *Accountants could go the way of coal miners! A mighty industry that once employed three-quarters of a million and helped bring down a government today employs fewer than SmithKline Beecham. I believe that accountants in industry could go the same way if they do not realise the fundamental changes they need to make.*

9 Outsourcing and shared service centres

59 Organisations have recognised that many of their non-core activities and processes can be operated more efficiently by an outside company that specialises in added-value outsourcing. Traditionally, service functions such as security and catering have been outsourced, but over the last 15 years IT and other services, driven by CCT in the public sector, have been widely outsourced. Mainstream finance outsourcing began in the early 1990s, with 50% of companies now outsourcing some part of their finance function.

60 Steps in outsourcing include gathering basic information; beginning dialogue with providers; preparing the ITT; providing assistance to outsourcers during

the bid process; evaluating the bids; making a decision; implementing, managing and monitoring the outsourcer.

61 In the last couple of years, outsourcing deals have moved into a second generation. The inevitable conflict of interests and lack of incentives to save money and add value, inherent in old-style deals, are being addressed. No longer is the emphasis on highly prescriptive contracts, but instead on risk-sharing partnerships and joint ventures.

62 Shared service centres (SSC) are a type of internal outsourcing, the focus being to provide non-core services to individual business units, but often they are set up and run by an external outsourcing partner. SSCs can contain one or several support activities or processes, from those that are high level and transaction based, like accounting and POP, to specialist services like legal. Cost savings from SSCs in Europe are reported to be as high as 30%.

63 Technical considerations to be taken into account when establishing an SSC include which processes should be incorporated; accounting and legal differences between countries; taxation problems and opportunities; and IT challenges.

64 The BBC case study is a good example of the way joint ventures are being formed to run outsourced SSCs. It describes the 18 month process of negotiation and the considerable amount of commitment that is required from both sides for the arrangements to be successful.

10 The finance function as facilitator of change, adding company-wide value

65 It is the role of the finance function to ensure that finances are used as efficiently and effectively as possible throughout the whole business. The implementation of these value-adding tools and techniques should therefore be driven by finance.

66 While finance no longer owns the information it provides within the business, it has a clear role to fulfil as information facilitator in training in the understanding of the tools and techniques; collecting and analysing information; acting as a catalyst for change across functions; assisting in the assessment of improvement ideas; assisting in planning, budgeting, performance measurement and monitoring; validating information.

67 The success of change utilising these tools and techniques will be dependent on effectively involving staff at all levels in the organisation, gaining their buy-in, selling the benefits and allaying their fears.

68 In the case study of company-wide ABC and BPR driven and facilitated by finance at Asea Brown Boveri (ABB), Volker Hevler said:

> *We set our sights very high from the start – ABC must cover the entire group and include full management buy-in and commitment. It is not sufficient to use ABC in your current cost accounting system or to use it as a parallel tool. Rather you must do it by the book and progressively.*

The objectives are to cost and price products better; to enable better management through insights into activities; to use ABC as a tool for change management; and to facilitate strategic decision making.

References

PART 1

1 Problems with the traditional finance function

1. Hackett Group, *Ongoing Benchmarking Survey*, 1996.

2. Banerjee, Jyoti and Kane, Wendy, Tate Bramald Consultancy, *CIMA/JBA Survey of Management Accountants' Use of IT*, October 1996.

3. Guy Clapperton, Bournemouth University, 'Research on management accountants for IBM', *Accountancy Age*, 17 October 1996.

4. Coopers & Lybrand, *Pan-European Finance Function Benchmarking Survey*, 1998.

5. Johnson, H.T. and Kaplan, R.S., Harvard Business School Press, 1987. *Relevance Lost: the rise and fall of management accounting*.

6. CAM-I, Consortium for Advanced Manufacturing International, is a not-for-profit group of companies, consultants and academics from around the world, undertaking research in the area of management accounting. Its UK base is in Poole, Dorset.

7. Johnson, H.T., *Relevance Regained*, Free Press, 1992.

8. Margaret May, 'An activity-based approach to resource accounting and budgeting in government', *Management Accounting*, July/August 1996.

2 The need for transformation of the finance function

1. The Society of Management Accountants of Canada, *Redesigning the Finance Function*, 1997.

2. Kaplan, R.S. and Norton, D.P., 'The balanced scorecard: measures that drive performance', *Harvard Business Review*, Jan/Feb 1992.

3. Janet Kersnar, 'Time to Bin the Budget', *CFO Europe*, May 1999.

4. CIPFA, *Accounting for Best Value Consultation Paper*, CIPFA, 1999.

PART 2

3 Value-based management

1. Price Waterhouse, *CFO, Architect of the Corporation's Future*, John Wiley 1997.
2. Alfred Rappaport, *Creating Shareholder Value*, Free Press, 1986.
3. EVA™ is a trademark of Stern Stewart & Co, USA.
4. Paul Nichols, 'Unlocking shareholder value', *Management Accounting*, October 1998.
5. CVA™, is a trademark of FWC AB, Sweden.
6. Case study VBM at British Aerospace contributed by Tony Bryan, former VBM Executive, Regional Aircraft Woodford, and Rogan Dixon, VBM Champion BAe Head Office, Farnborough.

4 Balanced scorecard

1. Kaplan, R.S. and Norton, D.P., 'The balanced scorecard: measures that drive performance', *Harvard Business Review*, Jan/Feb 1992.
2. Professor Lewy and Lex du Mee, *Management Control and Accounting*, KPMG Management Consultants, 1996.
3. Keasey, K., Aisthorpe, P., Hudson, R. and Littler, K., University of Leeds, 'Shareholder and stakeholder approaches to strategic performance measurement using the balanced scorecard', *CIMA Research Foundation Update*, Summer 1999.
4. Carolyn Fry, 'Rail renaissance', *Accountancy Age*, 21 January 1999.
5. Case study – Manchester City Council Housing Department's information strategy, written by Margaret May, with kind permission from Hilary Vaughan, Assistant Director (Finance), and the DMT at Manchester Housing.

5 Activity-based techniques

1. Friedman, A.L. and Lyne, S.R., *Activity Based Techniques – Real Life Consequences*, CIMA Research, 1995.
2. Ashworth, G. and Evans, H., 'The role of management accounting in business', *Management Accounting*, May 1996.

References

3 Michael Hammer, former professor of computer science at Massachusetts Institute of Technology, author with James Champy of *Reengineering the Corporation: a manifesto for business revolution*, Nicholas Brealey Publishing, 1994.

4 Steven Hronec, *Vital Signs*, AMACOM, 1993.

5 Case study – process-based performance improvement in Lund University Hospital, written by Andreas Johansson of QPR, Dr Morgan Andersson and Dr Ulf Hallgarde of University Hospital in Lund.

6 Case study – ABT and benchmarking at Metropolitan Housing Trust, written by Margaret May, with kind permission of George McMorran, MHT Finance Director.

6 Benchmarking

1 The Society of Management Accountants of Canada, *Implementing Benchmarking*, 1993. The Code of Conduct was co-authored by The American Productivity and Quality Center's International Benchmarking Clearinghouse and The Strategic Planning Council on Benchmarking, 3 January 1992.

2 Tower Hamlets benchmarking case study, written by Mike Howes, former Head of Benchmarking, and updated with information from Keith Luck, former Head of Finance, published in *Management Accounting* and by IFAC in 1997, as part of a piece of research, written by Margaret May, entitled *Preparing Organisations to Manage the Future*.

7 Information management

1 Kevin G. Dilton-Hill, 'Management information to support a world-class company', *Accountancy SA*, May 1993.

2 Rod Newing, 'Data warehousing', *Management Accounting*, March 1996.

3 Jeremy Rasmussen, 'The Internet – the Swiss army knife of business tools', *CMA Magazine*, March 1996.

4 Alan Perkins, 'Intra, not Inter', *Australian Accountant*, November 1996.

5 *Management Consultancy ERP Focus*, Winter 1998.

6 *Enterprise Resource Planning*, Butler Group.

7 *The European Software Market in 1997: Application Packages Lead the Way*, Gartner Group's Dataquest.

References

8   Friedman, A.L. and Lyne, S.R., *Activity Based Techniques – Real Life Consequences*, CIMA Research, 1995.

9   CostControl and Process Guide are products of QPR, Finland.

10 Hyper ABC, now renamed Metify, is a product of Armstrong Laing Limited, UK.

11 OROS is a product of ABC Technologies Inc, USA.

12 Sapling Corporation, Canada, produces NetPhrophet and NetScore.

13 Prodacapo AB, Sweden.

14 Anglian Water case study presented at IIR Utilities Conference in April 1998, with an extract appearing in *Management Accounting* in July/August 1998 entitled 'Advanced activity based management accounting', both by Margaret May, with the permission of Abhai Rajguru, former Anglian Water Services Finance and Planning Development Manager.

15 Nationwide case study written by Abhai Rajguru, former Nationwide Management Information Controller, published in *Management Accounting* and by IFAC in 1997, as part of a piece of research by Margaret May entitled *Preparing Organisations to Manage the Future*.

PART 3

8 How to plan and implement the necessary changes

1   John Fisher, 'Facing up to the 21st century', *CFO Magazine*, September 1995.

2   James Creelman, *Creating the Value-Adding Finance Function*, Business Intelligence, 1998.

3   The Hackett Group, *Best Practices Benchmark Study of Finance*, 1997.

4   Price Waterhouse, *CFO, Architect of the Corporation's Future*, John Wiley, 1997.

5   *Changing Work Patterns*, CIMA Research, 1996.

6   *Redesigning the Finance Function*, SMAC, 1997.

7   *Excellence in Finance*, written in cooperation with Arthur Andersen, Economist Intelligence Unit, 1998. There are extracts here from two of the 12 case studies contained in this book.

8   KPMG Management Consulting, *Finance of the Future*, 1998.

9 Outsourcing and shared service centres

1. Wilcocks, L. and Fitzgerald, G., *A Business Guide to Outsourcing IT*, Business Intelligence, 1995.
2. J. Brian Heywood, *Outsourcing the Finance Function*, Accountancy Books, 1996.
3. Walker International, *The Future of the Finance Function*, 1996.
4. James Creelman, *Creating the Value-Adding Finance Function*, Business Intelligence, 1998.
5. Matthew May, 'Stepping up the pace of change', *CFO Europe*, April, 1999.
6. Rodney Hobson, 'In-house is in vogue again', *The Times*, 13 April 1999.
7. John Barnsley, PwC, 'How to stay on top of the world', *Accountancy Age*, 11 February 1999.
8. Information in this section is drawn from a series of four articles in *Management Accounting* in 1998, written by KPMG staff and entitled 'Shared service centres'.
9. Price Waterhouse, *CFO, Architect of the Corporation's Future*, John Wiley, 1997.
10. *Outsourced Shared Services at the BBC* case study contributed by Richard Hartt, Quality Manager, MedAS and Penny Lawson, APOLLO Communications Manager, BBC.

10 The finance function as facilitator of change, adding company-wide value

1. Wilson, R.M.S. and Chua, W.F., *Managerial Accounting, Method and Meaning*, Chapman and Hall, 1993.
2. Nick Obolensky, *Practical Business Re-engineering*, Kogan Page, 1996.
3. Case study of company-wide ABC and BPR at ABB written by Andy Daniels, Manager UK, ABC Projects at Asea Brown Boveri Ltd.

Index

ABB (Asea Brown Boveri) 198–202, 214
ABC Technologies 138, 140
accounting operations 6, 21
activity analysis 73–8, 101, 102
activity-based budgeting (ABB) 92–3, 110, 209, 211
activity-based cost management 87–8, 208
activity-based costing 71, 77, 79–85, 107–8, 137–43, 195, 208–9, 214
   choice of drivers 82–3
   and customer profitability 83–4
   differences from traditional costing 79–80
   failure rates 189
   help desk costing 83, 84–5
   modelling software 85
   and pricing 84–5
   product costing 28, 80–2, 199
activity-based management (ABM) 87–8, 137–43, 211
activity-based management accounting (ABMA) 23, 91, 92, 137–43, 211
activity-based reporting 101–2, 208–9
activity-based techniques (ABT) 14, 22, 23, 28, 71–111, 115, 134, 137, 208–9
   CIMA Research publication 57, 72, 138
   data collection 76–7, 78
   hierarchical process/activity analysis 73–8
   performance improvement 72, 85–91
   performance management 72, 91–102
   software 137–43, 211
activity classifications 76, 85–6
actual activity analysis 102
Adidas-Salomon 170–1, 212
alternative service levels 28, 72, 76, 97, 209
Andersen Consulting 175, 177, 181
Anglian Water 143–8, 211
audits, for Best Value 27

BAAN 131, 135, 136, 137
balanced scorecard 22, 23, 24–5, 26, 28, 53–67, 115, 130, 134, 137, 138, 165, 206, 207, 208, 209, 210, 211
   implementation 56–7
   learning points for managers 57–8
   measures driving performance 53–4
   and quality frameworks 58–61
   weighted scorecard 54–6, 207
Barings Bank 40
Barnsley, John 182
BBC 186–92, 213
Beebe, Michael 180
benchmarking 20, 22, 23, 24, 28, 72, 108–9, 115–25, 130, 134, 159, 164, 165
   benefits 121
   code of conduct 120–1
   collaborative 116
   competitive 117
   data analysis 119
   data collection 117–18, 162
   documenting own processes 119
   ethics and etiquette 120
   external databases 115–16
   Hackett Group study 5
   implementing recommendations 119
   internal 115
   partners 119, 159
   process selection 118
   reviewing 119–20
   team organisation 118–19
Best Practice 20, 125, 150, 209
Best Value 12-13, 25–8, 72, 61–7, 125, 158, 206, 208, 209
   Accounting for Best Value Consultation Paper (CIPFA) 26
   Audits 28
   Local Government (Best Value and Capping) Bill 1998 26
   Fundamental Performance Reviews (FPRs) 27
   Local Performance Plans (LPPs) 27
   National Performance indicators (NPIs) 27
BMW 182

Index

Boston Consulting Group 35
bottom-up empowerment cycle 13, 38, 54, 205
Bournemouth University 6
BP Exploration 177, 182
BPR (business process re-engineering) 20, 28, 72, 77, 88, 89–91, 108–9, 134, 142, 164, 189, 195, 198–202, 208, 211, 214
brainstorming 90, 91, 162–3
Brassington, Keith 162
British Aerospace 43–9, 207
British Institute of Facilities Management (BIFM) 181
budgeting 6, 9–10, 23–4, 141
   activity based budgeting (ABB) 92–3, 110, 138
   priority-based budgeting (PBB) 28, 98–9
   process/activity based budgeting (ABB) 92–3, 110
budgeting panels 100
business analysts 19, 20, 23, 167–8
business consultants 19, 20, 23, 167
business intelligence tools 131–2, 164
Business Objects 61–7, 208
business process re-engineering (BPR) 20, 28, 72, 77, 88, 89–91, 108–9, 134, 142, 164, 195, 208, 211, 214
Butler Group 137

Caixa Catalunya 181
Cascading objectives 93–4, 209
case studies
   ABB 198–202, 214
   Adidas-Salomon 170–1
   Anglian Water 143–8
   British Aerospace 43–9
   BBC 186–92
   Chartermark 28
   Dell Computer 171
   Eurotunnel 61
   Lund University 102–6
   Manchester Council 61–7
   Metropolitan Housing Trust 106–11
   Nationwide 148–51
   SmithKline Beecham 171–2
   Tower Hamlets 121–5
cash drivers 34
cash value added (CVA™) 36

cashflow return on investment (CFROI) 35–6
cause and effect analysis 90
CAM-I 8, 75
CCT (Compulsory Competitive Tendering) 15, 26, 175, 206, 212
change 57, 195–202
   achieving success in 195–6, 213, 214
   in cost compositions 7–8
   impact of 196
   in the public sector 14–15
   resistance to 196
   and technology 21
   see also transformation project and facilitating change
Chua, W.F. 195
CIMA 5, 72
CIMA Research 57, 72, 138, 117, 166, 207
CIPFA 26
Citizens' Charter 14
Coca Cola 35
collaborative benchmarking 116
collaborative computing 133–4
Collum, Hugh 171, 206, 212
Common data model 25, 26
communication 159, 169, 185
Competing for Quality 14
competencies 22, 165–69, 212
competitive benchmarking 117
competitive environment 58
Compulsory Competitive Tendering (CCT) 15, 26, 175, 206, 212
computer and telephone integration (CTI) 134
Conoco 177
constraint removal 87, 88, 208
continuous improvement 135, 164, 209
contract management 177
control activities 6, 22, 165
   top down control cycle 11, 205
CorVu 140
Cost Control 140
costing systems 6, 7–9, 78–80, 205
   see also activity-based costing
costs
   activity-based management 87–8
   change in composition 7–8

costs *continued*
   direct 7–9
   of the finance function 5
   indirect 7–9
   reducing 9–10, 19, 138
   of software 142
   of transaction processing 5
Creating Shareholder Value (Rappaport) 34
Creelman, James 180
critical success factors (CSF) 24–5, 26, 53, 160, 207, 211
CFO Europe 24, 180, 211
CSC 180, 181
CTI (computer and telephone integration) 134
customer focussed 20, 21, 164, 165, 205
customers 160
   balanced scorecard perspective 53, 54, 206
   identification of 159
   profitability of 83–4, 138, 208
   satisfaction 150, 208
CVA (cash value added) 36

data collection 76–7, 78, 117–18, 161, 162
data warehousing 25, 131–2, 137, 148–51, 210
decision support 19, 22, 129, 134, 137–43, 164, 206, 210
decision support systems (DSS) 6, 22, 25, 129, 132
Dell Computer 171, 212
desktop information management tools 131
Diageo 24
discounted cash-flow (DCF) 39
document management 133–4
drivers 79, 80–5, 87, 137
DuPont 181

e-commerce 132–3, 164, 210
earned value activity analysis 101, 209
Ernst Young 72
Eastman Kodak 175
economic value added (EVA™) 35, 36–7
EDS 163, 187

EFQM Business Excellence Model 26, 28, 58–60, 162, 165, 208
electronic commerce 132–3, 164, 210
electronically funded transfers (EFT) 21
Elf Oil 181
EMU 129, 135
embedded VBM system 38, 207
(EIS) enterprise Information System 6, 25, 139, 140
enterprise resource planning (ERP) 6, 21, 22, 25, 129, 131, 135–7, 185, 210, 211
Eurotunnel 61, 208
EVA™ (economic value added) 35, 36–7
evaluation of alternative service levels 28, 72, 76, 97, 209
extranets 133

facilitating change 21, 195–202, 213–14
finance professionals 206, 212
   business analysts 19, 23, 167–8
   business consultants 19, 23, 167
   competencies 165, 212
   job roles 22–3
   job specifications 167–8
   people specifications 167–8
   retraining 22
   technical specialists 23, 168
Financial Managment Initiative 14
Financial Perspective (balanced scorecard) 53, 54, 206
financing activities 6, 22
Fisher, John 157, 211
force field analysis 119
Friedman, A.L. 72, 138
fundamental performance reviews (FPRs) 27

Gartner Group 137
Gattenio, Christine 162, 163
General Electric 24
Giozueta, Roberto 35
Global Benchmarks Alliance 116
groupware 134

Hackett Group 5, 19, 163
Hallgarde, Dr Ulf 102–6, 209

Harris Research 175
Hawkins, Dean 170
help desk costing 83, 84–5
Hevler, Volker 198, 199, 214
Heywood, J Brian 177
hierarchical process/activity analysis 73–8
 data collection 76–7, 78
 design and delivery subprocess 74–5
 model building 77–8
 and organisation structure 73–4, 165
HOLT Value Associates 35
Hoover 40–1, 42
Hronec, Steven (Vital Signs) 95, 96–7
Hyper ABC 140, 141

IBM 6
IDEF 142
impact of change 196
impact of technology 5, 21, 206
information management 22, 24, 25, 61–7, 79, 101, 129–51, 164, 210–211
 activity/process software 137–43, 211
 client/server 138, 140
 computer and telephone integration (CTI) 134
 continuous improvement 135
 data warehousing 25, 131–2, 137, 148–51, 210
 decision support systems (DSS) 6, 22, 25, 129, 132, 134, 137–143, 210
 desktop tools 131
 document management 133–4
 electronic commerce (e-commerce) 132–3,164, 210
 enterprise information system (EIS) 6, 25, 139, 140
 enterprise resource planning (ERP) 6, 21, 22, 25, 29, 131, 135–7, 185, 210, 211
 existing system analysis 130–1
 future needs analysis 134
 groupware 134
 impact of technology 5, 21
 legacy systems 21,129, 189, 210
 management information systems (MIS) 132

middleware 21, 210
millennium bug 41, 129, 135, 139, 210
on-line analytical processing (OLAP) 132
outdated systems 5–6, 7
project teams 130
role of 130
strategy 130
web-enabled 19, 20, 21, 210, 206
workflow systems 133
information overload 129
innovation
 balanced scorecard perspective 53, 54, 206
 stifling 12
integrated performance management 25, 26, 53, 91, 137, 165, 209
integrated risk management 41–2, 164, 207
inter-business unit charging 23, 39–40, 207
internal benchmarking 115
internal business perspective (balanced scorecard) 53, 54, 206
internal rate of return (IIR) 33, 36
International Accounting Standards (IASC) 184
Internet 132–3
intranets 62, 133, 145
Investors in People (IIP) 28
invitation to tender (ITT) 178–9
invoicing process 160–1

JBA 5
Jee, Susan 157, 2, 11
job roles 22–3
job specifications 167–8
Johnson, H.T. 8, 11, 13, 88

Kaplan, R.S. 7, 24, 53, 206
Kersnar, Janet 24
key performance indicators (KPIs) 24–5, 43–8, 53, 61, 207, 211
KPMG 56, 171, 207, 212

Legacy systems 21, 129, 189, 210
local performance plans (LPPs) 27
Lund University Hospital 102–6, 209
Lyne, S.R. 72, 138

Machiavelli 196
Malcolm Baldridge National Quality Awards 58–60
'Management Accounting' 7, 72, 183, 189
Management information systems (MIS) 132
Manchester Business School 177
Manchester City Council 61–7, 208
Market value added (MVA) 35
May, Matthew 180
measures of performance 10–11, 24, 53–4, 95–6, 109–10, 160
MedAS 186-92, 213
Meredith, Tom 171
Metify 140, 141
Metropolitan Housing Trust 106–11, 209
Middleware 21, 210
Millennium Bug 41, 129, 135, 139, 210
mission statements 163

Mobil 182
MVA (market value added) 35

national performance indicators (NPIs) 27
Nationwide 148–51, 211
Net Present Value (NPV) 33
Next Steps 14
Nichols, Paul 35
Norton, D.P. 24, 53, 206

Obolensky, Nick 196
on-line analytical processing (OLAP) 132, 136, 139
Oracle 131, 135, 137, 160, 161
organisation structure 73–4, 165
OROS 138, 140, 141
outsourcing 20, 22, 55–6, 175–81, 186–92, 164, 165, 182, 212–13
 BBC 186–92, 213
 benefits 175–6, 180
 bid evaluation 179
 contract management 177
 information gathering 178
 invitation to tender (ITT) 178–9
 partnerships 180–1
 problems of 176
 rejecting 176
 risks in 176, 180

Panoramic Business Views 140
PBB (priority-based budgeting) 23, 28, 72, 98–9, 100, 134, 209
people specifications 167–8
Peoplesoft 131, 135, 137
performance improvement 72, 85–91, 164
 activity-based cost management 87–8
 business process re-engineering (BPR) 20, 28, 72, 77, 88, 89–91, 108–9, 134, 142, 164, 195, 208, 211, 214
 core (value added) activities 86
 diversionary (non value added) activities 86
 support (secondary) activities 86
performance management 10–11, 33, 72, 91–102, 102–6, 134, 164, 206, 209
 activity-based reporting 101–2
 budgeting panels 100
 control of 25
 critical success factors (CSF) 24–5, 26, 53
 evaluation of alternative service levels 28, 72, 76, 97
 integrated 25, 26, 53, 91, 137, 165, 209
 key performance indicators (KPIs) 24–5, 43–8, 53, 61, 207, 211
 measures and targets 24, 53–4, 76, 95–6, 100, 109–10, 160
 objectives and responsibilities 93–4
 priority-based budgeting (PBB) 23, 28, 72, 98–9,100, 134, 209
 process/activity based budgeting (ABB) 92–3, 110, 209, 211
 quantum performance matrix (Hronec) 96–7
Perot Systems 181
Plan Compatable 184
Price/earnings ratio (P/E) 33
pricing 84–5
PriceWaterhouseCoopers (PWC) 33, 116, 166, 181, 182
priority-based budgeting (PBB) 23, 28, 72, 98–9, 100, 134
Process Guide 145–6

225

Index

process improvement lifecycle   90
process-based techniques *see* activity-based techniques (ABT)
Prodacapo   140, 198–202, 214
product costing   80–2, 199, 208
public sector
   Accounting for Best Value Consultation Paper (CIPFA)   26
   Best Value audits   28
   Best Value principles   12–13, 25–8, 72, 61–7, 125, 158, 206, 208, 209
   change and transformation   14–15
   Citizens' Charter   12
   Compulsory Competitive Tendering (CCT)   15, 26
   Continuity and Change   12
   Financial Management Initiative   12
   Best Value Fundamental Performance Reviews (FPRs)   27
   Local Government (Best Value and Capping) Bill 1998   26
   Best Value Local Performance Plans (LPPs)   27
   Next Steps   12
   Best Value National Performance indicators (NPIs)   27
   Resource Accounting and Budgeting   12

QPR   102–6, 140, 141, 143–8, 211
quality frameworks   25, 58–61, 97, 162
quantum performance matrix (Hronec)   96–7

Rappaport, Alfred, shareholder value formula   34, 207
Redesigning the Finance Function (SMAC)   22, 167–68
reducing costs   9–10, 19, 138
Regional Aircraft (BAe)   44, 207
Relevance Lost (Johnson)   8
Relevance Regained (Kaplan & Johnson)   11, 13, 88
reporting   101–2, 140
removal of constraints   87, 88, 208
resistance to change   196
resource accounting   14–15, 72, 205

resource allocation   9, 23, 206
risk management   40–2, 164, 207
Rover   182

sales invoicing process   160–1
SAP   131, 135, 136, 137, 138, 147, 187
Sapling Corporation   140
Sears   177
service levels   27, 28, 72, 76, 97, 115, 164
service-level agreements (SLAs)   19, 21, 23, 39–40, 160, 165, 169, 186, 207, 209
service-oriented   20, 21, 164, 186, 205
shared service centre (SSC)   20, 22, 164, 165, 168, 181–6, 212–13,
   accounting and legal differences   183–4
   BBC   186-92, 213
   implementation   185–6
   suitable processes   182–3
   and taxation   184
shareholder interests   12–13, 33, 57
shareholder value   13, 33–38, 40, 185, 205, 206, 207, *see also* value-based management (VBM)
SMAC   22, 167–68
Shell   41
skills requirements   22, 165, 166–9
Smith, John   187, 191, 192
SmithKline Beecham   171–2, 212
software   85, 137–48
   activity based 137-48
   budgeting features   141
   calculation features   141
   costs   142
   design considerations   138–9
   development of   138
   ERP   135-37
   implementation planning   143
   modularity   140
   reporting capability   140
   simulation features   141
   tailoring   141
   technological specification   140–1
   testing   142
spreadsheets   5–6
steering groups   158
stewardship activities   6, 19, 20, 22, 164
stifling innovation   12

strategy 10, 57, 26, 33, 39, 90, 137, 206, *see also* planning
Swiss Bank Corporation (SBC) 181

targets 95–6, 109–10
Tate Bramald Consultancy 5
taxation 6, 22, 33, 168, 183, 184, 213
teams 118–19, 130, 158
technical specialists 20, 23, 168
technological change 21
top down control cycle 11, 205
Tower Hamlets 121–5, 210
training 19, 22, 169
transaction processing 5, 6, 19, 206
transformation project 212
   benchmarking partners 159
   brainstorming sessions 162–3
   business case 158, 166
   communication 159, 169
   customer identification 159
   data collection 161, 162
   data validation 161
   documentation of activities 159–60
   implementation 169, 211–12
   monitoring 170
   need for change 205-6
   process map 160–1
   project plan 166
   skills requirements 22, 165, 166–9
   specification definition 164–5
   steering group 158
   team appointment 158
   training and development plans 169
   vision statements 163
transfer pricing 184
transition planning 169
treasury 6, 22, 41, 168
TUPE 188, 191

University of Leeds 57, 117

value drivers 34, 45
value statements 163
value-based management (VBM) 22, 23, 26, 33–49, 72, 134, 138, 164, 206–7
   cash value added (CVATM) 36
   cashflow return on investment (CFROI) 35–6
   economic value added (EVATM) 35, 36–7
   embedded VBM system 38
   inter-business unit charging 39–40
   market value added (MVA) 35
   Rappaport's theory 34, 207
   risk management 40–2, 164, 207
Vital Signs (Hronec) 95–7
VAT 185
vision statements 163

web-enabled 19, 20, 21, 206, 210
weighted average cost of capital (WACC) 34, 36
weighted scorecard 54–6
Welch, Jack 24
Wilson, R.M.S. 189, 195
workflow systems 133
world wide web 133

Xerox 117

Yea, Phillip 24
Yorkshire Water 41

Z charts 119